Hate Groups

Recent Titles in the
CONTEMPORARY WORLD ISSUES
Series

Torture and Enhanced Interrogation: A Reference Handbook
Christina Ann-Marie DiEdoardo

Racism in America: A Reference Handbook
Steven L. Foy

Waste Management: A Reference Handbook
David E. Newton

Sexual Harassment: A Reference Handbook
Merril D. Smith

The Climate Change Debate: A Reference Handbook
David E. Newton

Voting Rights in America: A Reference Handbook
Richard A. Glenn and Kyle L. Kreider

Modern Slavery: A Reference Handbook
Christina G. Villegas

Race and Sports: A Reference Handbook
Rachel Laws Myers

World Oceans: A Reference Handbook
David E. Newton

First Amendment Freedoms: A Reference Handbook
Michael C. LeMay

Medicare and Medicaid: A Reference Handbook
Greg M. Shaw

Organic Food and Farming: A Reference Handbook
Shauna M. McIntyre

Civil Rights and Civil Liberties in America: A Reference Handbook
Michael C. LeMay

GMO Food: A Reference Handbook, Second Edition
David E. Newton

Pregnancy and Birth: A Reference Handbook
Keisha L. Goode and Barbara Katz Rothman

Books in the **Contemporary World Issues** series address vital issues in today's society such as genetic engineering, pollution, and biodiversity. Written by professional writers, scholars, and nonacademic experts, these books are authoritative, clearly written, up-to-date, and objective. They provide a good starting point for research by high school and college students, scholars, and general readers as well as by legislators, businesspeople, activists, and others.

Each book, carefully organized and easy to use, contains an overview of the subject, a detailed chronology, biographical sketches, facts and data and/or documents and other primary source material, a forum of authoritative perspective essays, annotated lists of print and nonprint resources, and an index.

Readers of books in the Contemporary World Issues series will find the information they need in order to have a better understanding of the social, political, environmental, and economic issues facing the world today.

CONTEMPORARY WORLD ISSUES

Hate Groups

A REFERENCE HANDBOOK

David E. Newton

An Imprint of ABC-CLIO, LLC
Santa Barbara, California • Denver, Colorado

Copyright © 2021 by ABC-CLIO, LLC

All rights reserved. No part of this publication may be reproduced, stored in a retrieval system, or transmitted, in any form or by any means, electronic, mechanical, photocopying, recording, or otherwise, except for the inclusion of brief quotations in a review, without prior permission in writing from the publisher.

Library of Congress Cataloging-in-Publication Data

Names: Newton, David E., author.
Title: Hate groups : a reference handbook / David E. Newton.
Description: Santa Barbara, California : ABC-CLIO, an imprint of ABC-CLIO, LLC, [2021] | Series: Contemporary world issues | Includes bibliographical references and index.
Identifiers: LCCN 2021008702 (print) | LCCN 2021008703 (ebook) | ISBN 9781440877742 (hardcover) | ISBN 9781440877759 (ebook)
Subjects: LCSH: Hate groups.
Classification: LCC HV6773.5 .N49 2021 (print) | LCC HV6773.5 (ebook) | DDC 305.5/680973—dc23
LC record available at https://lccn.loc.gov/2021008702
LC ebook record available at https://lccn.loc.gov/2021008703

ISBN: 978-1-4408-7774-2 (print)
   978-1-4408-7775-9 (ebook)

25 24 23 22 21 1 2 3 4 5

This book is also available as an eBook.

ABC-CLIO
An Imprint of ABC-CLIO, LLC

ABC-CLIO, LLC
147 Castilian Drive
Santa Barbara, California 93117
www.abc-clio.com

This book is printed on acid-free paper ∞

Manufactured in the United States of America

Contents

Preface, xiii

1 BACKGROUND AND HISTORY, 3

Hate Groups and Hate Crimes, 4

Hate Groups and "the Other," 7

Hate Groups in History, 11
  Anti-Semitism, 15
  Anti-LGBT, 17

Ad Hoc, Informal, Spontaneous Hate Groups, 18
  Lynching, 18
  Other "Us" versus "Them" Violence, 23

Hate Groups in American History, 30
  The Know Nothings, 33
  The Ku Klux Klan, 35
  Violence against Aid Workers, 39

Trends in Hate Group Activity, 42

Conclusion, 44

2 PROBLEMS, CONTROVERSIES, AND SOLUTIONS, 57

Defining Hate Groups, 57

Categories of Hate Groups, 61

- Ku Klux Klan, 62
- Black Separatists and Nationalists, 65
- Neo-Nazism, 68
- White Nationalists, 71
- Racist Skinheads, 74
  - Anti-LGBTQ Hate Groups, 76
  - Anti-Muslim Hate Groups, 78
  - Anti-Immigrant Hate Groups, 82
  - Neo-Confederate Hate Groups, 84
  - Antigovernment Hate Groups, 85
  - Anti-Semitic Hate Groups, 88

How Hate Groups Operate, 88
- Birth and Growth, 91
- What Do Hate Groups Do?, 94
  - Violent Activities, 94
  - Socialization and Support, 95
  - Propagandizing, 96
  - Signs and Symbols, 98
  - The Internet, 99
  - Working within the System, 103
  - Other Activities, 104
- Fighting Back, 106
  - Education, 106
  - Legislation, 106
  - Court Cases, 107
  - Legal Actions, 108
  - Counteroffensive Actions, 109

Conclusion, 110

3 PERSPECTIVES, 131

Introduction, 131

Hate Groups in the History of the West, 131
Dawn A. Dennis and Jorge A. Munoz

Anti-LGBTQ Hate Groups in the United States, 136
Ellen Faulkner

Making a World of Difference, 143
Phil Fogelman

Some Medical Aspects of Hate, 147
Joel Grossman

Punish Crime, Not Thought Crime, 151
Jeff Jacoby

A Century of Resilience: The History of Anti-Sikh Hate in America, 156
Aasees Kaur and Nikki Singh

Descent, Dissent, and Rising Out: The Narrative Arc of the Ex-Hate Group Leader, 159
Jesse Kavadlo

Contemporary Anti-Semitism in American Higher Education, 164
Kenneth L. Marcus

Perpetuating Historical Genocide: Anti-Indian Groups Deserve Hate Group Designation, 168
Travis McAdam

Anti-Hispanic Immigrant Hate Crimes, 173
Michele Stacey, Kristin Carbone-Lopez, and Richard Rosenfeld

Unmasking "Antifa": More than Black Bloc, 178
Kitty Stryker

4 PROFILES, 183

Anti-Defamation League (ADL), 183
Zainab Al-Suwaij (1971–), 186
Heidi L. Beirich (1967–), 188
Morris Dees (1936–), 190
Gonzaga Institute for Hate Studies, 192
Human Rights Campaign, 193
Brian Levin, 195
Sigmund Livingston (1872–1946), 197
Not in Our Town, 199
Southern Poverty Law Center, 201
Stop AAPI Hate, 204
Ida B. Wells (1862–1931), 205

5 DATA AND DOCUMENTS, 211

Data, 211
- Table 5.1. Trends in Hate Crimes by Various Characteristics, 1996–2018, 211
- Table 5.2. Trends in Hate Crimes, 2004–2015, 213
- Table 5.3. Hate Crime Data by Group and Type, 2018, 214
- Table 5.4. Hate Crimes by Known Offender's Race and Ethnicity and by Bias Motivation, 2018, 215
- Table 5.5. Major Attacks on Aid Workers, 2008–2018, 220

Documents, 221

    Presidential Statements on Hate Violence (1868–2017), 221

    Third Enforcement Act (1871), 224

    Knights of the Ku Klux Klan v. Strayer (1928), 229

    Federal Hate Crime Law (1968), 232

    Hate Crime Statistics Act (1990), 234

    Violent Crime Control and Law Enforcement Act (1994), 235

    Church Arson Prevention Act (1996), 239

    The Matthew Shepard and James Byrd Jr. Hate Crimes Prevention Act (2010), 240

    Snyder v. Phelps et al. (2011), 244

    United States of America v. Paul Beebe, et al. (2011), 247

    Objective Evidence That the Crime Was Motivated by Bias (2015), 249

    Public Law 115–58 Joint Resolution (2017), 251

6   Resources, 257

Books, 257

Articles, 268

Reports, 280

Internet, 284

7   Chronology, 301

Glossary, 317
Index, 323

Preface

In 2020, two groups that issue annual reports on hate groups in the United States, the Anti-Defamation League (ADL) and the Southern Poverty Law Center (SPLC), listed a group known as Feuerkrieg Division (FD) as belonging to this category. ADL estimated that the group had about thirty members worldwide and announced that it "advocates for a race war and holds some of the white supremacist movement's most extreme views" (ADL n.d.). Both ADL and SPLC concluded that FD was a dangerous organization that espoused the most extreme interpretations of neo-Nazi political beliefs. In April 2020, the Estonian Internal Security Service announced that it had identified the leader of FD: a thirteen-year-old boy living on the island of Saaremaa. The island is otherwise best known for its fourteenth-century castle and spectacular ocean views. The boy identified himself on the popular gaming network Steam as "commander" of FD. Because of his age, the boy was not identified by name.

This story has a number of lessons for individuals interested in the problem of hate groups in the world today. First, it highlights the fact that groups still exist that promote the most violent, hateful political philosophies ever developed, namely, many varieties of racist, xenophobic, anti-Jewish, anti-LGBTQ, anti-Muslim, and other far-right organizations. Second, the story is a reminder that many of these organizations can exist in the deepest, darkest mists of human culture, largely unknown to both criminal investigators and the public at large. When information about especially troubling hate groups in existence today appears, it is often next to impossible to know who the leader(s) of that group might be, how they are funded, how many members they have, how serious a threat they might be, and, not the least important, whether they are actually hate groups at all.

Third, FD story illustrates the role of social media and the Internet in general in the work of hate groups. The thirteen-year-old Estonian boy had ready access to millions of men and women and boys and girls around the world. In addition to Steam, he had access to other popular platforms, such as Telegram and Wire, through which he was able to communicate in encrypted messages with his comrades and followers. With these mechanisms, he was able to propound a political view that might be completely false, or misleading at best, that could be attractive to enough people to allow "the group" to exist and plan actions to carry out its goals. The boy was also able to plan, provide information about, and attempt to carry out high-level crimes against targeted groups (such as Jewish sites in the city of Las Vegas, Nevada) without monitoring by external groups.

Hate groups are hardly a new phenomenon in history. In fact, if one accepts the Federal Bureau of Investigation's definition of a hate group as an organization whose "primary purpose is to promote animosity, hostility, and malice against persons belonging to a race, religion, disability, sexual orientation, or ethnicity/national origin which differs from that of the members of the organization" (CJIS 2015), hate groups have played a major role in human history as far back as written records exist. For most of that time, hate groups were largely religious organizations or organizations that sponsor attacks against individuals or groups who were different from the dominant group. Students of hate groups today generally do not deal in detail with Religion A who hates, attacks, and attempts to destroy Religion B or Nation A who has the same motives against members of Nation B. Yet, these endless events can serve as a lesson as to how modern hate groups arise, the reasons they exist, the goals they may seek, the actions they may follow, and the results of those actions.

Chapter 1 provides a general introduction to the topic of hate groups, with some attention to the history of religious, state-sponsored, and modern groups. Today, a great deal of research has been conducted on the nature of hate *crimes*; however, much less has been done on the nature of hate *groups*. One reason is the problem in discovering the connection between the two variables. Do hate groups themselves conduct, carry out, or just recommend specific acts of hate crime among their members or those influenced by their propaganda? The research on that topic is somewhat limited, with the general opinion being that specific hate crimes cannot generally be connected with specific hate groups.

Still, there can be little doubt about the influence of hate groups on the social and political aura of a nation. Perhaps the most recent example of that fact occurred as a result of the presidential election of 2016 in the United States. The new administration that resulted from that election had a significantly different view of the nature and importance of hate groups than did previous presidential administrations. Those effects can be seen in the number, type, size, influence, and activities of hate groups before and after that election.

Chapter 2 of this book focuses on the current status of hate groups in the United States. It discusses various categories of hate groups (e.g., Black separatist, white separatist, anti-Semitic, anti-LGBTQ, anti-Muslim, and neo-Nazi), with a review of some of the best known of groups in each of these categories. The chapter also provides a review of the nature of hate groups as organizations: the way they begin, how they are structured, how they carry out their activities, and how they fail.

The remaining chapters in this book provide resources for readers who would like to learn more about the subject of hate groups or to continue their own research on the topic. These chapters include an extensive annotated bibliography, a chronology of hate groups throughout history, a glossary of terms used in the field, a collection of essays about specific aspects of the topic, and a group of essays about important individuals and organizations in the field of hate groups.

References

ADL. n.d. "Feuerkrieg Division (FKD)." https://www.adl.org/resources/backgrounders/feuerkrieg-division-fkd

CJIS. 2015. *Hate Crimes Data Collection Guidelines and Training Manual.* Washington, D.C.: Criminal Justice Information Services Division, February 27, 2015. https://www.fbi.gov/file-repository/ucr/ucr-hate-crime-data-collection-guidlines-training-manual-v2.pdf/view

Hate Groups

1 Background and History

Westboro Baptist Church is located in Topeka, Kansas, founded in 1955 by Fred Phelps, the then associate pastor of the existing East Side Baptist Church. Membership in the church has historically been about forty, consisting primarily of members of Phelps' extended family. The church has achieved notoriety exceeding what might normally be expected from an entity of its size, largely because of the strong positions it has taken on various social and theological issues. Perhaps most familiar of these is its stand in opposition to same-sex relationships, which it deems sinful. So-called enablers of such practices are also seen as sinners. Church members picket on a regular basis at other churches, funerals, and other special occasions. The signs they carry during such events include comments such as "God Hates Fags," "No Tears for Queers," "God Gave Fags Up," and "Thank God for AIDS." The URL for the church's own website also carries the same message: godhatesfags.com (Brentlinger 2019; for more details on the church, also see "Westboro Baptist Church: Warriors for God?" 2013). Westboro's ire is directed not exclusively toward gay men and lesbians. It also pickets and protests on a regular basis against Catholics, Jews, military personnel, political leaders, victims of mass shootings, and, it sometimes seems, everyone who does not belong to the church itself (Sessions 2017).

Ku Klux Klan members attend an initiation ceremony in Baltimore, Maryland, in 1923. (The Illustrated London News Picture Library)

Organizations with strong negative feelings against other groups of individuals are often known as *hate groups*. According to the U.S. Federal Bureau of Investigation (FBI), a hate group is "[a]n organization whose primary purpose is to promote animosity, hostility, and malice against persons of or with a race, religion, disability, sexual orientation, ethnicity, gender, or gender identity which differs from that of the members or the organization, e.g., the Ku Klux Klan, American Nazi Party" ("Hate Crime Data Collection Guidelines and Training Manual" 2015).

Most hate groups direct their campaign against specific groups, such as Jews, Catholics, African Americans, Muslims, gay men and lesbians, or transgendered individuals. These groups can be broadly classified as being based on gender; gender identity; sexual orientation; religion; disability; or race, ethnicity, or ancestry ("2018 Hate Crime Statistics" n.d.). However, the FBI collects far more detailed statistical information on hate group victims, as shown in table 1.1.

One of the most characteristic features of hate groups is the symbolism they use in their operations. They may wear special kinds of clothing, have unique types of tattoos, employ recognizable hand or other gestures, and use distinctive symbols in their flags, banners, or other presentations. For example, some groups may use the symbol "14" on their materials. The symbol stands for the fourteen words in a group's statement of philosophy: "We must secure the existence of our people and a future for white children." The number may also be combined with other words, letters, and numbers by specific hate groups, such as 14/23, 14/88, or 14 Words. (For more details on the symbolism associated with hate groups, see "Hate on Display™ Hate Symbols Database" 2020.)

Hate Groups and Hate Crimes

A word of caution is appropriate at this point. One might reasonably assume that hate *groups* are closely associated with hate

Table 1.1 Bias Categories Used by the FBI in Hate Crime Reporting

General Category	Specific Biases
Race/Ethnicity/Ancestry	Anti-American Indian or Alaska Native
	Anti-Arab
	Anti-Asian
	Anti-Black or African American
	Anti-Hispanic or Latino
	Anti-Multiple Races, Group
	Anti-Native Hawaiian or Other Pacific Islander
	Anti-Other Race/Ethnicity/Ancestry
	Anti-White
Religion	Anti-Buddhist
	Anti-Catholic
	Anti-Eastern Orthodox (Russian, Greek, Other)
	Anti-Hindu
	Anti-Islamic
	Anti-Jehovah's Witness
	Anti-Jewish
	Anti-Mormon
	Anti-Multiple Religions, Group
	Anti-Other Christian
	Anti-Other Religion
	Anti-Protestant
	Anti-Atheism/Agnosticism/etc.
Sexual Orientation	Anti-Bisexual
	Anti-Gay (Male)
	Anti-Heterosexual
	Anti-Lesbian
	Anti-Lesbian, Gay, Bisexual, or Transgender (Mixed Group)
Disability	Anti-Mental Disability
	Anti-Physical Disability
Gender	Anti-Male
	Anti-Female
Gender Identity	Anti-Transgender
	Anti-Gender Non-Conforming

Source: "Hate Crime Statistics." n.d. Federal Bureau of Investigation. https://www.fbi.gov/services/cjis/ucr/hate-crime.

crimes. That is, it seems logical that individuals who carry out some type of action against another individual or individuals because of that person's or persons' race, religion, gender, sexual orientation, or other characteristics have some kind of connection with one or more hate groups. A person who sets fire to a church serving primarily African Americans, for example, might well be expected to belong to the Ku Klux Klan (KKK) or some other groups with professed disapproval of Black individuals. And one reads about that presumption from time to time. When an eighteen-year-old boy vandalizes a Jewish cemetery, law officials, media reporters, and others may well ask, "What caused him to take that action? Was he a member of some hate group who encouraged such actions?"

Interestingly enough, a somewhat limited body of research suggests that the connection between hate groups and hate crimes is much more tenuous than one might expect. Among the earliest such study was conducted in 2011 by researchers at Duquesne and George Mason universities. The researchers examined data in the Southern Poverty Law Center (SPLC) annual reports on hate crime between 2002 and 2008. They begin by acknowledging that "the potential connection between hate groups and hate crimes is obvious." They conclude from their study, however, that, surprisingly, "we find little evidence that hate groups are associated with hate crime in the United States." A connection between hate crimes and economic status appears to be weak, but tenuous, so they conclude by being somewhat mystifying as to what factors *are* predictive of hate crimes (Ryan and Leeson 2011, 256).

A somewhat more focused study using only "white supremacist" groups also found little empirical evidence for an association between hate groups and hate crimes but hypothesized some reasons that little or no connection might exist. The author suggested, for example, that groups provided individuals with a locus and opportunity to vent their feelings about sex, race, gender, religion, and other characteristics, thus reducing the likelihood of actual violent actions (Mulholland 2013). Perhaps the most extensive study completed thus far reported a correlation of 39.5 percent between locations where hate crimes are committed and hate groups are located, without finding clear evidence that the latter actually caused or were caused by the other (Jendryke and McClure 2019).

The safest conclusion to be made at this point, then, is that there is no clear conclusion as to the connection that exists, if any, between hate groups and hate crimes. That does not mean that experts in the field have no ideas as to such connections; just that almost no empirical evidence exists. For that reason, this book will, as its title suggests, focus on hate *groups*, with references to hate *crimes* only when that step seems necessary and proper for a review of the main topic.

A final word about the term *hate crimes*. Although several good definitions for this term have been proposed and are in use (see chapter 2, pp. 57), data on the topic are widely divergent. Those differences reflect the ways in which data are collected. For example, the Bureau of Justice Statistics (BJS) counts all hate crimes reported and not reported to law enforcement officers at every level. From 2013 to 2017, BJS estimated an annual average of 204,600 hate crime incidents (Oudekerk 2019, Figure 1). By contrast, the FBI counts only those crimes that have reached its own attention. This count is much smaller because only a small fraction of actual or suspected hate crimes are of sufficient consequence to reach this upper level of law enforcement. The number of hate crimes reported to the FBI in 2017, for example, was 6,370 ("2017 Hate Crime Statistics" n.d.). This distinction is important to understand when one encounters hate crime data that appear to be very different for the same or similar dates and events.

Hate Groups and "the Other"

Today, the vast majority of hate groups in the United States are made up primarily of white, Christian, heterosexual men. And such has been the case throughout the history of Western civilization wherever and whenever something like a "hate group" has existed. Probably the main difference between hate groups in the past and the present is that, until recently, such groups consisted of kings, princes, lords, members of the nobility, and religious leaders. One of the most famous of these events was the series of Inquisitions instituted by the Catholic Church from the thirteenth through the eighteenth centuries. During the Catholic, Roman, Spanish, and Portuguese Inquisitions, national rulers and leaders of the church searched out individuals thought to be guilty of any number of crimes, then punished, and often killed (Monter 2005).

Somewhat closer to home, white male (and, sometimes, female) emigrants to North America from Europe during the seventeenth century might also be thought of as a "hate group" in the sense that they looked upon Native American inhabitants of the continent as not very intelligent, dirty, bellicose, believers in strange religions, and generally inferior to the invading newcomers from Europe (Dunbar-Ortiz 2016). Indeed, the first colonists in North America were willing to employ the same methods used by the inquisitors and early North American missionaries to ensure purity in thought and deed of their neighbors. The legal system of the Massachusetts Bay Colony (and other early colonies), for example, included many of the same penalties for nonacceptable ideas or behaviors as those in Europe at the time: for example, the death penalty for same-sex behavior, adultery, and religious dissent ("Crime and Punishment in a Triangular Perspective: Assessing Theocracy and the Transfer of Culture" n.d.).

Some social scientists have attempted to explain this long history of establishing one group of people over another, a system of defining those who are "inferior" and "superior" in a culture. They use the concept of "us/them," "self/other," "belonging/othering," or some similar construct. "Othering" comes about when one group of people ("us") compares themselves to another group of people ("them") with a different color skin, with different physical attributes, speaking an unfamiliar language, and following a strange and incomprehensible religious tradition. These differences tend to cause "us" to wonder about "them," perhaps fear them, and almost certainly regard them as inferior to "us." (Among the many fine articles on "othering," see Brons 2015; Powell and Menendian 2016; Stabile 2016.)

Again, the process of "othering" has existed throughout the history of Western civilization, perhaps most visibly with regard to sex and gender. Until only recently, the vast majority of male political and religious leaders have made no secret of their belief that women are inherently and inevitably inferior to men. One need only read comments of the early Church Fathers and later Christian leaders to gain some sense of this attitude:

- "Woman is naturally of less strength and dignity than man" (Thomas Aquinas, thirteenth century).
- "You are the devil's gateway: you are the unsealer of that (forbidden) tree: you are the first deserter of the divine law: you are she who persuaded him whom the devil was not valiant enough to attack" (Tertullian, the Father of Latin Christianity, 155–245 CE).
- "woman was given to man [because] she was of small intelligence and who perhaps still lives more in accordance with the promptings of the inferior flesh than by superior reason" (Augustine, 354–430).
- "For as the sun is more glorious than the moon, though the moon is a most glorious body, so woman, though she was a most beautiful work of God, yet she did not equal the glory of the male creature" (Martin Luther, sixteenth century).
- "Nature I say, paints [women] further to be weak, frail, impatient, feeble and foolish: and experience has declared them to be inconstant, variable, cruel and lacking the spirit of counsel and regiment [or, leadership]" (John Knox, sixteenth century) (Mowczka 2013).

One might argue that hateful feelings such as these toward women no longer exist in modern society. It is probably true that such attitudes are rarely expressed with the vitriol characteristic of the preceding quotes. But that does not mean that women are no longer the victim of hate crimes. Instead, they are likely to experience offenses of a somewhat different nature, some of which are not reportable to law enforcement agencies. For example, women in most parts of the world are routinely paid less for doing the same job as a man. They find it difficult (sometimes impossible) to have the same opportunity for work advancement as do men. They are likely to encounter subtle forms of verbal disparagement, such as comments about their physical appearance. None of these behaviors is likely to qualify as a "hate crime."

Even obvious physical assaults, such as intimidation and vandalism, are unlikely to be recognized by the police as "hate crimes." Add to that fact the likelihood that many women are simply less inclined to report "hate crimes" because of their attachment to the offender, their perception that the offending act was not really a crime, that they did not want to make the offense a public issue, or that law enforcement officials did not think of the crime as being of sufficient import to act on (Li 2019).

For these reasons, a vast lacuna exists between the number of hate crimes based on gender, as reported by the FBI, and the true number of such crimes as determined by other means. For example, the FBI reported a total of twenty-five hate crime incidents as being "anti-female" in its most recent "Hate Crime Statistics" report. This number is less than 1 percent of all hate crimes reported to the FBI for the year ("2018 Hate Crime Statistics" n.d., Table 1). But a survey by the BJS from 2013 to 2017 found that the average number of antiwoman hate crimes annually was close to fifty thousand, about 30 percent of all hate crimes reported in those years. (Li 2019; these data illustrate the wide disparity between data presented in FBI reports, which include only crimes reported to that agency, and data from other sources, such as local, state, and regional agencies, as well as crimes that simply go unreported.)

One of the most interesting aspects of "othering" is the role of geography in the phenomenon. Granted that differences between "us" and "them" exist in many settings, it probably is much less important if the distance between the two groups is measured in hundreds or thousands of miles. Yes, the natives of Timor may look, act, and think differently from those of Brooklyn, but what difference does that make in one's everyday life? But the differences between the "us" who live in Queens and the "them" who live in Brooklyn—and who may interact with each other on many occasions—that difference may be very significant. As Sigmund Freud observed about this pattern when speaking about the importance of "small differences" between groups, "it is precisely communities with adjoining territories, and related to each other in other ways as well, who are engaged in constant feuds and ridiculing each other" (Alexander 2014).

So, perhaps the concept of a "hate group" is not a new one, beginning only with the Civil War or some later period in American history in the United States. Can we look for hints of the basic principles by which modern hate groups live in an earlier, even much earlier, period in Western civilization? Where does that question lead one?

Hate Groups in History

Our modern understanding of hate groups usually dates to the Civil War period, with the founding of the KKK, in Pulaski, Tennessee, in 1865. The organization primarily began as a social club for former Confederate soldiers before evolving into a terrifying and violent hate group. But the concept of an "us" versus "them" mentality existed long before the Klan's appearance. It probably dates to the dawn of human civilization, if not even earlier. Many of the beliefs held by hate groups today toward women, the disabled, and those of alternative sexual orientations and religious beliefs can be traced to social conventions and penalties displayed in Rome, the Middle Ages, the Renaissance period, and later eras, extending even to the present day.

One of the most characteristic features of hate groups is their opposition to diversity. A society in which all individuals had exactly the same physical, mental, emotional, psychological, and other characteristics would probably not have many (or any) hate groups. If everyone is the same, toward whom can one direct hate? It is for this reason that many nations and religions have themselves been hate-group-like entities. As many modern societies have discovered, acknowledging and adapting to individuals with different skin color, different physical features, different languages, different customs and rituals, and other differences can be an admirable effort but, at the same time, a stress on social institutions and practices.

It probably should not be surprising, then, to note that nation-states and religions have struggled to deal with such problems and, in that effort, behaved as if they were "hate groups." The term *hate group* would, of course, probably have no historical meaning when applied to the early Roman Catholic Church, eighth-century Spain, sixteenth-century France, or twenty-first-century China. But the history of those entities, along with countless other majority governing agencies in a country, illustrates ideas and behaviors that would not seem out of place among modern hate groups. They were just larger, more aggressive, more destructive, and more (or less) successful.

One of the most illuminating examples of this pattern is the growth of the Roman Catholic Church in the centuries following the death of Jesus. As it grew from an essentially small, persecuted group of believers, the church continuously struggled with what it was, that is, what doctrinal beliefs it held. Throughout the first ten centuries of the church's existence, it constantly fought against "outsider" groups that held views that leaders of the church found to be heretical and unacceptable. When heretics refused to renounce their beliefs and adopt traditional teachings, they often suffered severe penalties that ranged for excommunication and exile to burning at the stake. Among the early heretics who were attacked by the church were the Circumcisers, Gnostics, Montanists, Sabellianists, Ariansits, Pelagianists, and Nestorians ("The Great Heresies" 2020). The battles for which these groups fought might seem to be over minor matters of doctrine. But they were serious enough to the church's authority for them to suffer the fate of other hate group victims throughout history.

As specific heresies began to die out, the church turned its attention to individuals who appeared to be a heretic. The search for and punishment of such individuals became a major activity of the church throughout Europe during the period of the Inquisitions. Although reliable statistics are not available, some experts estimate that the number of people killed during the Inquisitions between the mid-thirteenth and mid-fifteenth century ranged into the high tens of thousands ("What Was the Death Toll During the Inquisition?" 2017; Deane 2011).

As the reign of the Inquisitors began to fail, the church faced yet another threat to its command of formal religion: the appearance of Protestantism in the sixteenth century. A new and violent period developed during which the Roman Catholic Church battled against Lutherans, Calvinists, Presbyterianism, and other "Reformist" groups. Again, the stakes were high, with eight separate wars between Catholics and Huguenots (Protestants) fought in France over religious freedoms between 1562 and 1598 ("The Eight Wars of Religion (1562–1598)" 2020).

Possibly the preeminent example of nation-state hate groups in recent history was the reign of the National Socialist (Nazi) Party in Germany during the 1930s and 1940s. From its earliest days of seeking power in the nation, the party's leader Adolf Hitler and his colleagues made no secret about their plan to make Germany a "racially pure" nation. To do so, Hitler focused on the destruction of all Jews living in the country, by one means or another. For example, as early as 1922, Hitler was quoted as saying:

> If I am ever really in power, the destruction of the Jews will be my first and most important job. As soon as I have power, I shall have gallows after gallows erected, for example, in Munich on the Marienplatz—as many of them as traffic allows. Then the Jews will be hanged one after another, and they will stay hanging until they stink. They will stay hanging as long as hygienically possible. As soon as they are untied, then the next group will follow and that will continue until the last Jew in Munich is exterminated. Exactly the same procedure will be followed in other cities until Germany is cleansed of the last Jew! (Stein 2000)

Of course, Hitler and the Nazi's image of racial purity extended beyond extermination of the Jews. Trains to the concentration camps were also filled with homosexuals, Roma and Sinti (gypsies), the unemployed and homeless, political opponents, welfare recipients, alcoholics, and those with physical and mental disabilities ("Who Were the Victims?" 2020). The goal of the last of these programs was the elimination of all individuals who had hereditary problems that the party decided should not be passed down to future generations. Ironically, the definition of who was "disabled" ran the gamut of individuals from those with identifiable physical or mental conditions such as epilepsy, dementia, and schizophrenia to less clear "defects," including those "not of German blood." This Euthanasia Program of both children and adults has been described by some experts as a "trial run" for the ultimate system of concentration camps and mass ovens for the destruction of "the unfit" ("Euthanasia Program" 2020).

One need not look back even seventy-five years to find examples of state-led hate groups. In the third decade of the twenty-first century, such examples are easy to find. In 2014, for example, the Chinese government began a program of rounding up and incarcerating members of the Uighur minority. As of 2020, an estimated million Uighurs had been sent to "reeducation camps" with little or no opportunity to communicate with those outside the camp and essentially no method of regaining their freedom. The reason for the Chinese action was said to protect the nation from politically dangerous Muslims who constitute the Uighur population. Worldwide response to these actions has been mild and, thus far, without noticeable impact on the Chinese policy (Maizland 2019).

Another prominent example of such actions is the campaign by the Buddhist government of Myanmar against its Muslim Rohingyas. Antagonisms between the two religious groups go back centuries in the area, but reached a climax in early 2010. In response to attacks by Rohingya groups on Myanmar police outposts, the government began a program of what can only be called annihilation or ethnic cleansing. Over the next decade, about 10 percent of the Rohingya population was displaced from their homes in Myanmar, while 60 percent were driven out of the country entirely. Again, international complaints against the Myanmar action have been largely ignored, and some experts warn that the Rohingya who remain in the country face the prospect of genocide ("Global Conflict Tracker" 2020).

Anti-Semitism

A seemingly endless number of examples of state and religious-sponsored hate group action can be cited over the centuries. However, a handful of hate crimes against some groups seem to reappear across the centuries. One of these long-term trends is anti-Semitism, the hatred and fear of, as well as the hostility toward, those of the Jewish faith. Some historians date the origins of anti-Semitism to the third century BCE when Jews were expelled from Egypt because they were thought of as "lepers" (although the story of "the exodus" is far more complicated than that; see Raspe 1998). Many studies have been conducted on the reasons for anti-Semitism. Most of the causes proposed sound familiar in the context of our earlier discussion here: the Jews were seen as somehow "different" from the cultures they joined because they were "inferior" to members of those cultures, or because they were "more clever" in business dealings, and therefore a threat to more "normal people" in the culture. A powerful excuse for the anti-Jewish sentiment was that "the Jews had killed Jesus" and, therefore, somehow deserved an unending and severe punishment from Christians. In addition, although seen by others as "inferior," Jews generally declared themselves to be "chosen by God" and, therefore, thought of themselves as superior to those around them (Shore 2020; possibly the best single source of information about anti-Semitism is Poliakov [1955/1975] 2003).

Whatever the causes, there can be little doubt that Jews have long been (except for women) the most consistent and severe victims of hate groups throughout the Western world. These troubles began in the Christian era as early as thirty-eight CE when rioters attacked and killed many residents of the city and created a restricted area within the city where they could live (Gambetti 2009).

Over the next twenty centuries, persecution of the Jews continued to occur frequently throughout most of the Christian world. This persecution consisted of mass killings (*pogroms*), destruction of temples and other properties, and wholesale expulsion of Jews from a nation. Just a summary of these events can take up numerous pages. (See, e.g., "A Brief Chronology of Antisemitism" 2015.) An important point about this review is that the events described in this history are not truly examples of modern hate group behavior. The actions that make up this review were not carried out by relatively small, single-purpose organizations, but were the results of concrete, intentional policies by leaders of a nation, a community, or a religious sect. Nonetheless, one need not search too far before finding somewhat similar stories—generally on a much smaller scale—carried out by anti-Semitic hate groups today.

Anti-Semitic hate crimes continue today. In fact, according to the most recent data available, these crimes have increased by about 40 percent between 2014 and 2018. In 2018, 351 violent crimes upon individuals included intimidation (69 percent), simple assault (18 percent), aggravated assault (7 percent), manslaughter and murder (31 percent), and other violent crimes (2 percent) ("2018 Hate Crime Statistics" n.d., Table 4).

In some ways, one of the most interesting features of these data is the number of crimes committed against property, rather than against individuals. For example, in 2018, nearly three times as many property crimes as personal crimes were committed against Jews. Of these, the vast majority were classified as destruction, damage, or vandalism (81 percent of all property crimes), followed by larceny or theft (6 percent), burglary and arson (3 percent each), and robbery (1 percent) ("2018 Hate Crime Statistics" n.d., Table 4).

Anti-LGBT

A somewhat similar story to that of the Jewish people can be told for those who engaged in same-sex behavior, so-called (but inappropriately so) homosexuals. The more common way of describing this type of hate is anti-LGBT, standing for opposition to lesbian (L), gay (G), bisexual (B), and transgender people (T). Although commonly accepted by many primitive cultures and especially in ancient Greece, same-sex behavior came under attack during the early Christian period (Donaldson et al. 2017; Norton [2002] 2012). Punishment for such behaviors ranged from fines to surgical procedures on the genitalia and other parts of the body to burning at the stake to death. Most such penalties had been removed or tempered by the end of the twentieth century, but not entirely so. For example, by 2020, more than seventy countries had retained laws punishing same-sex relationships, in eight of which the maximum penalty was death (Mendos 2019; #Outlawed: "The Love That Dare Not Speak its Name" 2020). At the time, government leaders in some nations were still pushing for death penalties in their own countries (Burke and Okiror 2019). The United States, and other countries with their own history of severe punishments for same-sex acts, has largely decriminalized such behaviors. Several antigay hate groups, on the other hand, have still called for actions of some type or another, including the death penalty, against same-sex behaviors (Skinner 2011).

Ad Hoc, Informal, Spontaneous Hate Groups

At the same time hate-based violence was being perpetrated on minorities by governmental and religious entities, similar events were being carried out by informal community groups for similar reasons. Imagine, for example, a town in the Middle Ages suddenly beset by an epidemic of measles. Humans at every stage of history have wondered and worried about the appearance of unexpected and unusual events, such as the occurrence of a disease. Long before the evolution of modern medicine, people looked for other reasons for such events, such as the presence of one or more heretics in the community who, intentionally or unintentionally, caused the abnormal event. Out of this line of thinking grew spontaneous, informal group actions to resolve the problem. One of the best-known and most widely cited examples of such events was the witch hunt, the search for a person (usually, but not always, a woman) who had cast a spell on the community. With or without the presence of a formal religion, such events often turned into hate-based violence that frequently resulted in the death of one or more witches or warlocks. The fact that we read and hear much more often about witches than about warlocks is, of course, an indication of the inherent antiwoman beliefs of most communities (Behringer 2008).

Lynching

The United States has its own long and troubled history of actions by spontaneous, ad hoc, informal hate groups formed exclusively for the punishment of some member or group of "others" in the community. One action perhaps best known of any in American history is the practice of *lynching*. Lynching can be defined as the act of putting to death an individual or individuals by mob action without legal approval or permission. According to one recent report, 4084 lynchings occurred in twelve Southern states between 1877 and 1950. Lynchings had not begun in 1877 but were a part of Southern history long before that time. In prior decades, however, whites were almost as likely as African Americans to be the victims of lynching. The major difference, however, was that Black lynchings were often accompanied by "extreme brutality such as burning, torture, mutilation, and decapitation of the victim" ("Lynching in America: Confronting the Legacy of Racial Terror" 2017; this report may be the best readily available resource on the topic of lynching in America).

Lynching in the United States reflected not only a powerful opposition to individuals of a different race but also an important tool in the evolution of American society following the Civil War. Freeing of the slaves and loss of the war left the American South with a new reality. Not only were Blacks now free to live and work on their own, but they were also free to take part in the political process. By the end of Reconstruction, some Southern states were governed and represented by Black governors, senators, and representatives. It was a situation that white Southerners could not tolerate. And lynching and other forms of violence provided just the tool needed to "keep Blacks in their place" (Olzak 1990).

The origin of the term *lynch* has been the subject of considerable scholarly research. Its etymology has been traced as far back as 1493, but is more reliably thought to reflect the philosophy and actions of an early American farmer. Exactly *which* that farmer is not known, but descriptions of possible contenders for the title provide a glimpse of the notion of extralegal actions taken by early colonists against malefactors. In general, those thought to be the correct "Mr. Lynch" all tended to use their own version of the law, holding on-the-spot trials and punishments ranging from tar-and-feathering to death by bludgeoning or hanging (Matthews 1904).

In any case, the use of lynching as an act against African Americans in general, rather than specific individuals, has now been well documented. According to one scholar of the topic, such events most commonly "carried a significance that transcended the specific act of punishment, turning the act into a symbolic rite in which the Black victim became the representative of his race and, as such, was being disciplined for more than a single crime." "Indeed," he went on, "the guilt or innocence of the victim was always far less important that the act of lynching itself." The act was intended, he continues, to be a "warning [to] the Black population not to challenge the supremacy of the white race" (Smead 1986, x).

Neither was lynching the only form of violence expressed by spontaneous hate groups against African Americans. Victims of white violence against Blacks also included beatings, burning at the stake, castration, torture, mutilation, decapitation, dismemberment, body piercing, flogging, and outright murder. Such events were frequently the focus of popular celebrations, with their time and place being announced in advance and then attended by crowds of hundreds or thousands of people celebrating the spectacle (Ifill 2003; "Lynching in America: Confronting the Legacy of Racial Terror" 2017, passim).

Lynching had largely died out by the middle of the twentieth century in the United States, although the last such event has been dated to 1981 (Blakemore 2019). Still, as will be discussed later in this text, African Americans are still subject to a variety of physical, mental, and emotional attacks in the United States today.

By no means was lynching a crime of violence reserved for African Americans. Indeed, recent research has shown that the act was performed routinely on members of other ethnic groups, often for classic reasons of the "us" versus "them" mentality. Along the southwestern border of the country, lynching and other violent acts against Mexicans and Mexican Americans was hardly an unknown phenomenon in the second half of the nineteenth century. One study documented 597 violent deaths of such individuals between 1848 and 1928. Of this, 267 died by lynching, 213 by shooting, 52 by physical mutilation, and 5 by burning. (No cause of death is known for the remaining 60 victims.) As with African Americans, the primary reason for these acts of violence was, according to the authors of this study, "an irrational prejudice towards racial minorities" (Carrigan and Webb 2003; the authors indicate that the numbers quoted in this article are "conservative estimates" because of the difficulties involved in obtaining accurate accounts of such events). As with attacks on African Americans by unruly crowds, various violent actions other than lynching was also possible. A sense of the brutality of these attacks is best obtained by a retelling of specific cases of hate group attacks on individuals (Esquivel 2019).

Animosities toward people of Latino or Hispanic heritage has by no means dissipated in a world supposedly more sensitive to the value of diversity and openness to individuals of other culture. In the United States, for example, the number of hate crimes against immigrants attempting to enter the United States from Mexico and Central America has increased rather dramatically in recent years. In addition to the traditional hatred of and fears about such individuals, more recent changes in American social and political life have apparently magnified these feelings. For example, as candidate for the presidency of the United States in 2016, Donald Trump spoke frequently and strongly about the dangers that Mexican immigrants posed to this country. Their continued arrival here, he said, would not only harm the nation's economy but would present new and dramatically serious crime problems for the country. He promised that the construction of a wall on the U.S.-Mexican border would be one of his priorities.

President Trump's views on immigration belong to a political philosophy known as *nativism*. This term refers to the belief that native inhabitants of a region are inherently superior to those from other regions and, therefore, deserve special recognition and treatment in their country. Nativist views are also known as *populism* (although the two differ from each other in some regards). As of 2020, the world appeared to be in the midst of a dramatic shift in political philosophies from a tendency toward more democratic regimes to ones with strongest nativistic and populist themes (Kyle and Gultchin 2018). Some observers have suggested that the views of President Donald Trump were influenced by and, in turn, influenced nativist (anti-immigrant) policies in the United States (Friedman 2017).

Since Trump's election, political scientists have explored the relationship (or lack of relationship) between Trump's open support of xenophobia, his election, and the growth of anti-immigrant violence in the United States. Most such studies suggest that the President's seeming support of anti-immigrant beliefs and actions played some role in the increase in anti-immigrant hate crime from at least 2016 to 2020. For example, one pair of researchers concluded from their studies that "we find compelling evidence to support the Trump Effect hypothesis. Using time series analysis, we show that Donald Trump's election in November of 2016 was associated with a statistically significant surge in reported hate crimes across the United States, even when controlling for alternative explanations. Further, by using panel regression techniques, we show that counties that voted for President Trump by the widest margins in the presidential election also experienced the largest increases in reported hate crimes" (Edwards and Rushin 2018, [1]).

This conclusion is reflected to some extent in the actual number of hate crimes committed against Latinos and Hispanics in the years preceding and during the Trump administration. In the early 2010s, those numbers were relatively constant at about 390 incidents per year. In 2015, for example, they stood at 392, increasing to 483 in 2016 and 552 in 2017. In

2018, they reached a total of 671, an increase over the previous year of almost 22 percent (data from "Hate Crime Statistics" for each year noted, Table 1).

An interesting phenomenon that has developed with regard to anti-immigration groups has been the development of loose, informal, ad hoc collections of individuals who are often protective of their own geographic area. Such groups may have one or more "leaders" who call upon members of the group to conduct extralegal activities to prevent immigrants from crossing into the United States. Such organizations are ephemeral, arising, surviving, and disappearing according to current circumstances (see, e.g., McCoy 2019). Little information is available on such groups, largely because they tend to be both disorganized and ephemeral.

Other "Us" versus "Them" Violence

In the far western part of the country, the unfortunate subjects of "us" versus "them" violence were immigrant Chinese, many of whom arrived in the United States to work in the gold mines or on the new transcontinental railway. Perhaps more "different" from Anglos than any other "out" group, the Chinese were subject to violent attacks from the moment of their arrival. They not only had the "wrong" skin color and the "wrong" language but also engaged in eating and drinking customs that were not comprehensible to the average American. It is hardly surprising, then, to read of the virtually nonstop series of attacks they experienced from white settlers in the region.

In 1871, for example, an unruly crowd was aroused by the shooting of a Los Angeles police officer by a Chinese man. In revenge for that act, a mob of about five hundred people (about 10 percent of the city population at the time) hauled Chinese men and women from their homes and hung them on hastily built gallows. One expert in the field has called this event "the largest mass lynching in U.S. history" (Lee 2015, 93). Four years later, another anti-Chinese attack occurred near Rock Springs, Wyoming. At the time, mixed crews of Anglo and Chinese workers were employed at a coal mine in the area. When problems began to arise between the mine owners, the Union Pacific Railroad, and the Anglo workers, the latter decided that Chinese workers were responsible for the impasse. Motivated by that belief, they attacked the small Chinese community at Rock Springs, killed twenty-eight men, wounded fifteen more, and essentially destroyed the Chinese enclave (Rea 2014). (As in previous cases described earlier, this handful of events cannot begin to describe the exposure of Chinese to hate group actions. For more details, see Pfaelzer 2007.)

The history of hate-inspired violence against Native Americans is much too long to be included in this chapter. That history began shortly after European settlers started to arrive in North America in the seventeenth century and continued well into the twentieth century (History.com Editors 2018). That violence took many forms, possibly the most important of which was the unintentional spread of diseases among Native Americans who were not immune to those diseases (primarily smallpox). But formal raids, battles, and wars by U.S., state, and local military forces were another expression of the white population's suspicion, jealousy, and hatred to the original inhabitants of the continent. Abundant citations are available that reflect the derogatory views of white explorers and settlers about their Native American neighbors. In many cases, the whites regarded Native Americans as dirty, unintelligent, combative, secretive, undependable, and generally inferior in every regard. One writer from the time described his Native American neighbors as "some of the least improved of the human Species, without any Learning or Knowledge in any of the politer Arts of Life" ("Becoming American. The British Atlantic Colonies, 1690–1763" 2009)

Such views, of course, fully justified (in the minds of whites) virtually any form of violence against Native Americans. Among the many examples of this attitude that might be cited is the so-called Sand Creek Massacre of November 29, 1864. That event was perpetrated under the authority of

Colonel John Chivington, already famous for his Civil War battle against a Confederate supply train at Glorieta Pass. Toward the conclusion of the war, Chivington, also a former Methodist missionary, was under some amount of criticism for his failure to pursue battles against Native Americans in Colorado. He decided to remedy that defect by ordering an attack against an otherwise peaceful collection of Cheyenne and Arapahoe peoples in the Sand Creek area. When some of his soldiers expressed concern about an attack with little or no military justification, Chivington declared, "Damn any man who sympathizes with Indians! . . . I have come to kill Indians, and believe it is right and honorable to use any means under God's heavens to kill Indians. . . . Kill and scalp all, big and little; nits make lice" ("The Sand Creek Massacre—8 Hours That Changed the Great Plains Forever 2020"; "Who Is the Savage?" 2001; for more information about such events, see Fixico 2019).

As with most other forms of hate crime, offenses against individuals and groups of individuals have not disappeared from the nation's crime scene. Indeed, as table 1.2 shows, such crimes continue to be reported to the FBI's Criminal Justice Information Services Division. In fact, some observers have noted the sudden increase in hate crime rates in 2016 and 2017. One possible explanation of this trend, they say, is the less rigorous opposition to hate crimes expressed in President Donald Trump's social policies (including his demand to build a wall to keep Mexicans and Central Americans out of the United States).

On October 3, 2010, a group of nine Latino youths kidnaped and tortured three men, ages seventeen, seventeen, and thirty, for being gay. The gang, who called themselves the Latin King Goonies, sodomized the three with the handle of a plunger and a small baseball bat, burned them with cigarettes, whipped the older man with a chain, and engaged in other acts of torture for more than three hours. Five gang members were later sentenced to prison terms of two to six years, while the gang leader's sentence was set at fourteen years in prison (Long 2010).

Table 1.2 Hate Crimes among Select Groups, 2013–2018

Year	Native American	African American	Asian	Arab	Hispanic
2013	129	1856	135	n/a	331
2014	130	1621	140	n/a	299
2015	131	1745	111	37	299
2016	154	1739	113	51	344
2017	251	2013	131	102	427
2018	194	1943	148	82	485

Source: "Hate Crime Statistics." Federal Bureau of Investigation. Criminal Justice Information Services Division. Table 1 for all reports. https://ucr.fbi.gov/hate-crime/2013/2014/2015/2016/2017/2018.

Anti-LGBT violent crimes conducted by hate groups, such as this one, are rare. Most beatings, murders, and other crimes are carried out by individuals or small groups of (almost always) men, often on a spur-of-the-moment lark (Parker 2016). Much more commonly, anti-LGBT hate groups work through the legislative process and the media to convince the general public of the threats posed to American society by the existence of gay men, lesbians, bisexuals, and transgender individuals. The work of the Westboro Baptist Church, mentioned earlier, is an indication of the most extreme of these views: God hates LGBT people, and they have no place in the Christian religion. Other Christian groups in the United States have taken similar positions, although not generally with the force expressed by Westboro. In many cases, these groups warn not only of an LGBT person's separation from God but also of the practical, everyday harm that comes from a same-sex lifestyle. For example:

- "Gaining access to children has been a long-term goal of the homosexual movement."
- "[Homosexuality] . . . embodies a deep-seated hatred against true religion."
- "One of the primary goals of the homosexual rights movement is to abolish all age of consent laws and to eventually recognize pedophiles as the 'prophets' of a new sexual order."

- "A little-reported fact is that homosexual and lesbian relationships are far more violent than are traditional married households."
- "Homosexuality is a poor and dangerous choice, and has been proven to lead to a litany of health hazards to not only the individuals but also society as a whole."
- "Your lifestyle—homosexuality—is always and forever, objectively and demonstrably wrong. It is never good, natural, right or praiseworthy. . . . In almost every category—disease, depression, drug and alcohol abuse, and suicide—those who call themselves 'gay' live and die with consequences that have nothing gay, in the true sense of the word, about them" (as cited in Anti-LGBT n.d.).

Actions of this kind illustrate a form of hate crime other than physical attacks on an individual or a group of individuals: psychological attacks. Anyone who listens to the preceding arguments may be inclined to view gay men, lesbians, bisexuals, and transgender as somehow inherently inferior to non-LGBT people. Children and young adults in particular may grow up knowing that they are "different" from others around them. And harmful comments by hate groups only reinforce this sense of being different and, more important, being of less value than friends, neighbors, and even family members.

One reflection of this environment is the high rate of suicide and suicide ideation among young LGBT individuals. (The term *ideation* refers to occasions on which a person thinks seriously about or begins to plan her or his own suicide.) The 2016 Youth Risk Surveillance Survey, conducted by the Centers for Disease Control and Prevention (CDC) found that LGBT youth were about three times more likely to contemplate or attempt suicide than were non-LGBT youth. That ratio increased to five times for LGBT and non-LBGT youth who had actually attempted suicide. Among those whose suicide attempt failed, somewhere between four and six times as many LGBT youth as non-LBGT youth required medical attention for poisoning, overdose, physical injury, or other serious condition (Kann et al. 2016). Data on the rate of suicide deaths among LGBT youth are not available, but most estimates say that suicide is among the top three causes of death among such individuals. The language promulgated by hate groups about sexual orientation, then, almost certainly has harmful effects at least as serious, and often more so, than physical attacks.

There may be a tendency, at times, to end a discussion of hate groups at about this point. Having discussed sexism, anti-Semitism, anti-LGBT, and racism (to come), are there any other hate philosophies and hate crimes worth considering? The answer to that question is a strong "Yes, there are." In some cases, hate crimes against other groups do occur, but they sometimes "get lost" in general discussions of the topic. In other cases, documented cases of hate crimes occur, without any "us" being identified or discussed.

One of these so-called "invisible" hate crimes includes those committed against disabled individuals ("The Invisible Hate Crime" 2018). One researcher has referred to such crimes as "minute" because their numbers are so small compared to other types of hate crime (McMahon, West, and Lewis 2004). Yet, recent studies suggest that these numbers are on the rise. They rose from 128 cases in 2017 to 177 crimes in 2018, an increase of nearly 40 percent. Of the 2018 cases reported, 110 were against individuals with mental disabilities and 67 against individuals with physical disabilities. The vast majority of cases involved either simple or aggravated assault (Heasley 2019; "2018 Hate Crime Statistics" n.d., Table 4). These numbers are especially troubling because people with physical or mental disabilities generally have fewer ways of protecting themselves against abusers than do other victims of hate crimes.

An interesting trend reported among antidisabled hate crimes is the use of social media to conduct such crimes. Obviously, they are not in-person physical assaults, but they have the capacity to cause mental and emotional distress among victims. A 2019 study conducted in Great Britain found, for example, that the number of online hate crimes committed against disabled individuals rose from 235 in 2016–2017 to 313 in 2017–2018, an increase of about a third. One respondent to the survey explained that individuals on social media took photographs of her and posted them online. The comments that appeared, she said, are "nasty, hurtful and leave me feeling frightened and angry. There is no escaping this online abuse if I want to use social media" (Walker 2019).

One group of individuals affected by hate crimes—but seldom mentioned in that context—is the homeless. According to one recent study of the problem, 1,758 acts of hate-inspired violence were committed against homeless individuals between 1999 and 2017. Given the problems of collecting data on this issue, that number is probably at least half that of the true number of such events. Among those crimes, the majority (82) were racially motivated, followed by antisexual orientation (38 cases), antiethnicity bias (27 cases), antiethnic bias (27 cases), and antireligious motives (15 cases). Only two of the crimes could specifically be designated as antihomelessness ("Vulnerable to Hate" 2018).

Although not covered by most hate crime legislation, such crimes against the homeless tend to be unusually violent and disturbing. Some of the examples mentioned in the report quoted earlier include:

- An elderly man was found dead in San Francisco's Golden Gate Park after apparently having been beaten for three days.
- A sixty-year-old homeless man in Riverside, California was intentionally struck and killed by a car.
- A fifty-three-year-old homeless man in San Diego was burned to death in a city park.
- A forty-two-year-old man in Albuquerque was found decapitated and naked, with his genitals having been removed near a WalMart store.

- A homeless woman was stabbed and beaten to death with a bat in Corona, California.
- A San Antonio police officer lost his job because he gave a sandwich made of dog feces "for laughs" with fellow officers ("Vulnerable to Hate" 2018, 12–14).

The pattern of hate crimes against the homeless is fairly clear. In the vast majority of cases, the perpetrator of a hate crime is a male (96 percent of the time) under the age of thirty (67 percent of the time). The victims in such cases are generally males (87 percent of the time) over the age of forty (69 percent of the time) ("Vulnerable to Hate" 2018, 11). Perhaps the most striking feature of hate crimes against the homeless is that such crimes are not designated as "hate crimes" by either federal or state laws. In fact, the first state to amend its hate crime laws to include the homeless as victims was Maryland, which adopted the change in 2009. The District of Columbia made a similar change in the same year. As of 2020, six states (Alaska, Florida, Maine, Maryland, Rhode Island, and Washington), the District of Columbia, and Puerto Rico have included homelessness in the hate crime statutes. Those numbers have not changed since 2014. Few cities have also taken that step. A few governmental entities have also recognized the problem of hate crimes against the homeless without necessarily altering their laws to any significant degree. In 2004, for example, California established a requirement that all law enforcement personnel view a two-hour telecourse on "crimes against homeless persons and on how to deal effectively and humanely with homeless persons, including homeless persons with disabilities" (California Code, Penal Code—PEN § 13519.64 2020).

Hate Groups in American History

The preceding sections of this chapter have illustrated the fact that hate crime can take one of two quite different forms: formal, legal acts and actions by governmental and religious agencies to enforce a single understanding of who is and is not an authentic member of society (such as laws against same-sex behavior and minority religious denominations); informal, spontaneous events aroused among local groups often by specific objectionable acts, such as lynchings and mob attacks on "others." Often these two expressions of hate have combined to create organizations and events that are a mixture of these two conditions. Such is very much the case with the history of hate groups in the United States.

Hate groups were an almost inevitable consequence of the founding of the earliest colonies in the seventeenth century. The vast majority of settlers arrived on these shores with a clear-cut idea as to what the new nation would look like. That idea has often been described as Manifest Destiny, the belief that "America was to be governed by White Anglo-Saxon Protestants, as ordained by 'God Almighty'" (Petrosino 1999, 26). Under such circumstances, hate crimes were bound to occur.

Fears about such a future were expressed by some leading politicians of the time. In 1753, for example, Benjamin Franklin wrote to his friend Peter Collinson about the dangers posed by non-Anglo Saxon immigrants. They were, he warned, "generally of the most ignorant Stupid Sort of their own Nation." "Not being used to Liberty," he went on, "they know not how to make a modest use of it; and . . . they are not esteemed men till they have shewn their manhood by beating their mothers, so these seem to think themselves not free, till they can feel their liberty in abusing and insulting their Teachers" ("From Benjamin Franklin to Peter Collinson, 9 May 1753" 1753). Franklin had also expressed his views on the topic in an earlier pamphlet, "Observations Concerning the Increase of Mankind" (1751). In the pamphlet, he asked, "Why should Pennsylvania, founded by the English, become a Colony of Aliens, who will shortly be so numerous as to Germanize us instead of our Anglifying them, and will never adopt our Language or Customs, any more than they can acquire our Complexion" ("Observations Concerning the Increase of Mankind" 1751).

The problem with regard to immigrants was that there would always be some individuals or groups of individuals who held different beliefs, arguing, for example, for other forms of religious expression or equality of the sexes. In such cases, it was essential for governing sectarian and religious bodies to describe such views as "heretical" and to find ways of punishing those who held those views. Such "deviant" views also had to be punished by spontaneous uprisings of local citizens against those who held such views.

Immigrants from Italy and other countries in southern Europe arrived in the United States in the late nineteenth century. As late as the early nineteenth century, Italians represented a vanishingly small fraction of the U.S. population. Between 1820 and 1829 for example, only 430 individuals from Italy were granted permanent residence status in the United States (Chiarello and Kerwin 2014, Table 4, pp. 22). But those numbers began to rise, and with that increase came stronger objections to the presence of Italian Americans within the existing population. The primary reason for this problem, of course, was that Italians were (and are) primarily Catholic, a religious denomination that did not fit into the concept of Manifest Destiny. As Italian immigration grew to nearly 50,000 in 1870–1879, 267,660 in 1880–1889, 603,761 in 1890–1899, and 1,930,475 in 1900–1909, hate crimes increased against the immigrants and their now-citizen predecessors by leaps and bounds.

One of the most famous of hate crimes against Italian immigrants occurred on March 14, 1891. The murder of New Orleans police chief David Hennessey was thought to have been the work of a group of Sicilian immigrants, and a mob surged into the street looking for revenge. The mob was even more outraged when some of the suspected individuals were found innocent of the crime, and it took out its anger on a small group of local Italian inhabitants. It gathered a group of eleven members, some of whom may or may not have been guilty, and carried out a mass lynching. It was, at the time, one of the largest such hate crime acts in American history (Blakemore 2018).

Anti-Italian hate groups had actually been preceded by a half century by similar groups opposed to arriving immigrants from Ireland. Opposition to the Irish was based largely on the same fears expressed about the Italians: that the Roman Catholic Church would replace existing Protestant churches and organizations and turn the United States into a Papist country. As is generally the case, new Irish Americans were generally regarded as "stupid," "lazy," "disreputable," and, in general, not worthy of becoming American citizens. One of the best known symbols of the time was the plethora of signs displayed at a host of work environments: "No Irish need apply."

The Know Nothings

In 1849, the strong anti-Irish feelings provoked the establishment of a new hate group in New York City, called the Order of the Star Spangled Banner (OSSB). Members of the group had to swear to a vow of secrecy, restricting its own beliefs and activities to a relatively small group of individuals with such feelings. The driving force behind the new society was a belief described in one popular American history textbook that "in due time the 'alien riffraff' would 'establish' the Catholic church at the expense of Protestantism and would introduce 'popish idols'" (Klein 2019).

The OSSB had a short history as an independent organization, but it became one of the nuclei for the formation of another xenophobic, anti-Catholic, anti-immigrant group, known at first as the Know Nothing Party. The name of the group arose out of the OSSB's policy of requiring its members to reply "I know nothing about" when asked about its activities. In a short period of time, the Know Nothing Party attracted a large membership with chapters located in most large cities of the country. The principles on which the party was based are contained in the party platform for the election of 1856. Among the planks of that platform were the following:

- The repeal of all naturalization laws
- The reservation of the suffrage and right to hold public office only to those born on American soil
- Opposition to foreign influence over the policies and programs of the United States
- More specifically, opposition to the Roman Catholic Church and the influence on the Pope in the United States
- Stronger and better enforced immigration laws
- Implementation of programs for protecting and promoting the interests of Protestantism
- The exile to their home countries of all immigrants who were paupers
- Enforced and expanded reverence for the life and works of George Washington
- Formation of organizations specifically for the advancement of true American ideals
- Death to all individuals who attempt to exert foreign influence on American policies and programs (Miller 2020)

By the time this platform was written, the Know Nothing Party had grown rapidly and experienced considerable success throughout the nation. In the off-year elections of 1854, the party had won major victories throughout the state of Massachusetts, including local elections in Boston and Salem. The party also elected 52 new members to the U.S. House of Representatives (one of whom was elected Speaker of the House) and five new members to the U.S. Senate (Ainsworth and Harward 2019, 457). Because of their severe penchant for secrecy, the full extent of the party's victories were not, and probably never will be, known. For example, Robert T. Conrad was elected mayor of Philadelphia in 1854 as a member of the Whig Party.

After his election, he acknowledged that he belonged to the Know Nothing Party and intended to carry out its platform in the city (Weigley 1982, 369).

Emboldened by its successes, the Know Nothings decided to abandon much of the secrecy inherent in its organization and, in 1849, adopted a new name, the American Party. By 1856, the party felt confident enough about its appeal to the U.S. electorate that it chose as its presidential nominee Millard Fillmore, who had already served as President from 1850 to 1853. The choice proved to be disastrous because Fillmore rejected some of the key elements of the American Party platform. That fact and internal arguments over the question of slavery doomed the party to failure in the election of 1856. Fillmore won only 21.5 percent of the popular vote and eight electoral votes. Not much of a success from some standpoints, but an acknowledgment that one in five Americans at the time subscribed to the party's anti-immigrant, anti-Catholic, xenophobic program.

By 1860, the Know Nothing/American Party had largely disbanded. The vast majority of those previously affiliated with those parties migrated to another new American political party, the Republican Party. Those decisions were made largely because the Republicans were comfortable with most of the policies of the Know Nothings and Americans. The move was fortuitous for the Republicans, giving them the margin to take over the Congress in 1858 and the presidency in 1860 (Landis 2018).

The Ku Klux Klan

Among those individuals concerned about hate crimes, the group whose name most commonly comes to one's attention is probably the KKK. The KKK was founded in Pulaski, Tennessee, on December 24, 1865. The founding members were six former officers of the Confederate army, which had been defeated in the Civil War earlier that year. The first leader of the organization was General Nathan Bedford Forest, who is perhaps otherwise best known for his leadership of a massacre of African American Union soldiers at Fort Pillow, Tennessee, on April 12, 1864 (Glaze 2020). The name selected for the organization is thought to have come from the Greek word *kyklos* (κύκλος; "circle") combined with the English word *clan*. The name also appeared in later years in other forms, most commonly as the Ku Klos Klan. That name is memorialized today by an existing descendant of the original KKK, the Ku Klos Knights ("Welcome to the Ku Klux Klan. Home of the Ku Klos Knights" n.d.).

The driving force behind the creation of the KKK was a series of events known as the Reconstruction. That term refers to a period from the last years of the Civil War to the end of the 1870s, during which the U.S. government attempted to right some of the wrongs associated with slavery and to ensure that newly freed slaves would have the full and unfettered rights of all American citizens. The period was marked by the passage of four Reconstruction Acts, three in 1867 and one in 1868. The acts provided clear and strict provisions designed to provide slaves with these rights and to protect them against retaliation by defeated and disillusioned members of the Confederate states (Stoner 2019).

Members of the former Confederacy were, of course, not very enthusiastic (to say the least) about the restrictions posed by the Reconstruction Acts. The divide between former Union and Confederate adherents was made far more combative because the division was also one of political parties. The newly formed Republican Party was the primary force behind the Reconstruction movement, while largely Democratic administrations were in control of the defeated Southern states. The formation of the KKK, then, was simply one of the many mechanisms by which Democratic Southerners attempted to resist the Reconstructionist Republics of the North.

For the most part, the KKK was a loose organization, often chartered within a state for charitable, benevolent, patriotic, fraternal, and similar purposes. It operated, however, under a strict and formal system with four classes of membership: probationary, primary order, the Order of American Chivalry, and the Superior Order of Knighthood and Spiritual Philosophies. It was ruled by individuals in various positions of authority, known by names such as the Grand, or Imperial, Wizard, Grand Titan, Grand Dragon, Grand Giant, Grand Cyclops, and Grand Turk. The organization also had a complex and detailed system of signs and symbols, perhaps best known of which were the characteristic white robes and caps and burning crosses they used at ceremonies (Illinois Legislative Investigating Commission 1976; Lester and Wilson 1905).

In contrast to its seemingly pacifist principles and goals, the vast majority of the Klan's activities were violent actions, at first against African Americans, and later, against other "others" groups, such as Jews, Roman Catholics, and immigrants. No brief summary can properly describe the depths of their terrorism. As just one example, a group of five hundred masked Klan members attached the Union County jail in South Carolina in January 1871. There, they removed eight Black prisoners from their cells and lynched them in a mass demonstration. The event was not interrupted by local law officials and, according to some accounts, may even been aided by those officials (Stagg 1974).

The Klan has actually gone through three different manifestations, dating from 1865 to 1871, again in 1915 to 1944, and then from 1946 to the present day. The end of the first period came about for a number of reasons. First, the Klan and other anti-Reconstructionists achieved some degree of success. Many former slaves who had had some political success with election to state and federal office had been killed, discouraged from running for office, or otherwise removed from the political stage. The anti-Reconstructionist Democrats throughout the South achieved an ascendancy in the area that they would retain until the civil rights movement and its accompanying legislation changed those Blue states Red, in a transformation that continues today. But the Reconstruction Acts of 1867,

1868, and later dates provided the federal government with powerful means for bringing the Klan's worst practices under control (Brister 2011; Ku Klux Klan 2020).

The second phase of the KKK originated in 1915 when a group of white supremacists led by one William Joseph Simmons met at Stone Mountain, Georgia. A common view is that Simmons's viewing of D. W. Griffiths's powerful motion picture *The Birth of a Nation* drove him to revive the anti-Black organization of the Reconstruction years. In its reincarnation, the Klan became a larger and more widespread organization. Although no dependable data exist, experts have estimated that, at its height, it had somewhere between three and eight million members in every state of the Union. The Klan also broadened its hate campaign beyond that of race to include Roman Catholics, Jews, most classes of immigrants, and organized labor. The organization also extended its appeal to groups beyond white men, developing special programs for women and children. Eventually, there developed a parallel organization to the men's movement, known as the Women's Ku Klux Klan or Ladies of the Invisible Empire. Adopting values of the Progressive movement in many regards, these groups continued to display powerful themes of racism, nationalism, and xenophobia (Blee [1991] 2009; Feldman 2003).

Children and young adults were also seen as ripe prospects for the new Klan. Some adult members of the group brought infants to be baptized at Klan events, while specific clubs and other groups were created for the very young and young adults. One such popular group was the Tri-K-Klub, which had its own theme song, slogans, and other ceremonies and symbols. An especially popular event was an annual Kool Koast Kamp, held in a coastal city such as Atlantic City or Palm Beach strictly for young members of the Klan (Onion 2013).

Enthusiasm for the Klan began to fall in the late 1930s, partly as a result of the Great Depression and the warning signs of a new world war in Europe. However, not long after that war ended, a third phase of the Klan began to appear. One powerful motive for this new iteration of the organization was the arrival of the civil rights movement, which reached its ascendancy in the 1960s. As demands for equality among the races grew, efforts to block such a drive arose in the South. Unlike its predecessor, the third phase of the Klan was largely a local phenomenon, often created in cities and towns with at least the acquiescence, and often the encouragement, of local government officials and law enforcement teams. Although united in a common philosophy of racial (and often religious) solidarity, these groups most commonly existed as individual associations with names such as the Alliance of American Klans, American Christian Knights of the Ku Klux Klan, East Coast Knights of the True Invisible Empire, Loyal White Knights of the Ku Klux Klan, Patriotic Brigade Knights of the Ku Klux Klan, and Church of the National Knights of the Ku Klux Klan (Ku Klux Klan n.d.). These groups today tend to exist in one or a few chapters in different communities, usually with a relatively small (but unannounced) membership.

With the movement toward greater equality in all fields in the United States over the past half century, these small, individual associations have largely constituted the third phase of the Klan's existence. However, at its height in the mid-twentieth century, the organization was able to claim a significant number of well-known and often highly respected lawyers, physicians, politicians at all levels, and, in general, members in good standing in the wider community. Among those individuals who are known or suspected to have been members of the Klan are federal and state senators and representatives, governors and mayors, members of the judiciary, and others in position of authority (Stockton 2015).

Violence against Aid Workers

One form of violence by hate groups that is especially difficult to understand involves actions against aid workers. An aid worker is someone who works for a charitable organization devoted to helping others, especially one who works in an international situation or conflict zone. An example of an aid worker is someone (usually) from a developed nation who travels to a (usually) developing nation to help individuals, governments, and other organizations there with any number of possible problems, such as developing more efficient agricultural methods, helping with a medical emergency, contributing to an improvement in the nation's educational system, or helping officials to develop more efficient systems of governance.

Aid workers are typically individuals who are willing or eager to share their own expertise with less fortunate individuals who can benefit from new knowledge or skills. A well-known form of this type of aid work in the United States is the Peace Corps. The Peace Corps was created by the executive order of President John F. Kennedy on March 1, 1961. The Peace Corps' mission was "to promote world peace and friendship by fulfilling three goals:

- To help the people of interested countries in meeting their need for trained men and women
- To help promote a better understanding of Americans on the part of the peoples served
- To help promote a better understanding of other peoples on the part of Americans." (Peace Corps 2020)

As of late 2019, there were 7,334 volunteers serving in sixty-one countries (all volunteers were withdrawn in 2020 because of the coronavirus pandemic) ("Fast Facts" 2020).

Examples of hate crimes against aid workers are abundant. Over the years, for example, Peace Corps volunteers have experienced a range of personal and property crimes, ranging from theft to aggravated assault. The most common of these events in 2018 was theft, reported by 28 percent of all departing volunteers in that year. More serious crimes included aggravated sexual assault and rape (5 percent for each category), aggravated physical assault (2 percent), and kidnapping (1 percent) ("2018 Annual Report of Crimes against Volunteers" 2019).

One of the most distressing examples of attacks by hate groups on aid workers involves the world's health agencies' effort to eradicate polio. Once one of the world's most serious and widespread diseases, polio has been all but eradicated in all countries with the exception of Afghanistan, Nigeria, and Pakistan. Health agencies are working to clear the disease in these three countries by sending volunteers across the nation teaching about polio and providing free vaccinations against the disease. In all three of these countries, hate groups have fought back against this effort by harassing and even killing volunteer workers. For example, three volunteers were shot to death in one week in 2019 in the city of Islamabad, Pakistan. The perpetrators were thought to be members of "Islamist militants and hard-line clerics" who believed that vaccination was a Western plot to sterilize Muslim children (Janjua 2019).

Hate violence against workers, in fact, appears to be a simple, if terrible, fact of life in aid programs. The Aid Worker Security Database maintains annual records of the number and type of violent acts performed each year. The most recent report from the organization contains data on eleven different variables (such as number of incidents, number of workers injured, total killed, and total kidnapped) from 2008 to 2018. In the last of those years, there were 226 reported and verified incidents involving 405 aid workers, including 131 murders, 131 other injuries, and 130 kidnappings. These numbers varied substantially over the ten-year period covered by the report ("Major Attacks on Aid Workers. Summary Statistics 2008–2018" 2020; the report also includes much more data on a variety of features of hate attacks against aid workers).

An increase in hate crimes against aid workers occurred in 2020 with the appearance of the coronavirus pandemic. Nurses in Mexico, for example, reported on the risks they faced in testing people for the virus and then for treating those infected with the disease. These risks included public taunting, removal from public modes of transportation, drenching with bleach on the streets, and other forms of verbal and physical harassment.

The perpetrators in such attacks appeared to be hate groups who (wrongly) believed that nurses, doctors, and other health workers were actually spreading the disease among the general population (Semple 2020). As long as lack of knowledge about the benefits of aid workers ring to a community and fear of such workers in general exist, hate crimes against aid workers are likely to continue (Nebehay 2020).

Trends in Hate Group Activity

One might like to have a report on hate group activities over the past years or decades. Are there more or fewer hate groups today than there were a decade ago? Were they more or less active then than they are today? How have their policies and practices changed over the years?

Unfortunately, data such as these are very difficult to come by. First, most hate groups are secretive organizations that do not publicize or report the number of members they have, the demographics of those members, the activities the group undertakes, its financial resources, and so on. In fact, there are only two major national organizations that attempt to keep track of the most basic information, namely, the number and names of hate groups in the United States in any one year. One of these groups is the SPLC, which has been conducting such research since 1999. In its first year of this research, SPLC identified 457 organizations that they could call hate groups. The number grew gradually and regularly until 2011, when the center listed 1,018 hate groups. After a short drop-off over the next three years (to a low of 784 in 2014), the number of hate groups listed grew to 1,020 in 2018, the highest number ever recorded by SPLC (see table 1.3). That number then fell substantially to 940 groups in 2019 ("The Year in Hate and Extremism 2019" 2020, 11). Although general descriptions of many of those groups are available on the SPLC website, those data are incomplete and do not cover demographic information ("Hate Groups Reach Record High" 2019).

Table 1.3 Trends in Hate Groups in the United States

Year	Number of Groups
1999	457
2000	602
2001	676
2002	708
2003	751
2004	762
2005	803
2006	844
2007	888
2008	926
2009	932
2010	1,002
2011	1,018
2012	1,007
2013	939
2014	784
2015	892
2016	917
2017	954
2018	1,020

Source: "Hate Groups Reach Record. High." 2019. Southern Poverty Law Center. https://www.splcenter.org/news/2019/02/19/hate-groups-reach-record-high.

Another organization that collects hate group data is the Anti-Defamation League (ADL). According to the most recent iteration of that data, there are 1,215 organizations that can be called "hate groups" as per ADL standards ("ADL H.E.A.T. Map™" 2020; see "All States 2018," "Download Selected Data"). ADL also keeps detailed records of the number of anti-Semitic hate crimes committed annually but provides no information on the number of anti-Semitic groups ("Audit of Anti-Semitic Incidents: Year in Review 2018" 2020).

Conclusion

Mention of the term "hate group" tends to provoke images of relatively well-known, tightly organized, very active groups of individuals with animosities toward specific groups of individuals, such as those of a different gender, skin color, ethnicity, nationality, or sexual orientation. As this chapter has attempted to show, such a definition does not begin to cover the range of hate activities that are and have always been a feature of human societies. Specific "hate groups" can range from worldwide religious dominations and dominant nation-states to informal, spontaneous groups of a handful of individuals with a very specific crime in mind. Despite this vast range of difference among "hate groups," certain common themes occur among them all. Perhaps the most basic of these is the conflict of views about our own family, friends, and neighbors ("us") and those who are different in any number of characteristics. But hate groups have other features that they tend to share in common, such as the way they form, the activities they hope to carry out, and the mechanisms by which they eventually fall apart and disband. Some of these common themes are the topic of chapter 2 of this book.

References

"ADL H.E.A.T. Map™." 2020. Anti Defamation League. https://www.adl.org/education-and-resources/resource-knowledge-base/adl-heat-map.

Ainsworth, Scott H., and Brian M. Harward, eds. 2019. *Political Groups, Parties, and Organizations That Shaped America*. Santa Barbara, CA: ABC-CLIO.

Alexander, Scott. 2014. "I Can Tolerate Anything but the Outgroup." Slate Star Codex. https://slatestarcodex.com/2014/09/30/i-can-tolerate-anything-except-the-outgroup/.

"Anti-LGBT." n.d. Southern Poverty Law Center. https://www.splcenter.org/fighting-hate/extremist-files/ideology/anti-lgbtq.

"Audit of Anti-Semitic Incidents: Year in Review 2018." 2020. Anti-Defamation League. https://www.adl.org/audit2018.

"Becoming American. The British Atlantic Colonies, 1690–1763." 2009. National Humanities Center. http://nationalhumanitiescenter.org/pds/becomingamer/peoples/text3/indianscolonists.pdf

Behringer, Wolfgang. 2008. *Witches and Witch-hunts: A Global History*. Cambridge, UK: Polity Press.

Blakemore, Erin. 2018. "The Grisly Story of America's Largest Lynching." History. https://www.history.com/news/the-grisly-story-of-americas-largest-lynching.

Blakemore, Erin. 2019. "The 1981 Lynching that Bankrupted an Alabama KKK." History. https://www.history.com/news/kkk-lynching-mother-justice.

Blee, Kathleen M. (1991) 2009. *Women of the Klan: Racism and Gender in the 1920s*. Berkeley and London: University of California Press.

Brentlinger, Rick. 2019. "Kill Gays Message from Hate-filled Baptist Kooks!" GayChristian 101. https://www.gaychristian101.com/Kill-Gays.html.

"A Brief Chronology of Antisemitism." 2015. The Jewish Agency for Israel. http://archive.jewishagency.org/jewish-history/content/36936.

Brister, Paul D. 2011. "Ku Klux Rising: Toward an Understanding of American Right Wing Terrorist Campaigns." Dissertation, Naval Postgraduate School. https://apps.dtic.mil/dtic/tr/fulltext/u2/a551880.pdf.

Brons, Lajos. 2015. "Othering: An Analysis." *Transcience* 6 (1): 69–90. https://www2.hu-berlin.de/transcience/Vol6_No1_2015_69_90.pdf.

Burke, Jason, and Samuel Okiror. 2019. "Ugandan MPs Press for Death Penalty for Homosexual Acts." *The Guardian*.

https://www.theguardian.com/world/2019/oct/15/ugandan-mps-press-for-death-penalty-for-homosexual-acts.

California Code, Penal Code—PEN § 13519.64. 2020. FindLaw. https://codes.findlaw.com/ca/penal-code/pen-sect-13519-64.html.

Carrigan, William D., and Clive Webb. 2003. "The Lynching of Persons of Mexican Origin or Descent in the United States, 1848 to 1928." *Journal of Social History* 37 (2): 411–438. https://www.sjsu.edu/people/ruma.chopra/courses/H170_MW9am_S12/s1/B2_Lynching_Mexicans.pdf.

Chiarello, Leonir Mario, and Donald Kerwin, eds. 2014. "International Migration, U.S. Immigration Law and Civil Society: From the Pre-Colonial Era to the 113th Congress." Scalabrini International Migration Network Inc. http://simn-global.org/wp-content/uploads/2018/10/InternationalMigration-US-Policies.pdf.

"Crime and Punishment in a Triangular Perspective: Assessing Theocracy and the Transfer of Culture." n.d. Project Albion. http://projetalbion.online.fr/memoire/crime1.html.

Deane, Jennifer Kolpacoff. 2011. *A History of Medieval Heresy and Inquisition*. Lanham, MD: Rowman & Littlefield.

Donaldson, Stephen R., et al. 2017. *The Encyclopedia of Homosexuality*. Abingdon, Oxon, UK: Routledge.

Dunbar-Ortiz, Roxanne. 2016. "Yes, Native Americans Were the Victims of Genocide." History News Network. http://historynewsnetwork.org/article/162804.

"The Eight Wars of Religion (1562–1598)." 2020. The Protestant Museum. https://www.museeprotestant.org/en/notice/the-eight-wars-of-religion-1562-1598/.

Esquivel, Paloma. 2019. "El Paso Massacre Was Just the Latest in Long Line of Anti-Latino Violence in the U.S." *Los Angeles Times*. https://www.latimes.com/california

/story/2019-08-16/el-paso-massacre-timeline-of-anti-latino-violence-in-united-states.

"Euthanasia Program." 2020. United States Holocaust Memorial Museum. https://encyclopedia.ushmm.org/content/en/article/euthanasia-program.

"Fast Facts." 2020. Peace Corps. https://www.peacecorps.gov/news/fast-facts/.

Feldman, Glen. 2003. "Keepers of the Hearth: Women, the Klan, and Traditional Family Values." In Bruce L. Clayton and John Salmond, eds. *Lives Full of Struggle and Triumph*. Gainesville, FL: University Press of Florida.

Fixico, Donald L. 2019. "When Native Americans Were Slaughtered in the Name of 'Civilization.'" History. https://www.history.com/news/native-americans-genocide-united-states.

Friedman, Uri. 2017. "What Is a Nativist? And is Donald Trump One?" *The Atlantic*. https://www.theatlantic.com/international/archive/2017/04/what-is-nativist-trump/521355/.

"From Benjamin Franklin to Peter Collinson, 9 May 1753." 1753. Founders Online. National Archives. https://founders.archives.gov/documents/Franklin/01-04-02-0173.

Gambetti, Sandra. 2009. "The Alexandrian Riots of 38 C.E. and the Persecution of the Jews. A Historical Reconstruction." *Supplements to the Journal for the Study of Judaism* 135. https://doi.org/10.1163/ej.9789004138469.i-336

Glaze, Robert L. 2020. "Fort Pillow Massacre." Encyclopedia Britannica. https://www.britannica.com/topic/prisoner-of-war.

"Global Conflict Tracker." 2020. Council on Foreign Relations. https://www.cfr.org/interactive/global-conflict-tracker/conflict/rohingya-crisis-myanmar.

"The Great Heresies." 2020. Catholic Answers. https://www.catholic.com/tract/the-great-heresies.

"Hate Crime Data Collection Guidelines and Training Manual." 2015. Criminal Justice Information Services (CJIS). Division Uniform Crime Reporting (UCR) Program. Federal Bureau of Investigation. https://ucr.fbi.gov/hate-crime-data-collection-guidelines-and-training-manual.pdf.

"Hate Groups Reach Record High." 2019. Southern Poverty Law Center. https://www.splcenter.org/news/2019/02/19/hate-groups-reach-record-high.

"Hate on Display™ Hate Symbols Database." 2020. ADL. https://www.adl.org/hate-symbols.

Heasley, Shaun. 2019. "Disability-Related Hate Crimes Up Sharply, FBI Data Shows." *Disability Scoop*. https://www.disabilityscoop.com/2019/11/14/disability-related-hate-crimes-up-sharply-fbi-data/27454/.

History.com Editors. 2018. "Native American History Timeline." History. https://www.history.com/topics/native-american-history/native-american-timeline.

Ifill, Sherrilyn A. 2003. "Creating a Truth and Reconciliation Commission for Lynching" *Law & Inequality: A Journal of Theory and Practice* 21 (2): 263–311. http://scholarship.law.umn.edu/lawineq/vol21/iss2/2.

Illinois Legislative Investigating Commission. 1976. "Ku Klux Klan." https://www.ncjrs.gov/pdffiles1/Digitization/46433NCJRS.pdf.

"The Invisible Hate Crime." 2018. Southern Poverty Law Center. https://www.splcenter.org/fighting-hate/intelligence-report/2018/invisible-hate-crime.

Janjua, Haroon. 2019. "Polio Vaccinator Is Shot and Killed in Pakistan." *The New York Times*. https://www.nytimes.com/2019/04/25/world/asia/polio-vaccine-pakistan.html.

Jendryke, Michael, and Stephen C. McClure. 2019. "Mapping Crime—Hate Crimes and Hate Groups in the USA: A Spatial Analysis with Gridded Data." *Applied Geography* 111: 102072. https://doi.org/10.1016/j.apgeog.2019.102072.

Kann, Laura, et al. 2016. "Sexual Identity, Sex of Sexual Contacts, and Health-Related Behaviors Among Students in Grades 9–12—United States and Selected Sites, 2015." *MMWR Centers for Disease Control and Prevention* 65 (9). https://www.cdc.gov/mmwr/volumes/65/ss/pdfs/ss6509.pdf.

Klein, Christopher. 2019. "When America Despised the Irish: The 19th Century's Refugee Crisis." History. https://www.history.com/news/when-america-despised-the-irish-the-19th-centurys-refugee-crisis.

"Ku Klux Klan." n.d. Southern Poverty Law Center. https://www.splcenter.org/fighting-hate/extremist-files/ideology/ku-klux-klan.

"Ku Klux Klan." 2020. History. https://www.history.com/topics/reconstruction/ku-klux-klan.

Kyle, Jordan, and Limor Gultchin. 2018. "Populists in Power around the World." Tony Blair Institute for Global Change. https://institute.global/sites/default/files/articles/Populists-in-Power-Around-the-World-.pdf.

Landis, Michael Todd. 2018. "How the Know Nothing Party Turned Nativism into a Political Strategy." Zocalo Public Square. https://www.zocalopublicsquare.org/2018/07/12/know-nothing-party-turned-nativism-political-strategy/ideas/essay/.

Lee, Erika. 2015. *The Making of Asian America: A History*. New York: Simon & Schuster Paperbacks.

Lester, J. C., and D. L. Wilson. 1905. *Ku Klux Klan: its Origin, Growth and Disbandment*. New York and Washington, DC: Neale Publishing Company. https://archive.org/details/kukluxklanitsor01flemgoog/page/n11

/mode/2up. Available in 2010 electronic version at http://www.gutenberg.org/files/31819/31819-h/31819-h.htm.

Li, Weihua. 2019. "Why Police Struggle to Report One of The Fastest-Growing Hate Crimes." *The Marshall Project*. https://www.themarshallproject.org/2019/11/26/why-police-struggle-to-report-one-of-the-fastest-growing-hate-crimes.

Long, Colleen. 2010. "Experts: Gang Taboos Fueled NYC Gay Bias Attack." *NBC News*. http://www.nbcnews.com/id/39691446/ns/us_news-crime_and_courts/t/experts-gang-taboos-fueled-nyc-gay-bias-attacks.

"Lynching in America: Confronting the Legacy of Racial Terror." 3rd ed. 2017. Equal Justice Institute. https://eji.org/wp-content/uploads/2019/10/lynching-in-america-3d-ed-080219.pdf.

Maizland, Lindsay. 2019. "China's Repression of Uighurs in Xinjiang." Council on Foreign Relations. https://www.cfr.org/backgrounder/chinas-repression-uighurs-xinjiang.

"Major Attacks on Aid Workers. Summary Statistics (2008–2018)." 2020. The Aid Worker Security Database. https://aidworkersecurity.org/incidents/report/summary.

Matthews, Albert. 1904. "The Term Lynch Law." *Modern Philology* 2 (2): 173–195.

McCoy, Micah. 2019. "Crossing the Line." ACLU New Mexico. https://www.aclu-nm.org/en/news/crossing-line.

McMahon, Brian T., Steven L. West, and Allen N. Lewis. 2004. "Hate Crimes and Disability in America." *Rehabilitation Counseling Bulletin* 47 (2): 66–75. https://doi.org/10.1177/00343552030470020101

Mendos, Lucas Ramón. 2019. "State-Sponsored Homophobia 2019." Geneva: LGA. https://ilga.org/downloads/ILGA_State_Sponsored_Homophobia_2019.pdf.

Miller, Laura M. 2020. "American Party Platform (1856)." Encyclopedia.com. https://www.encyclopedia.com/history

/dictionaries-thesauruses-pictures-and-press-releases
/american-party-platform-1856.

Monter, William. 2005. "Inquisition, The: The Inquisition in the Old World." Encyclopedia.com. https://www.encyclopedia.com/environment/encyclopedias-almanacs-transcripts-and-maps/inquisition-inquisition-old-world.

Mowczka, Marge. 2013. "Misogynistic Quotations from Church Fathers and Reformers." https://margmowczko.com/misogynist-quotes-from-church-fathers/.

Mulholland, Sean E. 2013. "White Supremacist Groups and Hate Crime." *Public Choice* 157 (1–2): 91–113. https://doi.org/10.1007/s11127-012-0045-7.

Nebehay, Stephanie. 2020. "Nurses must Be Protected from Abuse during Coronavirus Pandemic: WHO, Nursing Groups." Reuters. https://www.reuters.com/article/us-health-coronavirus-nurses/nurses-must-be-protected-from-abuse-during-coronavirus-pandemic-who-nursing-groups-idUSKBN21O317.

Norton, Rictor. (2002) 2012. "A History of Homophobia." http://rictornorton.co.uk/homopho1.htm.

"Observations Concerning the Increase of Mankind." 1751. Founders Online. National Archives. https://founders.archives.gov/documents/Franklin/01-04-02-0080.

Onion, Rebecca. 2013. "Going to Summer Kamp with the KKK." Slate. https://slate.com/human-interest/2013/03/the-ku-klux-klan-a-brochure-for-the-organization-s-summer-resort-photo.html.

Olzak, Susan. 1990. "The Political Context of Competition: Lynching and Urban Racial Violence, 1882–1914." *Social Forces* 69 (2): 395–421.

Oudekerk, Barbara. 2019. "Hate Crime Statistics." Bureau of Justice Statistics. https://www.bjs.gov/content/pub/pdf/hcs1317pp.pdf.

#Outlawed: "The Love That Dare Not Speak its Name." 2020. Human Rights Watch. http://internap.hrw.org/features/features/lgbt_laws/.

Parker, R. J. 2016. *Killing the Rainbow: Violence against LGBT*. Toronto, ON: RJ Parker.

Peace Corps. 2020. https://www.peacecorps.gov/about/.

Petrosino, Carolyn. 1999. "Connecting the Past to the Future: Hate Crime in America." *Journal of Contemporary Criminal Justice* 15 (1): 22–47. https://www.researchgate.net/publication/249713553_Connecting_the_Past_to_the_FutureHate_Crime_in_America.

Pfaelzer, Jean. 2007. "*Driven out: The Hidden War against Chinese America*. New York: Random House.

Poliakov, Léon. (1955/1975) 2003. *The History of Anti-Semitism*. 4 vols. State College: University of Pennsylvania Press.

Powell, John A., and Stephen Menendian. 2016. "The Problem of Othering: Towards Inclusiveness and Belonging." *Othering and Belonging* 1: 14–39. http://www.otheringandbelonging.org/the-problem-of-othering/.

Raspe, Lucia. 1998. "Manetho on the Exodus: A Reappraisal." *Jewish Studies Quarterly* 5 (2): 124–155.

Rea, Tom. 2014. "The Rock Springs Massacre." WyoHistory.org. https://www.wyohistory.org/encyclopedia/rock-springs-massacre.

Rushin, Stephen, and Griffin Sims Edwards. 2018. "The Effect of President Trump's Election on Hate Crimes." *SSRN Electronic Journal*. https://papers.ssrn.com/sol3/papers.cfm?abstract_id=3102652. (Access requires free enrollment at site.)

Ryan, Matt E., and Peter T. Leeson. 2011. "Hate Groups and Hate Crime." *International Review of Law and Economics*

31 (4): 256–262. https://doi.org/10.1016/j.irle.2011.08.004.

"The Sand Creek Massacre—8 Hours That Changed the Great Plains Forever." 2020. National Park Service (video). https://www.nps.gov/sand/index.htm.

Semple, Kirk. 2020. "'Afraid to Be a Nurse': Health Workers under Attack." *The New York Times*. https://www.nytimes.com/2020/04/27/world/americas/coronavirus-health-workers-attacked.html.

Sessions, David. 2017. "'Banished' Lauren Drain on Growing Up in the Westboro Baptist Church." *Daily Beast*. https://www.thedailybeast.com/banished-lauren-drain-on-growing-up-in-the-westboro-baptist-church.

Shore, Raphael. 2020. aish.com. https://www.aish.com/sem/wtj/.

Skinner, B. F. 2011. "Hating Gays Does not Make us a Hate Group." The Daily Kos. https://m.dailykos.com/stories/2011/04/03/963112/-Hating-gays-does-not-make-us-a-hate-group.

Smead, Howard. 1986. *Blood Justice: The Lynching of Mack Charles Parker*. New York: University Press.

Stabile, Susan J. 2016. "Othering and the Law." *University of St. Thomas Law Journal* 12 (2): 381–410.

Stagg, J. C. A. 1974. "The Problem of Klan Violence: The South Carolina Up-Country, 1868–1871." *Journal of American Studies* 8 (3): 303–318.

Stein, Stuart. 2000. "Statements by Hitler and Senior Nazis Concerning Jews and Judaism." Learning, Teaching and Researching on the Internet. https://phdn.org/archives/www.ess.uwe.ac.uk/genocide/statements.htm.

Stockton, Richard. 2015. "The Invisible Empire: Famous KKK Members in American Politics." All That's Interesting. https://allthatsinteresting.com/famous-kkk-members.

Stoner, James R. 2019. "(Why) Did Reconstruction Fail? Legislating and Constitutionalizing Civil Rights." *Perspectives on Political Science* 48 (4): 224–233.

"2018 Annual Report of Crimes against Volunteers." 2019. Peace Corps. https://s3.amazonaws.com/files.peacecorps.gov/documents/open-government/Annual_Report_of_Crimes_Against_Volunteers_2018.pdf.

"2018 Hate Crime Statistics." n.d. Federal Bureau of Investigation. https://ucr.fbi.gov/hate-crime/2018.

"2017 Hate Crime Statistics." n.d. Federal Bureau of Investigation. https://ucr.fbi.gov/hate-crime/2017/topic-pages/tables/table-1.xls.

"Vulnerable to Hate: A Survey of Bias-Motivated Violence against People Experiencing Homelessness in 2016–2017." 2018. National Coalition for the Homeless. https://nationalhomeless.org/wp-content/uploads/2019/01/hate-crimes-2016-17-final_for-web2.pdf.

Walker, Amy. 2019. "Online Hate Crime against Disabled People Rises by a Third." *The Guardian*. https://www.theguardian.com/society/2019/may/10/online-hate-against-disabled-people-rises-by-a-third.

Weigley, R. F. 1982. *Philadelphia: A 300-Year History*. New York: W.W. Norton & Company.

"Welcome to the Ku Klux Klan. Home of the Ku Klos Knights." n.d. http://www.kuklosknights.com/.

"Westboro Baptist Church: Warriors for God?" 2013. ABC News (video). https://www.youtube.com/watch?v=RUAH50hSCUg.

"What Was the Death Toll During the Inquisition?" 2017. History. Stack Exchange. https://history.stackexchange.com/questions/39443/what-was-the-death-toll-during-the-inquisition.

"Who Is the Savage?" 2001. PBS. https://www.pbs.org/weta/thewest/program/episodes/four/whois.htm.

"Who Were the Victims?" 2020. United States Holocaust Memorial Museum. https://encyclopedia.ushmm.org/content/en/article/mosaic-of-victims-an-overview.

"The Year in Hate and Extremism 2019." 2020. Southern Poverty Law Center. https://www.splcenter.org/sites/default/files/yih_2020_final.pdf.

2 Problems, Controversies, and Solutions

What is a hate group?
After spending more than fifteen thousand words in chapter 1 of this book talking about "hate groups," that may seem like a strange question to ask. Yet, the question is far more complex and more consequential than it may seem at first glance.

Defining Hate Groups

Many individuals and organizations have tried to develop their own definition of a hate group. These include researchers in the field of hate crimes and related topics, as well as law enforcement, civil rights, and other associations (see Blazak 2009 for a good discussion of this problem). As noted in chapter 1, the FBI defines a hate group as "an organization whose primary purpose is to promote animosity, hostility, and malice against persons of or with a race, religion, disability, sexual orientation, ethnicity, gender, or gender identity which differs from that of the members or the organization, e.g., the Ku Klux Klan, American Nazi Party" ("Hate Crime Data Collection Guidelines and Training Manual" 2015). In actual practice, the agency focuses much more on hate *crimes* than on hate *groups*.

A neo-Nazi skinhead attends a rally near the Capitol building in Washington, DC. "White power" skinheads such as neo-Nazis define themselves by a hatred of immigrants, Jews, and other minorities. (Rrodrickbeiler/ Dreamstime)

The two organizations most commonly associated with the study of hate groups are the Anti-Defamation League (ADL) and the Southern Poverty Law Center (SPLC), both of which use definitions similar to those of the FBI's:

ADL: "An organization whose goals and activities are primarily or substantially based on a shared antipathy towards people of one or more other different races, religions, ethnicities/nationalities/national origins, genders, and/or sexual identities. The mere presence of bigoted members in a group or organization is typically not enough to qualify it as a hate group; the group itself must have some hate-based orientation/purpose" ("Hate Groups" 2020).

SPLC: "An organization that—based on its official statements or principles, the statements of its leaders, or its activities—has beliefs or practices that attack or malign an entire class of people, typically for their immutable characteristics. We do not list individuals as hate groups, only organizations" ("Frequently Asked Questions about Hate Groups" 2020).

But defining a hate group is only the first, and not necessarily the most difficult, problem that scholars and organizations face. How does one decide if any one group in real life fits the conditions of any one of these definitions? For example, consider a group of evangelic Christians for whom the words of the Bible are accepted as entirely true in every respect. Such groups often believe that God has placed a prohibition on same-sex activities. Those groups may feel that they have an obligation to teach that such activities are sinful and harmful to those who practice them and to the general society. According to one interpretation of the definition of hate groups, such groups would fit that category because they "malign an entire class of people," those who are gay, lesbian, bisexual, and transgender. So, both ADL and SPLC list groups with such beliefs as hate groups.

But the groups themselves quite obviously object to that categorization. For example, in 2017, a Ft. Lauderdale, Florida, church group, D. James Kennedy Ministries, sued SPLC for religious discrimination because of its listing as a hate group.

That listing, the group said, prevented it from receiving certain economic rights and privileges (such as monetary grants) because of its being labeled as a hate group. (The church included Amazon in its suit because the company refused to allow the church to participate in its AmazonSmile program.) In promoting its views about same-sex activities, the church said, it was doing nothing more nor less than making its religious beliefs known and, therefore, was being persecuted for those beliefs. In 2019, a district judge in Florida rejected the suit, saying that SPLC was simply exercising its First Amendment rights of free speech in making its hate group designations. (He did not rule as to whether the church group was or was not a hate group.) The church then appealed that decision to the appeals level, with no decision from that appeal having been reached as of late 2020 (Man 2019).

Groups assigned the "hate" label by ADL or SPLC may object to this classification for reasons other than religious prejudice. One example is the lawsuit filed by the Center for Immigration Studies (CIS) against officers of the SPLC in 2019. CIS claimed that SPLC's listing as an anti-immigrant hate group had done irreparable harm to its fundraising capabilities. It said that it is the nation's only "independent, non-partisan, non-profit research organization . . . devoted exclusively to research and policy analysis of the economic, social, demographic, fiscal, and other impacts of immigration on the United States" ("Center for Immigration Studies Files a Civil RICO Lawsuit against the President of Southern Poverty Law Center" 2019). It claimed that the SPLC listing reflected a disagreement with CIS's work, findings, and public positions rather than any type of "hatred" by the group against immigrants themselves (Krikorian 2019). U.S. District Judge Amy Berman Jackson rejected the case because she said it did not fit into the provisions of the law under which it was filed, the Racketeer Influenced and Corrupt Organizations (RICO) Act (Kunzelman 2020).

Perhaps the most thorough and thoughtful analysis of the categorization systems used by ADL and SPLC can be found in a recent book, *The Manipulators*, by Daily Caller investigative reporter Peter Hasson. The main theme of Hasson's book is the way in which so-called Big Tech companies, such as Amazon, Facebook, Google, and Twitter, have adopted "a disturbing pattern of hostility to and silencing of conservative voices, which he links to an all-encompassing, far-left corporate monoculture" (From a review of the book at Lehman 2020). Lehman argues that hate group categorizations by the SPLC are not even intended to be fair and unbiased evaluations of the groups involved, but part of the overall scheme by liberal groups to denigrate and demonize the conservative right (Hasson 2020, 125–131).

At times, the ambiguity of the term *hate group* becomes particularly apparent. During the 2016 presidential campaign in the United States, for example, some of the comments made by candidate Donald Trump were taken to be racist, Islamophobic, or anti-immigrant. At least some members of some hate groups interpreted these comments as being supportive of their own goals and platforms. Well-known leaders of extremist hate groups, such as David Duke, Richard Spencer, and William Johnson, were all ecstatic by Trump's election, seeing the result as a validation of their own efforts. Duke, a former grand wizard of the Ku Klux Klan (KKK), explained his support for Trump after the Charlottesville, Virginia riots of August 2017. "We are going to fulfill the promises of Donald Trump," he said. "That's what we believed in. That's why we voted for Donald Trump, because he said he's going to take our country back" (Nelson 2017). Spencer, president of the National Policy Institute, agreed. In talking about the recent growth of hate groups in the country, he praised Trump for his role as an energizer and enabler of far-right hate groups. He has made it possible, Spencer said, for members of organizations like his own to run for office with a reasonable chance of success. They will be running, he said, "[n]ot as conservatives, but as Trump Republicans" (Altman 2016). In addition, a report on the relationship between Trump's election and hate groups reported that one of the most active hate groups on the Internet, The Daily Stormer, adopted a new name for Trump, "Our Glorious Leader," and initiated the formation of thirty-one new hate groups in the first few months of his presidency (Potok 2017).

Since Trump's election and his actions to reconfigure the party in his own image, some critics have become even more severe about the hate group features of the Republican Party. Articles in the online magazine *Salon* have attempted to make this point. In one such article, for example, the author wrote that "the post-civil rights GOP is our largest white identity group. Maybe we should thank Trump for making it so obvious" (Devega 2016; also see links to similar articles on Salon, including Denvir 2015).

The categorizations made by ADL and SPLC have enormous influence over the perception of hate groups in the United States and actions that may or may not be taken against those groups because of that classification. Each time one of the two groups publishes an update on its hate group numbers and listings, those results receive wide overage in almost every part of the country (see Hobbs and Byrd 2019). Although almost no data are available on the issue, it is difficult not to imagine how such publications would not affect public attitudes about the hate groups named, as well as legislative, economic, social, political, or other actions that might be taken with regard to a group's existence and activities.

Categories of Hate Groups

In 2020, the SPLC listed 940 organizations as hate groups. These groups ranged widely in purpose, history, membership, financial assets, and other features. This wide range of hate groups is often classified within one of a dozen-odd major categories, for example, Ku Klux Klan, Neo-Nazi, White Nationalist, Skinheads, Christian identity, Male Supremacy, Black Nationalist, Antireligionist, and Anti-LGBTQ. Groups within these categories are often remarkably similar to groups in another category. Yet, there are also some important differences among these categories. (Unless otherwise noted, all current data on hate groups come from the SPLC's most recent report on the subject ["The Year in Hate and Extremism 2019" 2020].)

Categorization of hate groups often involves some level of ambiguity. For example, a group listed by SPLC as "anti-Muslim" might also be thought of as "anti-immigrant." The classifications used here are those adopted by the SPLC.

Ku Klux Klan

In the United States, the term *domestic hate group* is attached perhaps most commonly with the KKK. As noted in chapter 1, the Klan was founded in Pulaski, Tennessee, in 1865 by a group of former Confederate army officers. Its purpose was to prevent the integration of former slaves into the mainstream life of the United States. The Klan survived less than a decade largely because of the actions of the federal government to monitor and control its activities. During this time, however, the Klan committed many unspeakable acts of violence against African Americans and white Americans who might have been supportive of efforts to achieve equality (Lester and Wilson [1905] 2010).

The Klan was reborn at a ceremony held at Stone Mountain, Georgia, on Thanksgiving Day, 1915. The event was inspired by a growing concern about the loss of traditional American life, meaning, to the Klan, the loss of a white Protestant hegemony in the country. The ultimate basis for this belief was the rapid increase in immigration to the United States from countries such as Ireland and Italy, often viewed as the source of "papist" teachings designed to undercut traditional American values. This version of the Klan was even more violent, if possible, than its predecessor, with lynchings, cross burnings, and other forms of violent action becoming almost a routine form of action throughout much of the country. At its height, in the mid-1920s, the Klan is thought to have had a national membership ranging between four and six million (McVeighn 1999). This version of the Klan also did not last very long. By 1930, its national membership had dropped to about thirty thousand. The organization finally disbanded in that year because of federal prosecution due to its failure to pay taxes. Some local groups remained in existence until the Klan disappeared almost completely during World War II (Lay [2005] 2016; Pegram 2011).

The third manifestation of the Klan occurred in the late 1950s with the rise of the civil rights movement. The peak moment of that movement was the adoption of the Civil Rights Acts of 1957 and 1960, which granted to citizens, regardless of their race or nationality, the right to vote, along with other protections of their civil liberties. This movement, as might be expected, spurred a renewed wave of racist and xenophobic feelings among some segments of the population. And, as had sometimes been the case in the past, the newly restored Klan routinely received the implicit and explicit support of law enforcement officers, government officials, and other politicians at the state and local (and, sometimes, national) level. Many of the most heinous crimes attributed to the Klan during its first and second phases occurred yet again during the third wave. In fact, the violence (including lynchings) attributed to the Klan during this period against civil rights workers and their supporters remains one of the darkest eras of American history (Etter, McElreath, and Quarles 2005).

No recognizable date exists for the disbandment of the Klan's third stage of existence. The organization has continued to operate, usually with a few dozen small, local groups, with small membership. Most estimates place membership in these groups at a few thousand ("Ku Klux Klan: A History of Racism" 2011). A more recent report on Klan activity concluded that "despite a persistent ability to attract media attention, organized Ku Klux Klan groups are actually continuing a long-term trend of decline. They remain a collection of mostly small, disjointed groups that continually change in name and leadership" ("Tattered Robes" 2016, 1).

Some observers have suggested that there is yet a fourth phase of the Klan, dating from the 1970s and 1980s to the present day. The leading figure in this movement was David Duke, a longtime white supremacist and former grand wizard of the Knights of the Ku Klux Klan. Duke's approach to racism and anti-Semitism was to discard the white robes and peaked caps of previous Klan groups, and to abandon that paraphernalia with business suits and a peaceful attempt to gain power through legal means. He withdrew from his original Klan connections in 1980 to form a new group, the National Association for the Advancement of White People. He ran successfully for state representative in Louisiana's 81st district in 1989, a seat he held until 1992. He was less successful in his campaigns for the U.S. presidency (1988, 1992), the governorship of Louisiana (1991), the U.S. Senate (1990, 1996, 2016), and the U.S. House of Representatives from Louisiana's 1st Congressional District.

In its Spring 2020 issue of *Intelligence Report*, SPLC listed forty-seven organizations that it classified as Klan hate groups. This number was down significantly from the 2016 total of 130 groups. The vast majority of these groups are small, independent club-like organizations or small chapters of larger national groups. As with most hate groups, relatively little is known about the structures and operation of these groups because of their own self-imposed policy of secrecy. The SPLC notes that the most visible Klan activities in 2019 were poorly attended and usually involved local rallies and the distribution of flyers. One rally it monitored had twelve attendees ("The Year in Hate and Extremism: Rage against Change" 2019, 44). Examples of some of the KKK groups named by SPLC are the American Christian Dixie Knights of the Ku Klux Klan, Christian American Knights of the Ku Klux Klan, East Coast

Knights of the True Invisible Empire, International Keystone Knights of the Ku Klux Klan, Oklahoma Knights of the Ku Klux Klan, Rebel Brigade Knights True Invisible Empire, Rocky Mountain Knights of the Ku Klux Klan, and United Northern and Southern Knights of the Ku Klux Klan. These groups generally do not have websites from which more information can be obtained, although their names sometimes show up in local news articles (see, e.g., Alvarez 2018; Bangert 2018; "Montana Klansman's Idea for 'Inclusive' KKK Elicits Derision" 2014; "United White Knights Talk about the Flyers Left in Sand Springs" 2011).

Among the Klan groups, the one claiming to have the largest membership is the Knights of the Ku Klux Klan, also just "the Knights." Their website provides a comprehensive, exhaustive, and lucid explanation of the group's beliefs about the genocide of whites that the Knights argue is now taking place in the United States. It is a useful introduction to the history of this particular group, as well as its goals and activities ("The Knights Party" 2018).

Black Separatists and Nationalists

The largest single group of hate groups, according to the 2020 SPLC *Intelligence Report,* is Black separatists. The number of such groups in the United States, according to this report, was 255, a decrease of 9 groups from the previous year. That number has been increasing gradually over the years, from a low of 81 in 2007 to 151 in 2012 to its present high point (SPLC *Intelligence Report* for relevant years; all group data of this type are from these sources). The SPLC attributes the recent rise in the number of Black nationalist and Black separatist hate groups to the policies and statements of President Donald Trump. Specifically, it argues that the growth is "a response to the current climate of racial divisiveness, specifically police violence and Donald Trump's derisive remarks about African Americans, including journalists and NFL players, and majority-black countries" ("The Year in Hate and Extremism: Rage against Change" 2019, 50).

The term *Black nationalists* is sometimes used as a synonym for Black separatists, although some significant differences exist between the two terms. A person can, for example, espouse anti-white, anti-Semitic, and anti-LGBTQ beliefs (fundamental to much of Black nationalism) without also recommending the creation of entirely separate Black facilities and governmental units (a common feature of Black separatism; Upchurch 2005).

The roots of Black nationalism date to the Revolutionary period in the United States. From time to time, spokespersons arose to suggest that one solution to the evils of slavery was the return of freed slaves to their original homes in Africa. One example is Prince Hall, believed to have been a freed slave, who founded the first Freemason lodge for Blacks, African Lodge #1 in Boston in 1784. In a 1787 speech to the Massachusetts State Legislature, Hall pointed out that conditions for Blacks in Boston "induce us earnestly to desire to return to Africa our native country . . . where we shall live among our equals and be more comfortable and happy, than we can be in our present situation" (Brooks 2000).

Hall's concept of an independent, self-sufficient Black society, either within the structure of American society or outside of it, reemerged on numerous occasions and in a variety of forms over the next two centuries or more. Prior to, during, and following the Civil War, the notion of Black nationalism or Black separatism became particularly appealing. It was arguably the first time in history during which Black slaves in the United States had any hope whatsoever of imagining a new and different future for the race. According to some authorities, one of the first (if not *the* first) promoter of this concept was Martin Delany (1812–1885), an African American abolitionist, journalist, physician, soldier, and writer. Delany suggested the return of freed American slaves to their original homes in Africa. Although he achieved no concrete success in bringing about such a change, his concept of Black separation became a model for later generations of Black nationalists and separatists.

In more recent times, Black nationalism and Black separatism have taken forms as benign as trying to convince American whites by verbal arguments of the need for equality among the races to outright violent events to achieve an equal, and, often, free and independent community of Blacks in America. The civil rights movement of the 1960s, for example, saw the rise of the Black Panthers, originally, the Black Panther Party for Self-Defense. The party adopted the position that violent action was sometimes needed to defend the rights of Blacks and to promote their integration into or increased separation from the majority white society. Over time, the Panthers augmented or replaced their policies of violence with a variety of social programs, such as health clinics and free food programs (Alkebulan 2012; for a good overall history of Black nationalism, see Van Deburg 1997).

Three groups on the SPLC list of hate groups continue to use the name "Black Panthers": the New Black Panther Party, the New Black Panther Party for Self Defense, and the Revolutionary Black Panther Party. Surviving members of the original Black Panther movement have gone out of their way to deny the presumption that any one of these groups is a legitimate heir of their party. They worry that the hateful and violent features of these new parties reflects poorly on the eventual positive programs developed by the original Panthers. In fact, some members of the original group have even sued the new groups to prevent their use of photos, quotations, symbols, and other memorabilia from the party of the 1960s (Murphy 2002).

Probably the oldest existing Black nationalist party to be listed by the SPLC as a hate group is the Nation of Islam. Founded in 1930 by an itinerant preacher, Wallace D. Fard Muhammad, the party's current leader is Louis Farrakhan, who took leadership of the group in 1977. The organization has expanded to nearly a hundred local mosques and other groups in almost every state of the United States. It has long been designated a hate group by both SPLC and ADL because of its supposed anti-Semitic, anti-Christian, anti-white, and anti-LGBTQ teachings ("The Nation of Islam" 2020; Nation of Islam n.d.). Its basic program calls for freedom, justice, and equality, and, lacking success in achieving those goals, "a separate state or territory of [our] own—either on this continent or elsewhere. We believe that our former slave masters are obligated to provide such land and that the area must be fertile and minerally rich. We believe that our former slave masters are obligated to maintain and supply our needs in this separate territory for the next 20 to 25 years—until we are able to produce and supply our own needs" ("What the Muslims Want" n.d.).

Another group of Black separatists are the so-called Black Hebrew Israelites. Members of this group subscribe to the belief that they are the descendants of the early Israelite tribes, and that many early Christian leaders, such as Jesus and the Apostles, were Black, not white. Various groups with somewhat different philosophies and practices fall within this category, including the African Hebrew Israelites of Jerusalem, Army of Israel, Commandment Keepers, Israel United in Christ, Israelite Church of God in Jesus Christ, Nation of Kings and Priests, Nation of Yahweh, True Nation Israelite Congregation, and Watchmen of Israel. Some, but not all, of these groups have been listed by the SPLC as hate groups, usually because of their anti-Semitic sentiments (Ben Levy 2012; Hoffman 2019; "Racist Black Hebrew Israelites Becoming More Militant" 2008).

Neo-Nazism

Neo-Nazism is a political and social philosophy that, as its name suggests, is a new version or revival of an ideology that had its origins in Germany in the early 1920s. The term *neo-Nazism* is actually an abbreviation for the official name of the belief and the party through which it is expressed, *National Socialism*. The best known spokesperson for the doctrine was Adolf Hitler, who outlined his beliefs in what is probably the movement's most famous treatise, *Mein Kampf* (*My Struggle* 1924). In the simplest terms, the doctrine held that the disastrous economic conditions suffered by the German people following World War I were largely caused by Communists, Jews, and other "enemies of the state." Hitler held that the nation would regain its original greatness only by returning to the ideal of a pure Aryan race. He argued that any means necessary could and should be used to "cleanse" the nation of its "impure" members. When Hitler was selected as Chancellor in 1933, he gained the pulpit from which he could put his political philosophy into action (Hett 2018).

The rise of neo-Nazism in the United States dates to 1959, when artist and politician George Lincoln Rockwell founded the American Nazi Party. This event produced widespread commentary and condemnation at the time, but not a particularly impressive recruitment of members ("Anti-Semitism: Neo-Nazism" 2020). After Rockwell was assassinated in 1967, the party began to fall apart, reappearing in the form of several splinter groups with a common philosophy, but slightly different modes of operation. According to the SPLC, the number of neo-Nazi parties in the United States has ranged in the twenty-first century from 94 to 207. The low point was reached in 2015 after a long decline in popularity, which began to increase again in 2016. The SPLC counted fifty-nine such groups in its latest report, among which were groups such as the American Nazi Party (with chapters in California, New Hampshire, Ohio, and South Carolina), Atomwaffen Division (active in eight states), Daily Stormer (one of the most active and influential groups, with a presence in ten states), and National Socialist Movement (ten states).

Today, only a small number of groups remain that explicitly call themselves "Nazi" or "National Socialist." The only such group recognized by the SPLC is the American Nazi Party, headquartered in Westland, Michigan. The party apparently has only a small membership, which it hoped to increase by the election of Donald Trump as president. Rocky Suhayda, chairman of the party, noted prior to the 2016 election that Trump's election would offer "a real opportunity for people like white Separatists" to start "acting intelligently," with the aim of building a mainstream political presence similar to that of the Congressional Black Caucus" (Pengelly 2016).

Among the groups retaining the "National Socialist" term in their name are the National Socialist German Workers Party, National Socialist Legion, National Socialist Liberation Front, and National Socialist Movement. The last of these claims to be the "largest and most active" National Socialist party in the United States today. Its platform calls for "defending the rights of white people everywhere, preservation of our European culture and heritage, strengthening family values, economic self-sufficiency, reform of illegal immigration policies, immediate withdrawal of our national military from an illegal Middle Eastern occupation, and promotion of white separation" ("America's National Socialist Party" n.d.).

The party's most recent appearance in the popular media occurred following the Unite the Right march at Charlottesville, Virginia, on August 11 and 12, 2017. Reacting to the violence that developed during that event, a group of citizens filed a lawsuit against twenty-one groups involved in planning the march, including the National Socialist Movement, and three other national socialist groups, the Traditionalist Workers Party, the League of the South, and Vanguard America (Smith 2018). (One of the ironies of this story is that, partially as a result of the lawsuits, the president of the National Socialist Movement, Jeff Schoep, resigned his post and was replaced by a white man, James Hart Stern, who pledged to turn the group into an educational tool for the Holocaust; Mettler 2019.)

White Nationalists

The mirror image of Black supremacist/nationalist groups is those based on the ideology of the White race over all other races (including Blacks). In the 2020 SPLC report, this category had the second largest number of hate groups listed, 155. That number has vacillated between 92 and 155 in the period from 2003 to 2019. As with other hate groups, the list of white nationalist groups had steadily decreased from a total of 146 in 2011 to 95 in 2015. It then began to rise in 2016 to 100 and to its current number of 155 in 2019. The term *white nationalist* or *white supremacist* can reasonably be extended to other groups with similar doctrines of white superiority over other races, such as those now listed among the KKK category, neo-Nazis, and skinheads.

When the term *white nationalist* or *white supremacist* is mentioned, the history of the KKK, discussed earlier, may be one of the first hate groups (and perhaps even, the *only* hate group) of that category. But white nationalists operating outside the Klan have been around since the end of the Civil War. As former slaves became integrated into society, gaining equal rights with their former masters, a reaction began among white politicians and ordinary citizens. The philosophy that made slavery possible in the first place, namely, that Blacks are inferior in all respects to whites, did not disappear with the war's end. Indeed, white groups were continuously active in attempting to reverse Black progress almost anywhere it began to appear.

Possibly the most egregious of all such actions, but one about which most Americans today know little or nothing, was the riots in Wilmington, North Carolina, in November 1898. An excellent history of that event is available in a new book, *Wilmington's Lie* (Zucchino 2020), which itself is well summarized by a recent article in the *New Yorker* magazine, "City Limits" (Crain 2020). Prior to the riots, the city of Wilmington had developed a successful postwar interracial government composed of Republicans and Populists, both Black and white. The city itself had a large, prosperous middle-class Black population. From their own political beliefs of the time, however, members of the Democratic Party decided to bring this coalition to an end and to take over all city offices. (It also attempted to take control of state government, which it did, a condition that remained until the Civil Rights Act of 1960 reversed political fortunes.) On November 18, a mob of Democrats attacked the city hall, Black-owned and white-supportive businesses, and a substantial part of the residential area. They forced the resignation of the mayor, the aldermen, and the chief of police. Fearing for their lives, most Blacks fled the city to an extent that the city's list of 125,000 voters in 1896 was reduced to 6,000 only six years later. The slaughter was so great that one eyewitness later said that "I nearly stepped on negroes laying in the street dead" (Crain 2020, 67).

Wilmington's story is by no means the only one of its kind. Indeed, it seems likely that several other similar tales could be told, and one goal of future historians might be to search out those tales. But glimmers of the attitudes that led to the Wilmington riots can easily be found in today's world. The most recent of such events was the Unite the Right rally held in Charlottesville, Virginia on August 11 and 12, 2017. The rally was proposed and organized by two prominent figures in the white supremacy movement, American neo-Nazis Jason Kessler and Richard Spencer. One purpose of the rally was to protest the removal of Civil War statues from Charlottesville streets. But the more important goal was to bring together a wide range of hate groups in a more concerted effort to advertise their common concerns about the structure and function of American society (Atkinson 2018; Kurtz et al. 2018). (A follow-up rally, Unite the Right II, was held in New York City on the first anniversary of the Charlottesville rally. It was attended by about two dozen followers of Richard Spencer and was opposed by more than a thousand opponents of the rally-goers; Fausett 2018.)

In some respects, the Unite the Right rally produced exactly the opposite effect than was intended. The criminal charges brought against some leaders of the rally and the widespread disapproval among the general public of the tactics used in the rally led to soul-searching among many of the groups involved in the event. Some leaders argued that groups should "back off" to some extent, avoid the use of violent protest, and at least appear to be more mainstream in their efforts to achieve their goal of white supremacy. Other leaders took a different view, suggesting that even more violent actions were needed to achieve their objectives. One result of this conflict was the splintering of some of the groups involved in the rally. In fact, according to the SPLC report for 2018, this fragmentation of groups may be one explanation for the growth in the number of white nationalist groups for its tally of hate groups for the year ("The Year in Hate and Extremism: Rage against Change" 2019, 46).

Among the groups that arose out of this debate, or that reemphasized their commitment to violent action, were the Proud Boys, Patriot Prayer, the Fraternal Order of Alt-Knights, and Hell-Shaking Preachers. As an example, the first two of these groups joined to organize a rally in Portland, Oregon, on August 4, 2018. A leader of the Proud Boys, Tusitala "Tiny" Toese, made no secret of the methods they intended to use at the rally. He advised his followers to be prepared for a "physical fight, whatever kind of fight—we're coming . . . and we're gonna raise hell" ("37 Organizations and a Regional Organization Representing over 50 Tribes Denounce Bigotry and Violence before Patriot Prayer and Proud Boys Rally in Portland on August 4 2018").

The Proud Boys is a group formed in 2016 by Canadian writer and political activist Gavin McInnes. McInnes claims that the group is a "pro-western fraternity, essentially a drinking club dedicated to male bonding, socializing and the celebration all things related to western culture." The group's history belies that description, however, with several instances in which members were arrested for violent behavior (Proud Boys 2020).

The largest white nationalist group, according to the SPLC, is the American Identity Movement, formerly known as Identity Evropa. The group was formed in 2016 by Marine veteran Nathan Damigo. He is said to have been influenced by the writings of former Klan Grand Wizard David Duke. Damigo relinquished his post as leader of the group in 2018, after he had been observed striking a female Antifa protester in the face. The new Evropa leader, Patrick Casey, has said that his group eschews violence in efforts to achieve their goal. It works, instead, he said, through the traditional political process which, in Evropa's case, involves a drive to "take over the GOP as much as possible" (Schecter 2018). His plan is to blanket college campuses with flyers and other information about the group's efforts, which are based on the principle that "we don't believe America needs to be 100.00 percent white, but we do think that America isn't going to be America if there isn't a European-America super-majority. . . . And in the future we would like to have immigration policies that favor high-skilled immigrants from, you know, Europe, Canada, Australia and so forth. And we also do want to have programs of re-migration wherein people who feel more of a connection to another part of the world, another race, another culture, even another religion in the case of Islam can return to their native homelands essentially" (Hannon 2018).

Racist Skinheads

The SPLC describes racist skinheads as "among the most dangerous radical-right threats facing law enforcement today." They constitute, the SPLC goes on, "a frequently violent and criminal subculture [that is] typically imbued with neo-Nazi beliefs about Jews, blacks, homosexuals and others [and] notoriously difficult to track" ("Racist Skinheads: Understanding the Threat" 2012, 1).

The skinhead movement did not begin that way. It first appeared in Great Britain in the late 1960s when lower-class groups of young British men and women began to become more aware of their often-disparaged lifestyle. They recognized that mainstream culture often looked down on such individuals as not leading the exemplary life that society expected of them. These individuals began to respond in a familiar way, by adopting and valuing the very characteristics for which they were being vilified. These actions included wearing the clothing of the lower class, to which many had been born, shaving their heads in order to disparage the style-conscious behavior of the middle and upper classes, and adopting an interest in certain types of Black music, such as soul music and reggae (Moore 1993; An excellent overview of the movement is available at Letts 2016). At this point in its history, the skinhead movement was not particularly racist, violent, or a hate group in any other sense. In fact, their activities often included Black Jamaican immigrants.

Over time, this characterization began to change, at least partially because of the increased number of immigrants from Pakistan and other Asian and African nations. Some skinhead individuals began to see people of color as no longer brothers and sisters in a common cause, but part of the problem against which they fought. By the early 1970s, this change was being reflected by the growing practice of "Paki-bashing," in which a person would "go up to them and bump into them, and then you nut [forehead bash] them right, and then you hit them, and as they go down you give them a kicking, bash them with an iron bar, and take their watches and rings and things like that" ("Racist Skinheads: Understanding the Threat" 2012, 4). Before long, one segment of the skinhead movement began to adopt most of the principles and practices of the Nazi and neo-Nazi movements. Members of skinhead groups can often be identified by characteristic features such as a shaved head, black Doc Martens boots, jeans with suspenders, and an array of typically racist tattoos ("The Year in Hate and Extremism: Rage against Change" 2019, 47).

The skinhead movement first appeared in the United States in the early 1980s. By 1988, the ADL estimated that about two thousand neo-Nazi skinheads were active in the country (Bishop 1988). At the same time, reports of violent crimes against people of color, Jews, homosexuals, and other minorities continued to grow. Although some skinheads advocated a more benign lifestyle, racist organizations grew in number and visibility throughout the nation.

In 2003, SPLC listed only 39 racist skinheads in its annual count of hate groups. This number began to grow rapidly by the end of the 2000s, reaching 136 in 2010. By the mid-2010s, the number had begun to fall off, reaching a low of 48 groups in SPLC's latest count. The SPLC sees these numbers as a trend in which the movement is beginning to die out. It says that such groups continue to pose a threat, however, because of the unusual level of violence with which they are associated. For no obvious reason, the largest number of skinhead groups are now found in California, which lists ACSkins, American Front, Crew 38, Golden State Skinheads (two chapters), and Western Hammerskins. Most of these organizations appear to have relatively modest memberships and come to popular attention only when they are involved in some act of violence against a minority to which they are opposed or a member of the general public ("Racist Skinheads: Understanding the Threat" 2012, 12–14).

Anti-LGBTQ Hate Groups

The SPLC first published a list of groups in this category in 2010. This late designation may seem a bit surprising, given the long history of hate crimes against LGBTQ people in the United States and around the world. Surprising also, perhaps, because of the SPLC's commentary in its original article on the topic that such individuals make up "by far the group most targeted in America for violent hate crimes" (Potok 2011b; data on which this claim is based can be found at Potok 2011a). The center listed seventeen anti-LGBTQ hate groups in 2010, increasing to forty-five in 2014. This number has remained fairly constant until 2019, when seventy anti-LGBTQ were listed ("Hate Over Time" n.d.).

As noted earlier, several groups within this SPLC category have offered strong objections to their listing as hate groups. Their argument tends to focus on freedom of religion and free speech rights for church groups. They point out that society in general and Christianity in particular have long stigmatized same-sex behavior. It is entirely within their rights, they say, to point out the flaws they see in such behavior without calling forth hateful reactions among their congregations.

The opposing side to this argument notes that most churches typically begin teaching their beliefs when individuals are quite young, for example, in regular Sunday School settings. They may then continue to teach that same-sex behavior is "sinful," "immoral," "unnatural," "abnormal," and "an abomination to God," and that "homosexuals" are usually child molesters, who "gave us Adolf Hitler, . . . the Brown Shirts, the Nazi war machine, and six million dead Jews," and intend to take over American society with their own hidden agenda which "represents the single greatest modern threat to freedom of religion and conscience" (The Propagandists 2011). Is it unreasonable to expect, then, that at least some small fraction of members of such churches would feel justified, and perhaps required, to deal with lesbians, gay men, bisexuals, and transgenders with verbal and physical actions, which may include physical attacks and even murder?

In its 2019 report on hate groups, SPLC made special mention of the influence of anti-LGBTQ hate groups on the administration of President Donald Trump. It listed several U.S. representatives and members of the executive branch with a long history of opposition to civil rights for LGBTQ individuals.

The one person who stood out in this analysis was Vice President Mike Pence, who has had a long history of anti-LGBTQ statements and activities ("The Year in Hate and Extremism: Rage against Change" 2019, 14–18; also see Drabold 2016; Fitzsimons 2019; "The Trump-Pence Administration's Crusade against LGBTQ Americans" n.d.).

As with most hate crimes, useful data about anti-LGBTQ events are in short supply, with the FBI and Bureau of Justice providing wildly divergent statistics. The best estimates available suggest that the rate of hate crimes against gay men and lesbians has remained about constant from 1996, when reporting to the FBI began (757 hate crimes against gay men and 150 hate crimes against lesbians) to 2017, the most recent year for which data are available (679 hate crimes against gay men and 126 hate crimes against lesbians) (Hauck 2019). But a troubling trend in LGBTQ hate crimes has developed since 2013. These crimes have involved violent actions against transgender and gender nonconforming individuals. In 2019, twenty-six deaths were reported for such individuals, crimes committed by acquaintances, partners, or strangers, and were, for the most part, Black women. The trend appears to have continued into 2020, with eleven more deaths having been reported in this category as of mid-May. One explanation for this trend may be the increasing visibility of transgender and gender nonconforming individuals in everyday life. This phenomenon appears to have deeply troubled some individuals, some of whom may have been hate group members or followers ("Violence against the Transgender and Gender Non-Conforming Community in 2020" 2020).

Anti-Muslim Hate Groups

One of the most recently created SPLC hate groups includes those organizations opposed to the religion of Islam and the people who practice that religion, the Muslims. No good data exist about the existence or numbers of anti-Muslim hate groups before the mid-2000s. According to available FBI records, the number of hate *crimes* against Muslims averaged in the high twenties from 1996 (when the agency started keeping records) and 2000, the year before the attacks of September 11, 2001 (see table 2.1). That number then skyrocketed in that fateful year to 481, after which it dropped off to the mid-100s. In the

Table 2.1 Hate Crimes against Muslims, 1996–2018

Year	Number of Crimes
1996	27
1997	28
1998	21
1999	32
2000	28
2001	481
2002	155
2003	149
2004	156
2005	128
2006	156
2007	115
2008	105
2009	107
2010	160
2011	157
2012	130
2013	135
2014	154
2015	257
2016	307
2017	273
2018	188

Source: "Hate Crime Data 1996–2014. 2016. The World. https://docs.google.com/spreadsheets/d/1OcBVU_H76qbKyPg8HUXxmOvfB4Odf76bTjn5pRhYav8/edit#gid=0; Data for 2016–2018 from "Hate Crime Statistics." appropriate year. Criminal Justice Information Services Division. Federal Bureau of Investigation. https://ucr.fbi.gov/hate-crime/2016.

most recent SPLC survey, the number of such hate groups fell from one hundred in 2018 to eighty-four in 2019. The SPLC claimed that some portion of that decrease was a result of "shake-ups at the White House [that] left the movement with far fewer allies in the halls of power" ("The Year in Hate and Extremism 2019" 2020, 16). SPLC had previously pointed to the policies of President Donald Trump, along with a handful of state governors and members of the Congress as having been a factor in the rise of anti-Muslim hate groups from thirty-five in 2015 to one hundred in 2016 and 114 in 2017 ("The Year in Hate and Extremism: Rage against Change" 2019, 37–40).

The largest anti-Muslim hate group identified by the SPLC was Act for America, which has thirty-nine chapters in twenty-three states and the District of Columbia. The organization claims to have more than a million members who stand for "the protection of the United States of America, and the Western values upon which our nation was built" ("Non-Discrimination and Anti-Violence Policy" 2019). Act for America's founder, Brigitte Gabriel, has outlined her organization's philosophy in two books, *Because They Hate: A Survivor of Islamic Terror Warns America* (Griffin, Godalming, 2008) and *Rise* (FrontLine 2018).

Criticism of anti-Muslim hate groups is generally based not so much on any violence they commit, encourage, or support, but on their characterization of the religion of Islam and Muslims. For example, these groups often warn that Islamic groups are attempting to undermine the American way of law and replace it with sharia, an Islamic religious law. They have been active in trying to pass state laws that would prevent this change from taking place. Another basis of concern is the groups' frequent attempt to characterize *all* Muslims as potential terrorists, rather than distinguishing peaceful members of the faith from their more extremist brothers and sisters (Elsheikh, Sisemore, and Lee 2017). One summary of 763 hateful activities against Muslims from 2012 to 2018 listed six types of acts deemed to be offensive by the authors: anti-sharia legislation; opposition to refugee resettlement; opposition to mosques, Muslim cemeteries, and schools; anti-Muslim actions and statements by elected and appointed officials; hate incidents against mosques and Islamic centers; and media reports of anti-Muslim violence and crimes ("Anti-Muslim Activities in the United States" 2018).

Some anti-Muslim hate groups base their efforts on the prevention of jihad in the United States (and, often, the rest of the world). *Jihad* is an Arabic word that can be translated as "struggle." It has many definitions, ranging from a person's efforts to live out the Islam faith to the maximum extent possible to a holy war to protect Islamic states from absorption and destruction to external forces. In this case, it also refers to an effort known as *civilization jihad*. This term generally refers to the efforts of Islamic forces to become the world's dominant power by overcoming other political systems. One familiar explanation for the concept comes from a document written by a major figure in the Islamist movement, Yusuf al-Qaradawi, "Explanatory Memorandum on the General Strategic Goal for the Group in North America." In the document, he said that all Muslims had to "understand that their work in America [was] a grand jihad in eliminating and destroying Western civilization from within and sabotaging its miserable house by their hands so that God's religion [Islam] is victorious over all religions" (May 2011).

Some hate groups take their names specifically from this concept of a jihadi threat, the Counter Jihad Coalition, Jihad Watch, and Radio Jihad, for example. Jihad Watch, for example, notes that its goal is "dedicated to bringing public attention to the role that jihad theology and ideology play in the modern world and to correcting popular misconceptions about the role of jihad and religion in modern-day conflicts" ("Why Jihad Watch" n.d.; see the "FAQ" section of this website for more information about this group). Several other anti-Muslim hate groups may hold similar positions on the battle against jihad, without actually including that term in their title. See, for example, a description of the Center for Security Policy for its outlook on the issue (Bridge Initiative Team 2017).

Anti-Immigrant Hate Groups

Among the terms most commonly used to describe American history is "melting pot." The term refers to a tendency of the nation to welcome peoples of all color, race, national origin, and ethnicity, and to bring them together in a single, homogenous culture. In this sense, it also referred to the willingness and even desire to invite immigrants from all over the world to join and become an integral part of American society. Immigration was regarded as a positive policy because it allowed the United States to take advantage of the finest qualities that people of all cultures had to add to the mix that was America. Even today, numerous articles, books, classes, curricula, and other educational media espouse the concept of an American melting point, usually praising the values it has held for the evolution of our society (Higgins 2015).

As chapter 1 of this book has shown that depiction of American attitudes toward immigration is only partially correct. In fact, it is often contradicted by the facts of the country's history. Some examples previously discussed include the expulsion of certain religious groups during Colonial times, acts of violence against Chinese immigrants during the late nineteenth century, and reactions against Irish and Italian immigrants in the early twentieth century. Even today, strong feelings against a liberal immigration policy, and against immigrants themselves is hardly an unknown factor. In the presidential campaign of 2016, one of Donald Trump's most frequently stated themes was the need for a wall along the border between Mexico and the United States. In describing Mexican immigrants, he said, "You wouldn't believe how bad these people are. These aren't people. These are animals" ("Remarks by President Trump at a California Sanctuary State Roundtable" 2018).

According to the SPLC, the number of anti-immigrant hate groups is second lowest (after Christian identity hate groups) of all groups surveyed. The center listed twenty such groups in 2019, up slightly from 2018 (seventeen groups). Yet, it suggests that such groups are still of considerable concern for two reasons. First, they are among the most violent of all hate groups, and second, as noted earlier, they have an impressive influence at the highest level of the federal government on U.S. policy about immigration.

Some specific examples of hate crimes against immigrants can be found in the Center for Investigative Reporting's "The Hate Report" for 2018. They involve numerous occasions when an individual shot at a person who appeared to be an immigrant because of her or his style of dress (Carless and Sankin 2018). Of particular interest is the possibility that some such hate groups are motivated by a somewhat less well-known philosophy known as *accelerationism*. According to this philosophy, dramatic, large-scale cultural changes are going to occur in the future. It is probably desirable, then, to take whatever actions are necessary to bring about those changes as quickly as possible, including the use of violence to accomplish that goal (Beauchamp 2019; "The Year in Hate and Extremism 2019" 2020, 10–12).

The majority of anti-immigrant hate groups listed by SPLC are single-chapter organizations located in widely distributed parts of the country. They include AZ Patriots and AZ Desert Guardians (not listed by SPLC), who apparently compete with each other for space and actions against illegal immigrants (Sommer 2019); Colorado Alliance for Immigration Reform, which argues that "immigration is the issue that determines every other issue" and, therefore, covers almost every aspect of immigration issues, including state, federal, election, and media topics (Colorado Alliance for Immigration Reform 2019); the Dustin Inman Society in Georgia, which quotes Plato on the masthead of its website to the effect that "one of the penalties for refusing to participate in politics is that you end up being governed by your inferiors" (The Dustin Inman Society 2020); and Help Save Maryland, whose mission statement describes itself as "a grassroots organization dedicated to preserving Maryland's Counties, Cities and Towns from the negative effects of Illegal Immigration" ("Welcome to Help Save Maryland" 2020).

Neo-Confederate Hate Groups

It probably is not especially surprising to know that some individuals and groups are still fighting the Civil War. These groups continue to believe in and espouse the principles on which the Confederate States of America (CSA) was founded in 1861. Neo-Confederate groups do not necessarily advocate for the creation of an independent sovereign state, such as the CSA. They may instead suggest a confederation of independent states, within the United States. One example they may point to is the status of Scotland in the United Kingdom. Scotland is in some ways an independent entity, with its own parliament and, to some extent, its own political system. But the country is still an integral part of a nation that also includes Northern Ireland, Wales, and England.

One such group, the League of the South, argues that a new political system is needed because "[o]ur culture is being sacked by an unholy crusade of leftist agitators and foreign religions and our very physical survival depends on us organizing and effectively defending ourselves from this enemy who seeks to eliminate us from the planet earth" (League of the South 2014). An important element of this threat, the League says, is its attack on important symbols of the former CSA, including its flag, monuments, and clothing. On its current website, the League lists active chapters in sixteen states: Alabama, Arkansas, Florida (two groups), Georgia, Kentucky, Louisiana, Maryland, Mississippi, Missouri, North Carolina, Oklahoma, South Carolina, Tennessee, Texas, Virginia, and West Virginia. Each chapter has its own state flag that may or may not include some element of the original CSA flag.

Activities of the League appear to be primarily commemorative of CSA traditions (such as visiting monuments and memorials) and educational (articles about its philosophy and work, as well as news about its annual convention).

Neo-Confederate groups appear to be in a state of decline at the moment. The number of such groups identified as hate groups by the SPLC has decreased from ninety-one in 2003 to twenty-six in 2019. The strongest period across this date range was in 2003–2008, when an average of about one hundred chapters a year were so designated by the Center. Since 2010, that number has dropped to less than forty chapters annually. The most recent decline in the movement may be due, at least in part, to its participation in the Unite the Right rally in Charlottesville, Virginia, in November 2017 (Antifa.atl 2020).

Antigovernment Hate Groups

In addition to the relatively specialized hate groups discussed earlier, several other types of hate groups exist. SPLC has classified these "other" groups in different ways over the years. At some times in history, it has used a category known as General Hate Groups for these "other" groups. Groups included in that list change, however, being added in some years and redefined in other years. In its most recent report, for example, the center has classified hate music labels, Holocaust denial groups, radical traditional Catholic groups (which reject core Catholic teachings and espouse anti-Semitism), and various other groups that endorse various hate doctrines ("The Year in Hate and Extremism 2019" 2020, 23). The Center listed 165 such groups in its most recent report.

The center has also introduced a new category of hate groups in its 2020 report on the topic: antigovernment hate groups. The reason for this change, it has said, is the rising visibility of such groups in the last few years as dominant political philosophies in the United States have changed. Many organizations listed as antigovernment hate groups have also been classified as Patriot Groups. Patriot Groups are those that, in general, subscribe to a philosophy that American democracy is being attacked by forces designed to change its existence in fundamental ways. By some accounts, this movement originated in a speech before Congress by President George H. W. Bush. In that speech, Bush expressed his hopes for a "new world order." Some individuals took that remark to suggest that behind-the-scenes forces were working to overthrow the American way of life (Bush 1990).

Antigovernment hate groups now exist in every state of the United States, with the largest number in California (forty-six), Texas (thirty-eight), and Ohio (thirty-two). Some examples of these groups are the California State Militia (seven chapters), Citizens Militia of Mississippi (seven chapters), State of Jefferson Formation (fourteen chapters), and III% United Patriots (many chapters in forty-five states).

One common element of the antigovernment movement has been the acceptance of several conspiracy theories about the workings of the U.S. government. One such theory holds that a "deep state" exists that works behind the scenes in the American government, attempting to bring about the fundamental changes mentioned by President Bush. Such theories became particularly popular during the presidency of Barack Obama, which resulted in an increase in antigovernment groups (as measured by SPLC) from 149 in the last year of George W. Bush's presidency (2008) to 512 in the first year of Obama's term (2009) and then to 824 in 2010, 1,274 in 2011, and 1,380, the highest point ever, in 2012 ("Antigovernment Movement" 2020). Although President Donald Trump has himself advanced several conspiracy theories about the "deep state," the number of antigovernment hate groups has fallen off from 690 in the first year of his term (2017) to 612 in 2018 and 576 in 2019. By some accounts, this decrease may reflect the acceptance of "deep state" theories by the Trump administration (Clark 2020).

A subdivision within the Antigovernment Hate Group category, according to SPLC, consists of militias. Historically, the term *militia* generally refers to a military force consisting of civilians designed to assist or supplement the activities of a regular army force in case of an emergency. Today, the term may have a somewhat different meaning in that it might also refer to civilian groups that may, in fact, find it necessary to oppose existing governments, including their military arms. As such, some of the groups listed within this category may be viewed as being the most likely to take violent action to achieve their aims. When participating in a rally, for example, members may tend to wear military uniforms and carry weapons, such as assault rifles (for images, see, e.g., Walters 2017). Over the past half decade, about one-quarter to one-third of all antigovernment hate groups have been militia groups ("The Year in Hate and Extremism 2019" 2020, 43).

Another subgroup of antigovernment hate groups is the Oath Keepers Movement, started in 2009 by a former U.S. paratrooper, Stewart Rhodes. The organization consists primarily of current and former members of the armed forces, police, and first responders. Members of the group tend to accept various conspiracy theories that predict the overthrow of American society by a number of forces both within and outside the government. Its manifesto explains that members owe an allegiance to the U.S. Constitution, but not necessarily to politicians. The organization is especially concerned about efforts to promote gun control legislation, seeing such acts as only the first step in vastly reducing personal and property rights in the country. A defining document for the Oath Keepers is its Declaration of Orders We Will Not Obey, which includes ten specific occasions in which they will not follow directions from the federal, state, or other governmental agencies. These items include any orders to disarm Americans, to conduct warrantless searches, to impose martial law or a state of emergency, to invade or subjugate any state that asserts its own sovereignty, and to force any American citizen into any type of detention camp ("Declaration of Orders We Will Not Obey 2020").

Yet another subgroup of antigovernment hate groups consists of the so-called Three Percenters (also, III% groups). The name "Three Percenters" is based on the contention that only that fraction of the population was engaged in the battle against England in the Revolutionary War. The organization sees itself as being "the last defense to protect the citizens of the United States if there ever comes a day when our government takes up arms against the American people." The group has adopted three principles on which it operates: moral strength, physical readiness, and no first use of force ("What Is the Three Percenters?" 2020).

Anti-Semitic Hate Groups

The SPLC does not list a category with this title, and the ADL produces only an annual "Audit of Antisemitic Incidents." In its 2019 report, ADL listed 2,107 anti-Semitic incidents in the United States, an increase of 12 percent over 1,879 incidents in 2018. That number is the highest total of incidents since the ADL started keeping records in 1994 (2,066 incidents). The majority of those incidents (1,127) were some form of harassment, such as the use of spoken or written statements or physical acts against a person or group of people. The second most common type of incident was vandalism, such as the painting of a swastika or physical destruction of an object. A total of 919 such incidents were recorded by the ADL. The last category of incidents were physical assaults, of which sixty-one cases were listed. Of these, eleven involved the use of a deadly weapon such as a knife or gun. These sixty-one cases resulted in ninety-five injuries, including five deaths (all data from "Audit of Antisemitic Incidents 2019" 2020). Descriptions of specific events of anti-Semitic incidents and statistical trends over time can be found in this report at https://www.adl.org/audit2019#themes-and-trends.

How Hate Groups Operate

One way to think of hate groups is as collections of individuals (neo-Nazis, skinheads, Three Percenters, black separatists, etc.) with strong feelings about (against) other groups of individuals (African Americans, Jews, Catholics, Asians, LGBTQ individuals). That is the view of hate groups used in this book so far. But there is another way of looking at hate groups: as organizations. According to this view, a hate group has a beginning, a corporate history, officers and members, a mission statement, certain types of activities, a history of successes and failures, and, in some cases, a record of disbandment or dissolution. In this regard, the Black Riders Liberation Party may be similar in some ways (but certainly not all ways) to Alphabet, Ford Motor Company, or Mrs. Fletcher's Aerial and Janitorial Services. For someone who would like to have a better idea as to how hate groups work, this second approach to the question can often be useful. (One of the most valuable articles on this aspect of hate groups is Woolf and Hulsizer 2004.) The approach is somewhat handicapped by the fact that many hate groups tend to be secretive or less than forthcoming about their structure and function. Some observations reported here, then, must be viewed with a measure of uncertainty.

Hate groups arise because of at least two basic factors: (1) a context in which some justification can be provided for the organization of a hate group and (2) the appearance of an individual or small group of individuals who have the traits needed for the creation of such a group. Sometimes, the setting out of which a hate group arises can be some very specific, often dramatic, event that calls widespread attention to a conflict between "us" and "them." Perhaps the best known example of such an event in recent history was the attack on the World Trade Center and the Pentagon by a small group of Islamic terrorists on September 11, 2001. One of the immediate responses to this event was the message that not just these individuals but possibly *all* Muslims are radical terrorists whose goal is to destroy the United States and against whom, then, organized opposition must be created. Despite efforts by government officials and other people in authority to reduce the alarmist responses to this event, several new anti-Muslim groups were formed in the years following the attack, and other groups refocused their efforts to include Muslim among their targets ("Extremist Groups React to the 9/11 Attacks" 2001).

Of course, in many instances, no distinct event is required to provide the atmosphere for the formation of a hate group. For example, as earlier sections of this book have shown, Jews, LGBTQ individuals, Blacks, Asians, and other minority groups have been seen for centuries as outsiders or "enemies of the people." So, the animosity against Jews, for example, evidenced by the actions of hate groups today does not derive from opposition to some specific action by Jewish individuals or groups: It has existed for two thousand years and, at some times and in some places, it is at least as strong today as it has ever been (Dreier 2020; Goldstein 2012).

More than just an opportunity to create an anti–hate group is necessary, however. At least as important to such an event is an individual or small group of individuals with the imagination, skills, and charisma capable of bringing people of like interests together to form a hate group. Numerous examples of this feature of hate groups are available online and in published literature. Just one of the many possible examples is William H. Regnery II. Regnery is the grandson of William H. Regnery, who made a fortune in textile manufacturing and banking. After his grandfather's death, Regnery took control of his business operations, but proved to be less than successful as a businessman. Instead, he turned his attention to conservative politics, developing a system of belief that includes anti-Semitic, anti-immigrant, and racist political philosophy. In 2001, he founded the Charles Martel Society, which publishes the racist quarterly magazine, *The Occidental Quarterly*. Four years later, he also founded the National Policy Institute, also devoted to a study and promotion of his hate-based philosophy. In 2011, Regnery hired Richard Spencer, one of the leading figures in extremist conservative thought in the United States and Europe. Some critics have said that Regnery, Spencer, and NPI were singularly unsuccessful in promoting the ideas of white nationalism until the election of President Donald Trump in 2016. Since then, they say, Trump's political policies and decisions have legitimized the causes for which Regnery, Spencer, and NPI have long been working (Roston and Anderson 2017; Williams 2017).

Birth and Growth

Like most businesses, hate groups tend to lead complex histories, from birth to periods of growth and diversification to, in many cases, decay and decline. ADL has summarized these stages for the hate groups it has studied in its own work ("How Hate Groups Form" 2020; all examples in this section are adapted from this publication). The first step most commonly occurs when one or a small number of individuals from an existing hate group break away to form their own organization. He, she, or they learn the skills of running a hate group and decide to go off in a new direction, a process that the ADL calls *graduating*, as when one "graduates" from one educational level to the next. The ADL offers the name of Billy Roper as an example of this process. Roper, who describes himself as a "biological racist," started out as a member of the Neo-Nazi National Alliance in the 1990s and 2000s before breaking off and forming his own group, the White Revolution, in 2002. When that group failed, he joined a KKK group, called the Knights Party, before moving on once again to form a Christian identity hate group, the Divine Truth Ministries, in 2016, and then, in 2017, yet another new group, the Shield Wall Network, where he remains today (Billy Roper n.d.; Dentice 2013; Shield Wall Network [SWN] 2020).

A second way by which hate groups form is familiar to graduating, in that members of a parent group break off and form their own new group, but adopt much of the philosophy and program of the original group. One example is the formation of Outlaw Hammerskins from the parent Hammerskins group in the early 2000s. The Hammerskin Nation had been formed in the 1980s and grew rapidly in popularity. A decade later, they were called "the most violent and best-organized neo-Nazi skinhead group in the United States" by the ADL ("The Hammerskin Nation" 2002). Only a few years later, fissures began to appear within the group, with some members arguing that it had begun to drift from its original mission and activities, that is, it was less "pure" than it ought to have been. By 2006, a handful of members from the group had formed two offspring groups, Northern Hammerskins and Arizona Hammerskins, designed to return to the movement's original objectives. By 2006, these groups had combined and taken in more new members from the original Hammerskin Nation, forming yet another new group, Outlaw Hammerskins. At that point, the original group had disbanded and disappeared from the hate scene (Brien James 2018; Holthouse 2006).

A third way in which hate groups form is the complete breakup of an existing group into splinter groups with more or less the same philosophy and program of action as the parent group. One good example of this case is the Aryan Nation, which was founded in 1977 by American engineer and white supremacist Richard Butler. The group was based on the belief that Christians, not Jews, are God's "chosen people." More to the point, perhaps, it taught that the Jewish race was born through the union of Eve and Satan. For many years, the Aryan Nation was quite successful, especially in the creation of chapters in prisons. It began to experience problems, however, partly because of the increasingly poor health of the founder, with the consequent debate over succession of leadership (Butler died in 2004), as well as a court case won by the SPLC against the Aryan Nation in the amount of $6.3 million for violent actions of the group's members. That award drained the group's financial resources and was instrumental in its demise in 2010. By that time, the group had lost a large part of its membership to new groups, with new names and new leaders, but with principles and programs similar to those of the original group. A handful of groups formed as a result of the Aryan Nation's demise, generally with relatively small memberships, modest visibility, and relatively short times of survival. They have included The Order, New Order, the Phineas Priesthood, White Aryan Resistance, 1st SS Kavallerie Brigade Motorcycle Division, United Church of Yahweh, Church of Jesus Christ Christian/Aryan Nations, and Aryan Republic Homeland ("Aryan Nations" n.d.; Kushner 2003, passim).

Yet another appearance of new groups arises on the adoption of formerly popular names. The best known of these instances is probably that of the KKK. Once a robust national organization with a very large membership and strong influence on the media, legislators, and other aspects of society, the Klan that was so well known in the 1860s and 1920s had largely collapsed by the end of World War II. The name persisted, however, as, time after time, some individual or small group of individuals appropriated that title into their own new hate group. Today, the SPLC lists more than two dozen "Klan" groups, most with no more than a handful of members and modest programs of action. Some such groups are the Alliance of American Klans, American Christian Knights of the Ku Klux Klan, Exalted Knights of the Ku Klux Klan, Patriot Brigade Knights of the Ku Klux Klan, United Dixie Whites of the Ku Klux Klan, and White Knights of Texas ("The Year in Hate and Extremism 2019" 2020, 26; this list of Klan groups varies from year to year so that more recent reports may list new groups or omit groups that have disbanded).

The ADL also identifies the role of "copycatting" in starting and naming a new hate group. Thus, if Blood Brothers happens to be the name of a particularly successful hate group (no such group actually exists), then other groups might decide to use a take-off of that name, such as Blood Brothers Club, Kingdom of Blood Brothers, or Blood Brothers for Peace. These names do not necessarily indicate subdivisions, such as chapters, of a larger group (in this case, "Blood Brothers"), but independent groups that have appropriated that name.

Another pathway for the development of hate groups is through evolutionary change. The discussion of the skinheads movement earlier shows how a group that starts out as a benign, even constructive, collection of individuals can evolve over time to become one of the most violent hate groups in existence today. Another example cited by ADL is the organization known as the Foundation for the Marketplace of Ideas, which grew out of a conservative Republican group at Michigan State University, Young Americans for Freedom, a legitimate mainstream proponent for conservative ideas. When activist Kyle Bristow became leader of that group, he had more ambitious plans for the group. In 2016, he and a group of others founded a more radical, violent organization that is now known as The Foundation for the Marketplace of Ideas (Balleck 2019, 125–127; it was listed as a hate group by SPLC in 2019 but has since been removed from that list. For more background on the organization, see Tanner and Burghart 2018).

What Do Hate Groups Do?

What is it that hate groups actually *do*? A range of answers is possible for that question.

Violent Activities

One possible answer is that hate groups carry out violent crimes against individuals or groups of individuals against whom they hold an animosity. Public accounts of hate group activities often depict crowds of individuals with characteristic dress and symbols (such as swastikas and Nazi flags) waving rifles and other types of firearms. In fact, there are virtually no data showing that hate groups carry out violent crimes, *as a group*, in this fashion. The evidence that does exist suggests that individuals who may or may not be members of hate groups *do* carry out some crimes.

For example, in May 2017, eighteen-year-old Devon Arthurs was accused of the murder of two roommates at an apartment complex in Tampa, Florida. All three individuals were at the time members of the neo-Nazi Atomwaffen group (Thompson

2018). In another example of such a crime, forty-year-old Russell Courtier and his girlfriend, both white, were found guilty of intentionally running over nineteen-year-old Larnell Bruce Jr., a Black man, in their jeep. Courtier was a member of the hate group European Kindred, which he had joined while incarcerated in prison ("How an Oregon Murder Trial Reflected the True Face of America" 2019). Courtier was later given a death sentence in the crime. (For a more detailed discussion of such crimes, see especially "New Hate and Old: The Changing Face of American White Supremacy" 2020.)

Much more common are crimes committed by individuals who are inspired by, but not members of, one or another hate group. One of the most famous of such cases in recent years involved the murder of nine African Americans at the Emmanuel African Methodist Episcopal Church in Charleston, South Carolina, by twenty-two-year-old Dylann Roof in June 2015. Detailed reviews of Roof's life found that he had become inspired to carry out his actions by studying various hate group online sites about Black-on-white crimes (Collins 2017). There has been a significant increase in the number of crimes like those committed by Roof in years. Such crimes have become known as *lone wolf* (if one person is involved) or *leaderless resistance* (generally, two men) (Lenz et al. 2015). One recent study of the phenomenon has concluded that crimes of this type pose "a significant threat to public safety" (Chermak, Freilich, and Suttmoeller 2011, 2). The same study attempted to show how hate groups have been involved in such events, which claimed more than 560 lives between 1990 and 2010 alone (Chermak, Freilich, and Suttmoeller 2011, 4).

Socialization and Support

Humans have a tendency to spend time with others who have the same interests. People who enjoy the use of firearms, for example, tend to join gun clubs. Others who like to read may join book clubs. And individuals with strong political leanings may become Democrats, Republicans, or some other designation. So, it should hardly be surprising that at least one motivation for joining a hate group is the opportunity to meet with others of the same persuasion, providing an opportunity to share ideas, plans, and hopes with others about Jews, LGBTQ folks, Muslims, or other minorities. Neither should it be surprising that these get together may often be the most important single reason for becoming member of a group and that a group might go out of its way to provide social events to strengthen bonds among people.

The KKK has an especially long history in this respect. Some historians have argued, for example, that the primary reason for the founding of the Klan was just for this purpose: a social club for like-minded individuals (although its early history largely belies this argument). Even today, Klan chapters have developed and offer a host of social events that mimic social gatherings that occur in any neighborhood or community, such as backyard barbecues. These gatherings generally appear to have no element of violence, but are simply an opportunity for like-minded people to get together. They often have, however, a distinctly Klan (or other hate group) tone to them, such as Klan-sponsored "kookouts" or Christmas-themed "Klanta Klaus" parties for children of a group ("How Hate Groups Form" 2020; Palmer 2012). (Of course, these events often serve the additional purpose of recruitment opportunities for Klan chapters.)

Some hate groups that have been more successful recently have also made a point of explaining that they are primarily fraternal organizations interested in the protection of Western culture. They tend to especially eschew violence as part of their platforms, although outside observers sometimes point to actions that contradict those claims (Morlin 2017; Sommer 2017).

Propagandizing

One of the most important functions of any hate group (as with most other nonhate groups) is propagandizing, the distribution of information about some particular organization or cause, often presented in a biased or misleading manner. Propagandizing is important not only to explain a group's position on some topic (such as Muslim activities) but also to gain greater understanding and acceptance of this position. Even more important is the recruitment of new members to the group as a result of this type of publicity.

Throughout most of the history of hate groups, one of the most common forms of propagandizing is with printed materials, such as newspapers and newsletters, posters, banners, stickers, and flyers. Indeed, for many Americans, the most common contact one has with a hate group is a flyer found attached to the windshield of one's car.

ADL conducts an annual survey of propagandizing by organizations that it has designated as hate groups. The 2020 report found a total of 2,713 events or actions in 2019 that could be considered to be propagandizing, more than double the number listed for 2018 (1,214) and more than six times the number reported for 2017. About a quarter of events in 2019 occurred on college and university campuses, a number about the same as in 2018. Three hate groups—Patriot Front, American Identity Movement, and New Jersey European Heritage Association—were responsible for 90 percent of all propagandizing events. The themes most often used by Patriot Front (responsible for two-thirds of all events overall) were "One Nation Against Invasion," "For the Nation Against the State," "America is Not for Sale," "Revolution is Tradition," "Reclaim America," and "Deport Them All" ("Year-Over-Year. White Supremacists Double Down on Propaganda in 2019" 2020, 5).

The ADL report also draws attention to events it calls "flash demonstrations." These events are marches, gatherings, or similar events that take place without advance notice, make their statement, and then disburse fairly quickly (thus giving protesters little or no opportunity to respond to an event). ACL counted twenty-seven such events in 2019, the majority of which were Klan rallies of one or two dozen participants.

Perhaps the most notable such event occurred at a Holocaust memorial meeting in Russellville, Arkansas, at which members of the Shield Wall Network assembled, chanting "6 million more," waving swastika flags, and holding signs with message such as "The Holocaust didn't happen, but it should have" ("Year-Over-Year. White Supremacists Double Down on Propaganda in 2019" 2020, 11).

Signs and Symbols

Among the most treasured of resources for a hate group are signs and symbols that "belong" to the group. These signs and symbols can occur in a number of formats, including acronyms supposedly known primarily or only to group members, numbers with special significance, phrases that may be associated only with group membership, logos, flags, and hand signals. The most complete summary of these items has been published by ADL, which lists more than two hundred such items (for a complete list of signs and symbols, see "Hate on Display™ Hate Symbols Database" 2020).

As an example, the numeric symbol "100%" generally has the meaning "100% white," used by white supremacist individuals or groups. As with other types of symbols, this number is often tattooed on a person's body to indicate his or her membership in a specific group. Another popular numerical symbol is "14," "14 words," or some variation of the number. It stands for the fourteen words that occur in a popular white supremacist slogan, "We must secure the existence of our people and a future for white children."

Signs and symbols have two primary roles in the function of a hate group. First, they are visible evidence of a person's membership in and commitment to some specific group and the ideals for which it stands. This role is not trivial. A member who leaves the group or otherwise offends the group leadership may be required to remove any symbolic tattoos carrying that symbol. There have been cases in which the offending member (or previous member) has had his tattoo removed either by burning (on occasions, with a blow torch) or by excision with a knife (Schiller 2014).

Signs and symbols can also be used as scare tactics to nonmembers and non–hate group individuals. The noose and swastika both have frightening aspects for nonwhites and Jews, respectively, over long periods of time. The use of such a symbol as a tattoo, part of a uniform, on a flag or banner, or in some other ways can be regarded as very threatening for individuals of various minorities ("Swastikas and Other Hate Symbols" 2017).

Hate symbols often have more concrete roles to play for those planning to commit hate crimes. For example, Dylann Roof, who shot to death nine worshipers at a church in Charleston, South Carolina, in 2015, carried with him eighty-eight bullets for the crime. The number "88" is used by hate groups to stand for the eighth letter of the alphabet, "H," so that its double use is intended to stand for "Heil Hitler." The 88 symbolism was also used by two men who planned to assassinate President Barack Obama in 2008. The "88" goal would be accomplished by killing 88 Blacks, among whom fourteen would be decapitated (Willingham 2019).

The Internet

Until less than about a decade ago, hate groups relied on only two methods to communicate with their members and the general public: the written and spoken word. If a group wanted to get its message out, it used speeches, rallies, leaflets, newsletters, and similar ways of contacting other people. Today, that reality has changed dramatically. Probably the most common tool that hate groups use is the Internet. It is now possible simply to type the name of a hate group into a browser to find its home page (or some other reference) on which one can find out details about the organization, such as its history, purpose, officers, membership rules, activities, and available resources, as well as ways of joining the group or making a financial donation.

How has the Internet benefited the existence and operation of hate groups? First, the Internet allows a user to remain anonymous. So, if one finds a web page for the Ku Klox Klun, one has no way of knowing who the owners of that website might be. It might very well *not* be any hate organization with that name. It might instead be owned by some other type of group in Russia or China. Thus, the site may contain statements that have no contact with reality in any way that may or may not be legitimate expressions of the views of the Ku Klox Klun, whether it exists or not. Of course, anonymity of web users has been a fundamental principle of the Internet since its origin in the 1980s. The original, and persistent, concept was and has been to guarantee a person's right of free speech in his or her use of the web. Removing the mask of anonymity might be a way of dealing with the unhealthy use of the Internet by hate groups. But it might also pose a serious threat to the right of individuals to carry on free and unrestricted discussions on the web (Mondal et al. 2018).

The Internet also provides individuals and groups with an opportunity to reach large groups of users across wide geographical areas in essentially real time. The push of a button can release one's website or other web message to millions of users in virtually every country in the world. An additional feature of this tool has been revealed only recently. An argument has been made that one way of reducing a hate group's access to the Internet is simply for an Internet service provider to close down that group's website. For social media companies such as Facebook or Twitter, for example, technology permits the company to prohibit an organization from having access to its site. The troubling discovery, however, is that the electronic technology associated with the Internet allows a "disappeared" site to reappear almost instantaneously at almost any location in the world. A consequence of this discovery is the realization that closing down one site may only exacerbate the problem, allowing not one new site, but perhaps multiple sites, to take the place of the banned hate group site (for the breakthrough research on this topic, see Johnson et al. 2019).

The Internet also provides a tool by which hate groups can easily raise money. First, the geographic reach of the Internet makes it possible for a hate group to reach out to an almost endless list of users who may be interested in contributing to the group. The potential pool of contributors is, thus, expanded almost beyond imagination. Hate groups can also make use of a host of existing Internet resources to increase their donor base. For example, a group can open an account on GoFundMe, FundRazr, Indiegogo, Kickstarter, or some other crowdfunding site to collect funds for their operation. One example that has been cited is a GoFundMe campaign created by the American Freedom Party ostensibly created to protect white South Africans from "genocide." But, as it turns out, some of the money collected went to a commemoration of Adolf Hitler's birthday ("Funding Hate: How White Supremacists Raise Their Money" 2017).

Many other online platforms are available for legitimate methods for collecting donations for hate groups. For example, Amazon provides an ad hoc method for fundraising for hate groups (and many other kinds of groups) both through its normal business models and through special contributory programs designed to help philanthropic agencies. In the first instance, books and other materials whose sale profits can help a hate group may be as readily available to the general public online as is virtually any other type of products. Thus, the company, probably unknowingly and maybe unwillingly, may be helping to promote hate campaigns in the United States and around the world (Breland 2019; Kotch 2020a).

The Internet is also a powerful tool for hate groups' efforts to increase their own membership. Without this tool, such groups would have to rely on word of mouth, print media, radio and television, and other systems with relatively limited reach (Proud Boys and the like are unlikely to take out advertisements on national television to promote their cause). All an

Internet promotion needs for a recruiting campaign is a relatively modest financial investment and the push of a button to send out its messages to millions of people around the world. As with mass marketing, the return rate of such a campaign can easily be less than 0.1 percent, still large enough to increase membership numbers for one or another hate group (Kamenetz 2018; Keneally 2018).

Perhaps the most revealing success with regard to the use of the Internet involved planning for the Unite the Right rally in Charlottesville, Virginia, in November 2017. Several groups were able to communicate with each other via the web platform Discord, a primary hub for more than 150 million gamers worldwide. The hate groups were able to share and carry out plans for the rally on Discord, including arranging for speakers, reserving and booking hotel rooms, and obtaining necessary permits from the city. When Discord found out about the event, it blocked a number of hate group accounts, announcing that the site's goal was to bring people together, not tear them apart (Glaser 2018; Weill 2018).

The value of the Internet was revealed once more after Discord's action. In planning for the second Unite the Right march planned for Washington, D.C., in November 2018, planners simply switched to other platforms, especially Facebook Messenger and Signal, an encrypted texting app familiar to many of the groups.

Several organizations have attempted to find ways in which the problematic use of the Internet by hate groups can be reduced or eliminated. The fundamental problem, as noted earlier, is the conflict between finding ways of preventing speech that can actually have verifiable and harmful effects on individuals or society and the right to free speech guaranteed by the U.S. Constitution (although not necessarily so guaranteed in other nations). One of the most thorough of these studies is a report produced by the Center for American Progress in 2018, *Curbing Hate Online: What Should Companies Do?*. The report reviews the main points presented here, along with a set of recommended changes in policies and practices that will achieve an effective balance between rights of free speech and protection against hate group harm (Fernandez 2018).

Working within the System

Another, less common, form of activism involves working within the system to achieve a group's goals. Possibly the earliest expression of this approach can be traced to the early 1970s with the work of white supremacist David Duke. A college-educated, intelligent, attractive young man, Duke was as committed to the goals of the KKK as many other men and women of the time were. In fact, he was eventually elected grand wizard of the national group.

But Duke argued that the way the Klan was going about its business was counterproductive with the general public. The average person, he said, was so turned off by the clothing, tattoos, rhetoric, and other aspects of white supremacism that they could never take seriously, less accept, the message that the Klan was trying to deliver. In one of his most memorable quotes in his early career, he advised his followers to "get out of the cow pasture and into hotel meeting rooms" (Wade 1987, 368). This advice later evolved into a form of hate actions sometimes referred to as "coat-and-tie" activity.

Duke himself took this advice seriously, and almost always appeared as a well-dressed, seemingly well-behaved lobbyist for a particular viewpoint in political debate. His concept of political activism has been at least partly vindicated by his modest success in the political field, most importantly his election to the U.S. House of Representative from the state of Louisiana in 1989. Duke's approach eventually gained more or less acceptance in at least some parts of the hate group universe. For example, in the Unite the Right march of November 2017 in Charlottesville, Virginia, several participants were dressed in conventional clothing that would, under other circumstances, have made their presence unremarkable (Wolf 2017). Today, a significant number of hate groups acknowledge to a greater or lesser degree the value of eschewing violence as a way of achieving their objectives and frame their work within the context of just a point of view that is part of the political mainstream in the United States today ("U.S. White Supremacy Groups" 2020).

An example of some of the most effective use of "coat-and-tie" action by hate groups is the spread of anti-sharia laws in the states. An anti-sharia law is a piece of legislation that prevents the introduction of any type or aspect of law from some foreign country, most commonly, sharia law that is predominant in many Islamic states. A model statute for this type of law has been produced by the Center for Security Policy, a group that SPLC has labeled a hate group in its 2020 report. Some form of the law has been introduced at least forty times in seventeen states between 2011 and 2018. It has been passed in eleven states during that period. These actions appear, however, to be largely symbolic, with little or no identifiable impact on the legal system of any state. They are then, for the most part, an effort by the Center for Security Policy to "draw attention to their anti-Muslim beliefs" (Olalde and Gardiner 2019).

Other Activities

Experts on hate groups have taken note of the fact that such organizations will seize upon almost any type of activity to gain new members and further their cause. A particularly striking example of the fact can be traced to the coronavirus pandemic of 2020. At a midpoint of that event, questions began to arise as to when some types of "normal" activity could be restored. After being confined to their own homes for at least two months, many citizens were eager to have governmental permission to return to restaurants, beauty parlors, department stores, athletic events, and other events that had been closed down for an extended period of time. Some individuals who felt most strongly about this problem eventually began to organize protests at state capitols and other governmental buildings to make their case. Generally, such protests were peaceful, exhibiting little or no violence.

One of the most interesting features, however, was the presence of members from hate groups that have not typically been associated with everyday political or social issues, such as Proud Boys, and groups such as militias that make up a large part of the patriot movement. The presence of such individuals has been easily confirmed because of their characteristic uniforms, banners, symbols, and other representations. In addition, notice of upcoming protests and calls for hate group participation have been readily available on social media, especially 4chan, QAnon, Reddit, and similar sites (Farivar 2020). Much of the evidence for the involvement of hate groups in reopening protests has come from internal documents that outline the rationale and plans for disruptive activities from the groups themselves (Kotch 2020b; an unconfirmed report of possible hate group protesters against a march held in honor of George Floyd, killed by police officers in Minneapolis, can be found at "White Bystanders Armed with Rifles Watch Floyd Protesters March in Indiana" 2020).

Not all authorities blame hate groups for hijacking protests, marches, and riots. In May 2020, for example, Attorney General William Barr suggested that "far left extremist groups" were pursuing their own objectives distinct from coronavirus issues in these protests. Barr did not immediately refer to the evidence he had for making such a statement, although President Donald Trump shortly thereafter repeated and endorsed Barr's claims ("Barr Blames 'Far-Left Extremist Groups' for Violence amid George Floyd Protests" 2020).

Why, the question is, would hate groups have any interest in reopening the U.S. economy during a time of the pandemic? The answer appears to be that many such groups are eager to take advantage of any opportunity of any time to take advantage of public dissatisfaction or distrust of the government, possibly encouraging them to join with the hate movement, in spirit, if not in actual membership. This approach holds special appeal to accelerationists, who hope to take advantage of any chance to encourage opposition to traditional governmental structure and function, and bring about a second civil war in the United States (Reid and Valasik 2020). (Some members of hate groups label such an uprising as "the boogaloo," an armed rebellion against the government; Zadrozny 2020.)

Fighting Back

Several approaches have been suggested for dealing with the harm that can be caused by the activities of hate groups: educational programs, legislation dealing with hate crimes, court action against offending groups, and counteroffensive actions against such groups.

Education

One example of a program for teaching about hate groups is the "Confronting White Nationalism in Schools" toolkit developed by the Western States Center. The program makes use of possible scenarios involving hate crimes with methods for dealing with such events for students, parents, staff, and administration. Some scenarios used in the program include the appearance of hateful symbols and speech in a school, evidence of white nationalist organizing outside of the school environment, and organizational efforts for white nationalist groups within the school (Flanagan, Acee, and Schubiner 2019; also see "After Charlottesville: Teaching about Racism, Antisemitism and White Supremacy" 2020; "Don't Be a Puppet" n.d.; "Hate Crimes" n.d.; O'Neill n.d.).

Legislation

Some people might suggest that hate groups be more closely monitored by the adoption of laws that limit or prohibit their activities. In fact, no such laws referring to *groups* exist in the United States or other parts of the world. The main reason for this situation is that hate crimes today are almost never committed by organized groups who carry out violent activities against other groups. Some members of such groups *are* involved in such activities, and those actions can be described and punished by statutes. Some of the laws dealing with hate *crimes* include The Matthew Shepard and James Byrd Jr. Hate Crimes Prevention Act of 2009 (18 U.S.C. § 249); Criminal Interference with Right to Fair Housing Act of 2015 (42 U.S.C. § 3631); Damage to Religious Property, Church Arson Prevention Act of 1996 (18 U.S.C. § 247); Violent Interference with Federally Protected Rights Act of 1968 (18 U.S.C. § 245); and Conspiracy Against Rights Act of 1968 (18 U.S.C. § 241) ("Hate Crime Laws" 2019).

Court Cases

The absence of laws against the existence or actions of hate groups has long made it difficult to those affected by such groups to bring legal action against them. There is some precedent for such suits, however, in legal actions by individuals and organizations against specific hate groups, such as the KKK, in the early and mid-twentieth century. Those cases have been few and far between, however, until the most recent times. An example of this kind of action is a case filed against two hate groups, Patriot Movement AZ and AZ Patriots, in 2019 by a coalition of Arizona churches. The churches argued that the hate groups had harassed volunteers attempting to aid migrants seeking refuge from federal immigration officials. The case was eventually settled in 2020 when the patriot groups agreed to a settlement with the churches (MacDonald-Evoy 2020).

Similar cases have been filed in the last few years, most of which have not yet been resolved in the courts. Perhaps the most famous of these cases was a tort action taken by the organization Integrity First for America against several hate groups involved in the Charlottesville, Virginia, riots of November 2017 and the leaders of those groups. The groups named in the action include Vanguard America, Traditionalist Worker Party, League of the South, and National Socialist Movement ("324

F.Supp.3d 765 (2018)" 2018). A somewhat similar action was also taken in 2019 by the city of Dayton, Ohio, against a KKK-related group, the Honorable Sacred Knights. The suit claimed that while the Knights' actions were probably protected by the First and Second Amendments of the U.S. Constitution, the city had proof that the group was likely to carry out paramilitary actions during its march in the city scheduled for May 25, 2019 (Schaefer and Reed 2019).

Legal Actions

Why, one might ask, is some type of legal action against hate groups not a sensible and common procedure? The main problem with this approach is that the actions for which hate groups are almost always best known are some form of speech, either verbal, print, or electronic. And the courts have confirmed several times that these forms of action are protected by the First Amendment of the U.S. Constitution. Only if a hate group carries out some type of illegal behavior, such as setting fire to a church, is it likely to face investigation and criminal proceedings from law enforcement agencies.

It is for that reason that several arrests by federal law enforcement officers in early 2020 drew so much attention in the public media. Those arrests involved members of a hate group known as "The Base." The group had adopted many of the principles espoused and used by the Arabic group, Al Qaeda, whose name in English is also "The Base." Its purpose has been to bring about radical revolution and the ultimate demise of the United States government. It especially encourages actions by independent "lone wolves" and "accelerationists" attempting to hasten the government's demise.

The measures against The Base are fundamentally different from earlier efforts to control hate speech by hate groups. Federal agents had obtained recordings among Base members describing specific acts of terror, such as the derailing of trains, poisoning of water supplies, and murder of individuals. As Robert K. Hur, U.S. attorney for Maryland said, these defendants "did more than talk. . . . They took steps to act and act violently on their racist views" ("The Base" 2020; MacFarquhar and Goldman 2020). As of late 2020, it is still too early to know how extensively this tool will be used against terrorists and the success it may have for the purpose of controlling hate groups.

Counteroffensive Actions

Among the most successful efforts to combat the activities of hate groups has been the formation and actions of groups created especially for this purpose. This book has already highlighted the activities of two of the most important of these groups, the ADL and the SPLC (for more details on the groups themselves, see their entries in chapter 4 of this book).

Perhaps the most visible of current anti–hate group organization is Antifa, an abbreviation for the term *antifascist*. Antifa is not a typical organization, with leaders, chapters, official membership roles, mission statements, and the like. Instead, it is a collection of fluid groups of individuals who subscribe to a common goal: to react aggressively to far-right political movements. It is sometimes referred to as an "organizing strategy." One expression of this mission is a quote from an early proponent of the movement, Spanish revolutionary José Buenaventura Durruti Dumange (1896–1936), who said, "Fascism is not to be debated, it is to be destroyed" (Bray 2017, 1).

Although its earliest history dates to the late nineteenth century, Antifa became particularly popular in the 1930s with the rise of fascist governments in Germany, Italy, and Spain. The movement was slow to move to the United States because, of course, no fascist government of any significance existed in this country. In fact, Antifa was largely moribund in the United States until about 2016, when Donald Trump was elected as the president of the United States. With Trump's accession to power and the subsequent rise of far-right hate groups, Antifa achieved its first awakening in this country. As rallies by hate groups became more common and more violent, the same occurred with Antifa groups. Today, almost any hate group event that occurs in public is likely to be countered by a similar action from Antifa supporters. Probably the most dramatic example of this conflict between groups occurred at the Unite the Right rally held in Charlottesville in 2017 ("Watch: Here's What You Need to Know about Antifa" 2017; "Seven Things You Need to Know about Antifa" 2020).

Antifa activities have often drawn as much criticism as that of hate groups themselves. The complaint is that violence by hate groups cannot be overcome by equivalent violence by Antifa groups. As an example, President Trump announced on May 31, 2020, that "the United States of America will be designating ANTIFA as a Terrorist Organization" (Perez and Hoffman 2020). His administration later produced evidence for the validity of this action (which, some scholars said, was probably unconstitutional). That evidence was later shown to be inaccurate (Mackey 2020). The debate over Antifa actions is, however, hardly over and can be expected to continue into the foreseeable future.

Conclusion

In recent years, the SPLC and ADL have tried to count the number of hate groups active in the United States. Those efforts have been challenging because most hate groups tend to be small, often poorly organized, and usually secretive in their operation. Given these research problems, both groups have estimated that about one thousand hate groups appear to be active in the United States at any one time.

Most of these groups are evanescent with brief histories and modest activity at any one time. They hardly represent a major threat to American society. On the other hand, some of these hate groups have been in existence in some form or another for decades, with ambitious programs in opposition to Jews, LGBTQ people, Muslims, immigrants, and other minorities. These groups feel strongly enough that many have developed active programs through which they make known their goals and work to achieve those goals by one means or another, often with violent attacks. The election of a new president in 2016 appears to have altered the dynamics of this hate group movement. Whether the changes one currently sees in the hate group movement are a temporary and nonthreatening challenge to American society or they represent the outward expression of a deeper political philosophy in the nation's soul is a question that probably will not be answered for many years.

References

"After Charlottesville: Teaching about Racism, Antisemitism and White Supremacy." 2020. ADL. https://www.adl.org/education/resources/tools-and-strategies/after-charlottesville-teaching-about-racism-antisemitism.

Alkebulan, Paul. 2012. *Survival Pending Revolution: the History of the Black Panther Party.* Tuscaloosa: The University of Alabama Press.

Altman, Alex. 2016. "The Billionaire and the Bigots." *Time.* https://time.com/4293564/the-billionaire-and-the-bigots.

Alvarez, Alma Rosa. 2018. "Guest Opinion: KKK Fliers Are Anything but Harmless." *Mail Tribune.* https://mailtribune.com/news/top-stories/guest-opinion-kkk-fliers-are-anything-but-harmless.

"American Border Patrol/American Patrol." n.d. Southern Poverty Law Center. https://www.splcenter.org/fighting-hate/extremist-files/group/american-border-patrolamerican-patrol.

"America's National Socialist Party." n.d. National Socialist Movement. https://www.nsm88.org/aboutus.html.

"Anti-Muslim Activities in the United States: Violence, Threats, and Discrimination at the Local Level." 2018. New America. https://www.newamerica.org/in-depth/anti-muslim-activity/.

"Anti-Semitism: Neo-Nazism." 2020. Jewish Virtual Library. https://www.jewishvirtuallibrary.org/neo-nazism-2#5.

Antifa.atl. 2020. "Paul Townsend of LaFayette, Georgia: League of the South Member and 'Unite the Right' Participant Advocates Genocide." Atlanta Antifa. https://atlantaantifa.org/2020/04/27/paul-townsend-of-lafayette-georgia-league-of-the-south-member-and-unite-the-right-participant-advocates-genocide.

"Antigovernment Movement." 2020. Southern Poverty Law Center. https://www.splcenter.org/fighting-hate/extremist-files/ideology/antigovernment.

"Aryan Nations." n.d. Southern Poverty Law Center. https://www.splcenter.org/fighting-hate/extremist-files/group/aryan-nations.

Atkinson, David C. 2018. "Charlottesville and the Alt-right: A Turning Point?" *Politics, Groups, and Identities* 6 (2): 309–315.

"Audit of Antisemitic Incidents 2019." 2020. ADL. https://www.adl.org/audit2019#major-findings.

Balleck, Barry J. 2019. *Hate Groups and Extremist Organizations in America: An Encyclopedia*. Santa Barbara, CA: ABC-CLIO.

Bangert, Dave. 2018. "KKK Recruiting Fliers Found on Cars, Businesses Downtown Lafayette." Journal & Courier. https://www.jconline.com/story/news/2018/01/12/kkk-recruiting-fliers-found-cars-businesses-downtown-lafayette/1028824001/.

"Barr Blames 'Far-Left Extremist Groups' for Violence Amid George Floyd Protests." 2020. YouTube. https://www.youtube.com/watch?v=RaWrHPBdqXE.

"The Base." 2020. ADL. https://www.adl.org/resources/backgrounders/the-base.

Beauchamp, Zack. 2019. "Accelerationism: The Obscure Idea Inspiring White Supremacist Killers Around the World."

Vox. https://www.vox.com/the-highlight/2019/11/11/20882005/accelerationism-white-supremacy-christchurch.

Ben Levy, Sholomo. 2012. "The Black Jewish or Hebrew Israelite Community." Jewish Virtual Library. https://web.archive.org/web/20120709012354/https://www.jewishvirtuallibrary.org/jsource/Judaism/blackjews.html.

"Billy Roper." n.d. Southern Poverty Law Center. https://www.splcenter.org/fighting-hate/extremist-files/individual/billy-roper.

Bishop, Katherine. 1988. "Neo-Nazi Activity is Arising among U.S. Youth." *The New York Times*. https://archive.nytimes.com/www.nytimes.com/library/national/race/061388race-ra.html.

Blazak, Randy. 2009. "Toward a Working Definition of Hate Groups." In Barbara Perry, et al., eds. *Hate Crimes*, 4 vols., 133–162. Westport, CT: Praeger Publishers.

Bray, Mark. 2017. *Antifa: The Antifascist Handbook*. Brooklyn, NY and London: Melville House Publishing.

Breland, Ali. 2019. "How Facebook and Amazon Help Hate Groups Raise Money." *Mother Jones*. https://www.motherjones.com/politics/2019/03/facebook-amazon-smile-fundraising-hate-discrimination/.

Bridge Initiative Team. 2017. "Factsheet: Center for Security Policy." Bridge. https://bridge.georgetown.edu/research/factsheet-center-for-security-policy/.

"Brien James." 2018. One People Project. http://onepeoplesproject.com/2018/08/21/brien-james/.

Brooks, Joanna. 2000. "Prince Hall, Freemasonry, and Genealogy." *African American Review* 34 (2): 197–216. https://doi.org/10.2307/2901249.

Bush, George. 1990. "Address before a Joint Session of the Congress on the Persian Gulf Crisis and the Federal Budget Deficit." The American Presidency Project. https://www

.presidency.ucsb.edu/documents/address-before-joint-session-the-congress-the-persian-gulf-crisis-and-the-federal-budget.

Carless, Will, and Aaron Sankin. 2018. "The Hate Report: The State of Anti-immigrant Hate, 2018." Reveal. https://www.revealnews.org/blog/the-hate-report-the-state-of-anti-immigrant-hate-2018/.

"Center for Immigration Studies Files a Civil RICO Lawsuit against the President of Southern Poverty Law Center." 2019. Center for Immigration Studies. https://cis.org/Litigation/CIS-RICO-Lawsuit-SPLC.

Chermak, Steven M., Joshua D. Freilich, and Michael Suttmoeller. 2011. "The Organizational Dynamics of Far Right Hate Groups in the United States: Comparing Violent to Non Violent Organizations." Final Report to Human Factors/Behavioral Sciences Division, Science and Technology Directorate, U.S. Department of Homeland Security. College Park MD: START. https://www.dhs.gov/sites/default/files/publications/944_OPSR_TEVUS_Comparing-Violent-Nonviolent-Far-Right-Hate-Groups_Dec2011-508.pdf.

Clark, Charles S. 2020. "Deconstructing the Deep State." Government Executive. https://www.govexec.com/feature/gov-exec-deconstructing-deep-state/.

Collins, Cory. 2017. "The Miseducation of Dylann Roof." Teaching Tolerance. https://www.tolerance.org/magazine/fall-2017/the-miseducation-of-dylann-roof.

Colorado Alliance for Immigration Reform. 2019. cairco.org.

Crain, Caleb. 2020. "City Limits: What a White Supremacist Coup Looks Like." *The New Yorker*. April 27, 2020, 67–71.

"Declaration of Orders We Will Not Obey." 2020. Oath Keepers. https://oathkeepers.org/declaration-of-orders-we-will-not-obey/.

Dentice, Dianne. 2013. "The Demise of White Revolution: What's Next for Billy Roper?" *Social Movement Studies*

12 (4): 466–470. https://doi.org/10.1080/14742837.2013.807729.

Denvir, Daniel. 2015. "The Republican Party is Now America's Largest Hate Group." *Salon*. https://www.salon.com/2015/11/27/the_republican_party_is_now_americas_largest_hate_group/.

Devega, Chauncey. 2016. "Donald Trump Has Dropped the GOP's Mask: Conservatism and Racism Now Officially the Same Thing." *Salon*. https://www.salon.com/2016/03/01/donald_trump_has_dropped_the_gops_mask_conservatism_and_racism_now_officially_the_same_thing/.

"Don't Be a Puppet." n.d. Federal Bureau of Investiation. https://cve.fbi.gov/home.html.

Drabold, Will. 2016. "Here's What Mike Pence Said on LGBT Issues over the Years." *Time*. https://time.com/4406337/mike-pence-gay-rights-lgbt-religious-freedom/.

Dreier, Peter. 2020. "Why Anti-Semitism is on the Rise in the United States." *Dissent*. https://www.dissentmagazine.org/online_articles/anti-semitism-rise-trump.

The Dustin Inman Society. 2020. https://www.thedustininmansociety.org/.

Elsheikh, Elsadig, Basima Sisemore, and Natalia Ramirez Lee. 2017. "Legalizing Othering: The United States of Islamophobia." Haas Institute for a Fair and Inclusive Society, University of California, Berkeley. https://haasinstitute.berkeley.edu/sites/default/files/haas_institute_legalizing_othering_the_united_states_of_islamophobia.pdf.

Etter, Greg W., Sr., David H. McElreath, and Chester L. Quarles. 2005. "The Ku Klux Klan: Evolution towards Revolution." *Journal of Gang Research* 12 (3): 1–16. https://www.researchgate.net/publication/292621352_The_Ku_Klux_Klan_Evolution_towards_revolution.

"Extremist Groups React to the 9/11 Attacks." 2001. Southern Poverty Law Center. https://www.splcenter.org/fighting-hate/intelligence-report/2001/extremist-groups-react-911-attacks.

Farivar, Masood. 2020. "How Far-Right Extremists Are Exploiting the COVID Pandemic." *VOA News*. https://www.voanews.com/covid-19-pandemic/how-far-right-extremists-are-exploiting-covid-pandemic.

Fausett, Richard. 2018. "Rally by White Nationalists Was over Almost before It Began." *The New York Times*. https://www.nytimes.com/2018/08/12/us/politics/charlottesville-va-protest-unite-the-right.html.

Fernandez, Henry. 2018. "Curbing Hate Online: What Companies Should Do Now." Center for American Progress. https://www.americanprogress.org/issues/immigration/reports/2018/10/25/459668/curbing-hate-online-companies-now/.

Fitzsimons, Tim. 2019. "Pence Praises Rule That Would Let Adoption Agencies Exclude Gay Parents." NBC News. https://www.nbcnews.com/feature/nbc-out/pence-praises-rule-would-let-adoption-agencies-exclude-gay-parents-n1081821.

Flanagan, Nora, Jessica Acee, and Lindsay Schubiner. 2019. "Confronting White Nationalism in Schools: A Toolkit." Western States Center. https://www.westernstatescenter.org/2020-white-nationalism-in-schools-trainer.

"Frequently Asked Questions about Hate Groups." 2020. Southern Poverty Law Center. https://www.splcenter.org/20200318/frequently-asked-questions-about-hate-groups#hate%20group.

"Funding Hate: How White Supremacists Raise Their Money." 2017. ADL. https://www.adl.org/media/10761/download.

Goldstein, Phyllis. 2012. *A Convenient Hatred: The History of Antisemitism*. Brookline, MA: Facing History and Ourselves.

Glaser, April. 2018. "White Supremacists Still Have a Safe Space Online." Slate. https://slate.com/technology/2018/10/discord-safe-space-white-supremacists.html.

"The Hammerskin Nation." 2002. ADL. https://www.adl.org/education/resources/profiles/hammerskin-nation.

Hannon, Elliot. 2018. "White Nationalist Leader Posts Pictures of Casual White House Visit a Day after Midterms." Slate. https://slate.com/news-and-politics/2018/11/white-nationalist-identity-evropa-patrick-casey-white-house-twitter-pictures.html.

Hasson, Peter. 2020. *The Manipulators: Google, Facebook, and Silicon Valley's War on Conservatives*. Washington, DC: Regnery Publishing.

"Hate Crime Data Collection Guidelines and Training Manual." 2015. Criminal Justice Information Services (CJIS). Division Uniform Crime Reporting (UCR) Program. Federal Bureau of Investigation. https://ucr.fbi.gov/hate-crime-data-collection-guidelines-and-training-manual.pdf.

"Hate Crime Laws." 2019. United States Department of Justice. https://www.justice.gov/crt/hate-crime-laws.

"Hate Crimes." n.d. Teachers Pay Teachers. https://www.teacherspayteachers.com/Browse/Search:hate%20crimes.

"Hate Groups." 2020. ADL. https://www.adl.org/resources/glossary-terms/hate-group.

"Hate on Display™ Hate Symbols Database." 2020. ADL. https://www.adl.org/hate-symbols.

"Hate over Time." n.d. Southern Poverty Law Center. https://www.splcenter.org/hate-map?ideology=anti-lgbt.

Hauck, Grace. 2019. "Anti-LGBT Hate Crimes Are Rising, the FBI Says. But It Gets Worse." *USA Today*. https://

www.usatoday.com/story/news/2019/06/28/anti-gay-hate-crimes-rise-fbi-says-and-they-likely-undercount/1582614001/.

Hett, Benjamin Carter. 2018. *The Death of Democracy: Hitler's Rise to Power and the Downfall of the Weimar Republic.* New York: Henry Holt and Company.

Higgins, Julia. 2015. "The Rise and Fall of the American Melting Pot." *The Wilson Quarterly.* https://www.wilsonquarterly.com/stories/the-rise-and-fall-of-the-american-melting-pot/.

Hobbs, Stephen, and Caitlin Byrd. 2019. "A Deeper Look at South Carolina's Hate Groups." *The Post and Courier.* https://www.postandcourier.com/a-deeper-look-at-south-carolinas-hate-groups/article_ae2d8092-4752-11e9-8296-2fd276592369.html.

Hoffman, Rafael. 2019. "Who Are the Black Hebrew Israelites?" Hamodia. https://hamodia.com/prime/black-hebrew-israelites/.

Holthouse, David. 2006. "Motley Crews: With Decline of Hammerskins, Independent Skinhead Groups Grow." Southern Poverty Law Center. https://www.splcenter.org/fighting-hate/intelligence-report/2006/motley-crews-decline-hammerskins-independent-skinhead-groups-grow.

"How an Oregon Murder Trial Reflected the True Face of America." 2019. *Independent.* https://www.independent.co.uk/arts-entertainment/tv/features/mobeen-azhar-black-and-white-killing-bbc-larnell-bruce-jr-russell-courtier-portland-oregon-a9078386.html.

"How Hate Groups Form." 2020. ADL. https://www.adl.org/resources/backgrounders/how-hate-groups-form.

Johnson, N. F., et al. 2019. "Hidden Resilience and Adaptive Dynamics of the Global Online Hate Ecology. *Nature*

573 (7773): 261–265. https://www.nature.com/articles/s41586-019-1494-7.pdf.

Kamenetz, Anya. 2018. "Right-Wing Hate Groups Are Recruiting Video Gamers." NPR. https://www.npr.org/2018/11/05/660642531/right-wing-hate-groups-are-recruiting-video-gamers.

Keneally, Meghan. 2018. "Hate Groups Using Similar Online Recruiting Methods as ISIS, Experts Say." ABC News. https://abcnews.go.com/US/hate-groups-similar-online-recruiting-methods-isis-experts/story?id=53528932.

"The Knights Party." 2018. https://kkk.bz/.

Kotch, Alex. 2020a. "Funding Hate: How Online Merchants and Payment Processors Help White Nationalists Raise Money." Center for Media and Democracy. https://www.exposedbycmd.org/wp-content/uploads/2020/04/Funding-Hate-Report-by-CMD.pdf.

Kotch, Alex. 2020b. "Secretive Right-Wing Nonprofit Plays Role in COVID-19 Organizing." PR Watch. https://www.prwatch.org/news/2020/05/13581/secretive-right-wing-nonprofit-plays-role-covid-19-organizing.

Krikorian, Mark. 2019. "Nobody Expects the SPLC Inquisition!" Center for Immigration Studies. https://cis.org/Oped/Nobody-Expects-SPLC-Inquisition.

"Ku Klux Klan: A History of Racism." 2011. Southern Poverty Law Center, 6th ed. https://www.splcenter.org/sites/default/files/Ku-Klux-Klan-A-History-of-Racism.pdf.

Kunzelman, Michael. 2020. "Judge Tosses out Lawsuit over Law Center's Hate Group Labels." AP. https://apnews.com/a5cabf26f1c1487baf7d4997f7139972.

Kurtz, Hilda E., et al. 2018. "Special Forum: In the Aftermath of the Hate Rally in Charlottesville." *Southeastern Geographer* 58 (1): 6–38.

Kushner, Harvey W. 2003. *Encyclopedia of Terrorism*. 2003. Thousand Oaks, CA: Sage Publications.

Lay, Shawn. [2005] 2016. "Ku Klux Klan in the Twentieth Century." New Georgia Encyclopedia. https://www.georgiaencyclopedia.org/articles/history-archaeology/ku-klux-klan-twentieth-century.

League of the South. 2014. https://leagueofthesouth.com/.

Lehman, Charles Fain. 2020. "Review: 'The Manipulators' by Peter Hasson. Washington Free Beacon. https://freebeacon.com/culture/review-the-manipulators-by-peter-hasson/.

Lenz, Ryan, et al. 2015. "Age of the Wolf: A Study of the Rise of Lone Wolf and Leaderless Resistance Terrorism." Southern Poverty Law Center. https://www.splcenter.org/sites/default/files/d6_legacy_files/downloads/publication/lone_wolf_special_report_0.pdf.

Lester, J. C., and D. L. Wilson. [1905] 2010. *Ku Klux Klan: Its Origin, Growth and Disbandment*. New York: Neale Publishing Company. http://www.gutenberg.org/ebooks/31819.

Letts, Don. 2016. "The Story of Skinheads." YouTube (video). https://www.youtube.com/watch?v=SemmTRV_fnw.

MacDonald-Evoy, Jerod. 2020. "Extremist Group Patriot Movement Az Agrees to Settle Federal Lawsuit with Valley Churches." *AZ Mirror*. https://www.azmirror.com/blog/extremist-group-patriot-movement-az-agrees-to-settle-federal-lawsuit-with-valley-churches/.

MacFarquhar, Neil, and Adam Goldman. 2020. "A New Face of White Supremacy: Plots Expose Danger of the 'Base.'" *The New York Times*. https://www.nytimes.com/2020/01/22/us/white-supremacy-the-base.html.

Mackey, Robert. 2020. "White House Forced to Retract Claim Viral Videos Prove Antifa Is Plotting Violence." *The Intercept*. https://theintercept.com/2020/06/04/white

-house-forced-retract-claim-viral-videos-prove-antifa-plotting-violence/.

Man, Anthony. 2019. "Worldwide Christian Ministry Based in Fort Lauderdale Fights 'Hate Group' Label." *South Florida Sun-Sentinel.* https://www.sun-sentinel.com/local/broward/fort-lauderdale/fl-ne-kennedy-ministries-splc-hate-group-ruling-20190920-yyzvi6zp2rgvzatlkwcgsll37u-story.html.

May, Clifford D. 2011. "Among the Believers." Foundation for Defense of Democracies. https://www.fdd.org/analysis/2011/08/25/among-the-believers/.

McVeighn, Rory. 1999. "Structural Incentives for Conservative Mobilization: Power Devaluation and the Rise of the Ku Klux Klan, 1915–1925." *Social Forces* 77 (4): 1461–1496. https://doi.org/10.2307/3005883.

Mettler, Katie. 2019. "How a Black Man "Outsmarted" a Neo-Nazi Group—and Became Their New Leader." *Denver Post.* https://www.denverpost.com/2019/03/02/black-man-leads-national-socialist-movement/.

Mondal, Mainack, et al. 2018. "Characterizing Usage of Explicit Hate Expressions in Social Media." *New Review of Hypermedia and Multimedia* 24 (2): 110–130. https://homepages.dcc.ufmg.br/~fabricio/download/tham_mondal2018.pdf.

"Montana Klansman's Idea for 'Inclusive' KKK Elicits Derision." 2014. *Orcinus.* http://dneiwert.blogspot.com/2014/11/montana-klansmans-idea-for-inclusive.html.

Moore, Jack B. 1993. *Skinheads Shaved for Battle: A Cultural History of American Skinheads.* Madison: University of Wisconsin Press.

Morlin, Bill. 2017. "New "Fight Club" Ready for Street Violence." Southern Poverty Law Center. https://www.splcenter.org/hatewatch/2017/04/25/new-fight-club-ready-street-violence.

Murphy, Dean E. 2002. "Graying Black Panthers Fight Would-Be Heirs." *Global Action on Aging*. http://globalag.igc.org/ruralaging/us/blackpanthers.htm.

"The Nation of Islam." 2020. ADL. https://www.adl.org/resources/profiles/the-nation-of-islam.

"Nation of Islam." n.d. Southern Poverty Law Center. https://www.splcenter.org/fighting-hate/extremist-files/group/nation-islam.

Nelson, Libby. 2017. "'Why We Voted for Donald Trump': David Duke Explains the White Supremacist Charlottesville Protests." *Vox*. https://www.vox.com/2017/8/12/16138358/charlottesville-protests-david-duke-kkk.

"New Hate and Old: The Changing Face of American White Supremacy." 2020. ADL. https://www.adl.org/media/11894/download.

"Non-Discrimination and Anti-Violence Policy." 2019. ACT for America. https://www.actforamerica.org/policy.

Olalde, Mark, and Dustin Gardiner. 2019. "The Network Behind State Bills 'Countering' Sharia Law and Terrorism." *Public Integrity*. https://publicintegrity.org/politics/state-politics/copy-paste-legislate/many-state-bills-one-source-behind-the-push-to-ban-sharia-law/.

O'Neill, Patrice. n.d. "When Hate Happens Here." Not in Our Town Northern California. https://www.niot.org/sites/default/files/KQEDNIOT-LearningGuideWeb.pdf.

Palmer, Brian. 2012. "Ku Klux Kontraction." *Slate*. https://slate.com/news-and-politics/2012/03/ku-klux-klan-in-decline-why-did-the-kkk-lose-so-many-chapters-in-2010.html.

Pegram, Thomas R. 2011. *One Hundred Percent American: The Rebirth and Decline of the Ku Klux Klan in the 1920s*. Chicago: Ivan R. Dee.

Pengelly, Martin. 2016. "American Nazi Party Leader Sees 'A Real Opportunity' with a Trump Presidency." *The*

Guardian. https://www.theguardian.com/us-news/2016/aug/07/american-nazi-party-leader-trump-opportunity.

Perez, Evan, and Jason Hoffman. 2020. "Trump Tweets Antifa Will Be Labeled a Terrorist Organization but Experts Believe That's Unconstitutional." CNN Politics. https://www.cnn.com/2020/05/31/politics/trump-antifa-protests/index.html.

Potok, Mark. 2011a. "Anti-gay Hate Crimes: Doing the Math." Southern Poverty Law Center. https://www.splcenter.org/fighting-hate/intelligence-report/2011/anti-gay-hate-crimes-doing-math.

Potok, Mark. 2011b. "Gays Remain Minority Most Targeted by Hate Crimes." Southern Poverty Law Center. https://www.splcenter.org/fighting-hate/intelligence-report/2011/gays-remain-minority-most-targeted-hate-crimes.

Potok, Mark. 2017. "The Year in Hate and Extremism." Southern Poverty Law Center. https://www.splcenter.org/fighting-hate/intelligence-report/2017/year-hate-and-extremism.

"The Propagandists." 2011. Southern Poverty Law Center. https://www.splcenter.org/20110930/propagandists#in-their-own-words.

"Proud Boys." 2020. ADL. https://www.adl.org/resources/backgrounders/proud-boys-0.

"Racist Black Hebrew Israelites Becoming More Militant." 2008. *Intelligence Report.* 131. https://web.archive.org/web/20150302073703/http://www.splcenter.org/get-informed/intelligence-report/browse-all-issues/2008/fall/ready-for-war.

"Racist Skinheads: Understanding the Threat." 2012. Southern Poverty Law Center. https://www.splcenter.org/sites/default/files/d6_legacy_files/downloads/publication/Skinheads_in_America_0.pdf.

Reid, Shannon, and Matthew Valasik. 2020. "Why Are White Supremacists Protesting to 'Reopen' the US Economy?" *The Conversation.* https://theconversation.com/why-are-white-supremacists-protesting-to-reopen-the-us-economy-137044.

"Remarks by President Trump at a California Sanctuary State Roundtable." 2018. The White House. https://www.whitehouse.gov/briefings-statements/remarks-president-trump-california-sanctuary-state-roundtable/.

Roston, Aram, and Joel Anderson. 2016. "This Man Used His Inherited Fortune To Fund The Racist Right." BuzzFeed.News. https://www.buzzfeednews.com/article/aramroston/hes-spent-almost-20-years-funding-the-racist-right-it.

Schaefer, Christina, and Molly Reed. 2019. "City of Dayton Filing Lawsuit against KKK-affiliated Group Planning Rally." Dayton 24/7 Now. https://dayton247now.com/news/local/city-of-dayton-filing-lawsuit-against-kkk-affiliated-group-planning-rally.

Schecter, Anna. 2018. "White Nationalist Leader Is Plotting to 'Take over the GOP.'" *NBC News.* https://www.nbcnews.com/politics/immigration/white-nationalist-leader-plotting-take-over-gop-n920826.

Schiller, Dane. 2014. "Aryan Gangsters Use Blow Torches to Burn off Sacred Tattoos." Chron. https://blog.chron.com/narcoconfidential/2014/10/aryan-gangsters-use-blow-torches-to-burn-off-sacred-tattoos/.

"Seven Things You Need to Know about Antifa." 2020. BBC Radio 4. https://www.bbc.co.uk/programmes/articles/X56rQkDgd0qqB7R68t6t7C/seven-things-you-need-to-know-about-antifa.

"Shield Wall Network (SWN)." 2020. ADL. https://www.adl.org/resources/backgrounders/shield-wall-network-swn.

Smith, David. 2018. "After Charlottesville: How a Slew of Lawsuits Pin down the Far Right." *The Guardian.* https://

www.theguardian.com/world/2018/may/29/charlottesville-lawsuits-heather-heyer-richard-spencer-alt-right.

Sommer, Will. 2017. "The Fratty Proud Boys Are the Alt Right's Weirdest New Phenomenon." *Medium.* https://medium.com/@willsommer/the-fratty-proud-boys-are-the-alt-rights-weirdest-new-phenomenon-7572b31e50f2.

Sommer, Will. 2019. "Border Livestreamers Feud over Prime Spots to Catch Migrant Crossings." *The Daily Beast.* https://www.thedailybeast.com/border-livestreamers-feud-over-prime-spots-to-catch-migrant-crossings.

"Swastikas and Other Hate Symbols." 2017. ADL. https://www.adl.org/sites/default/files/documents/swastikas%20and%20ther%20hate%20symbols.pdf.

Tanner, Chuck, and Devin Burghart. 2018. "What is the Foundation for the Marketplace of Ideas?" Institute for Research & Education on Human Rights. https://www.irehr.org/2018/03/02/foundation-marketplace-ideas/.

"Tattered Robes: The State of the Ku Klux Klan in the United States." 2016. Anti-Defamation League. https://www.adl.org/sites/default/files/documents/assets/pdf/combating-hate/tattered-robes-state-of-kkk-2016.pdf.

Thompson, A. C. 2018. "An Atomwaffen Member Sketched a Map to Take the Neo-Nazis Down. What Path Officials Took Is a Mystery." *ProPublica.* https://www.propublica.org/article/an-atomwaffen-member-sketched-a-map-to-take-the-neo-nazis-down-what-path-officials-took-is-a-mystery.

"324 F.Supp.3d 765 (2018)." [aka Sines v. Kessler]. 2018. District Court for the Western District of Virginia.

"37 Organizations and a Regional Organization Representing over 50 Tribes Denounce Bigotry and Violence before Patriot Prayer and Proud Boys Rally in Portland on August 4." 2018. The Skanner. https://www.theskanner.com/news/newsbriefs/27253-37-organizations-and-a-regional-organization-representing-over-50-tribes-denounce

-bigotry-and-violence-before-patriot-prayer-and-proud -boys-rally-in-portland-on-august-4.

"The Trump-Pence Administration's Crusade against LGBTQ Americans." n.d. Human Rights Campaign. https://assets2.hrc.org/files/assets/resources/Trump-Pence-Administration-Anti-LGBTQ-Actions-10.21.pdf.

"United White Knights Talk about the Flyers Left in Sand Springs." 2011. 8ABC Tulsa. https://ktul.com/archive/united-white-knights-talk-about-the-flyers-left-in-sand-springs.

Upchurch, Thomas Adams. 2005. "Black Separatism." In Rodney P. Carlisle, ed. *Encyclopedia of Politics: The Left and the Right*, vol. 1. Thousand Oaks, CA: Sage Reference.

"U.S. White Supremacy Groups." 2020. Counter Extremism Project. https://www.counterextremism.com/content/us-white-supremacy-groups.

Van Deburg, William L. 1997. *Modern Black Nationalism: From Marcus Garvey to Louis Farrakhan*. New York: New York University Press.

"Violence against the Transgender and Gender Non-Conforming Community in 2020." 2020. Human Rights Campaign. https://www.hrc.org/resources/violence-against-the-trans-and-gender-non-conforming-community-in-2020.

Wade, Wyn Craig. 1987. *The Fiery Cross: The Ku Klux Klan in America*. New York: Simon & Schuster.

Walters, Joanna. 2017. "Militia Leaders Who Descended on Charlottesville Condemn 'Rightwing Lunatics'." The Guardian. https://www.theguardian.com/us-news/2017/aug/15/charlottesville-militia-free-speech-violence.

"Watch: Here's What You Need to Know about Antifa." 2017. Medium Timeline. https://timeline.com/antifa-origins-anti-fascist-nazi-germany-hitler-mussolini-history-1a5c44e2f723.

Weill, Kelly. 2018. "Chat Site for Gamers Got Overrun by the Alt-Right. Now It's Fighting Back." *Daily Beast*. https://www.thedailybeast.com/chat-site-for-gamers-got-overrun-by-the-alt-right-now-its-fighting-back.

"Welcome to Help Save Maryland." 2020. https://www.helpsavemaryland.org/.

"What Is the Three Percenters?" 2020. The Three Percenters. https://www.thethreepercenters.org/.

"What the Muslims Want." n.d. Nation of Islam. https://www.noi.org/muslim-program/.

"White Bystanders Armed with Rifles Watch Floyd Protesters March in Indiana." 2020. *Politico*. https://www.politico.com/news/2020/06/05/george-floyd-protests-armed-white-bystanders-indiana-303143.

"Why Jihad Watch." n.d. Jihad Watch. https://www.jihadwatch.org/why-jihad-watch.

Williams, Lance. 2017. "Meet the Ex-GOP Insider Who Created White Nationalist Richard Spencer." *Reveal*. https://www.revealnews.org/article/meet-the-gop-insider-who-created-white-nationalist-richard-spencer/.

Willingham, A. J. 2019. "These are the New Symbols of Hate." CNN. https://www.cnn.com/2019/09/28/us/hate-symbols-changing-trnd/index.html.

Wolf, Cam. 2017. "The New Uniform of White Supremacy." *GQ*. https://www.gq.com/story/uniform-of-white-supremacy.

Woolf, Linda M., and Michael R. Hulsizer. 2004. "Hate Groups for Dummies: How to Build a Successful Hate-Group." *Humanity and Society* 28 (1): 40–62. https://doi.org/10.1177/016059760402800105.

"The Year in Hate and Extremism: Rage against Change." 2019. *Intelligence Report*. https://www.splcenter.org/sites/default/files/intelligence_report_166.pdf.

"The Year in Hate and Extremism 2019." 2020. Southern Poverty Law Center. https://www.splcenter.org/sites/default/files/yih_2020_final.pdf.

"Year-over-Year. White Supremacists Double Down on Propaganda in 2019." A Report from the Center on Extremism." 2020. https://www.adl.org/media/14038/download.

Zadrozny, Brandy. 2020. "What Is the 'Boogaloo?' How Online Calls for a Violent Uprising Are Hitting the Mainstream."NBC News. https://www.nbcnews.com/tech/social-media/what-boogaloo-how-online-calls-violent-uprising-are-getting-organized-n1138461.

Zucchino, David. 2020. *Wilmington's Lie: The Murderous Coup of 1898 and the Rise of White Supremacy*. New York: Atlantic Monthly Press.

3 Perspectives

Introduction

The study of hate groups is surrounded by a host of theoretical and technical questions. It is also the subject of more personal concerns and debates. This chapter provides an insight into both aspects of this topic. The essays presented here range from a scholarly analysis of physical and neurological changes that may occur in the body and mind of a person engaged in hate activities to a personal plea for openness to all kinds of hate speech, whether they are designed concretely to lead to hate crimes or not. The essays are designed to allow readers to think of hate group issues in a new light on a variety of fronts.

Hate Groups in the History of the West
Dawn A. Dennis and Jorge A. Munoz

When people think of hate groups in American history, the Western landscape is not always the first place to think of as a hotbed of white supremacist groups and activity. States in the West, such as California, Oregon, Washington, and Nevada, have a long history of racial violence and vitriol; and following the election of 2016, hate groups in the Western states increased in membership numbers and moved into virtual

---

A memorial outside the gay rights landmark Stonewall Inn in New York City, for the victims of the mass shooting inside Pulse, a nightclub in Orlando, FL, in June 2016. (Zhukovsky/Dreamstime.com)

space on forums such as 4chan and sites dedicated to Donald Trump that provide anonymity on discussion boards that are violent, misogynistic, and grounded in religious myth that provide legitimacy to white supremacy ideology and praxis. White supremacist extremist groups in the Western states have connected with other hate groups across the nation, Europe, and Latin America via the Internet to spread hate and organize for an impending race war. In 2019, the Southern Poverty Law Center (SPLC) tracked more than seventy-five hate groups in California, fifteen organizations in Oregon, thirty groups in Washington, and about seven in Nevada. As antiracist educators at a public institution in California, our pedagogy and research is grounded in unmasking racist ideologies in the United States. Through innovative assignments, specific readings, and showing films like *American History X*, we create space for engaging in critical dialogue about racial rhetoric and racial violence with our students. This essay seeks to discuss the Christian extremist roots of hate groups in the West, as part of the larger network of hate in the world landscape, in both the physical and virtual world.

Christian extremist groups rely upon religious myth making to legitimize beliefs, racial bias, and violence. A religious story conveys divine authority that civil discourse does not, adding religious legitimacy to social beliefs. Craig Prentiss argues that, "When a community sees a story as authoritative, the story is understood as setting a paradigm for human behavior" (Prentiss 2003, 21; Lincoln 1992, 24–26). For example, the myth of the Curse of Canaan where Noah curses Ham's son Canaan to be the servant of humanity was used to justify slavery (Glaude 2003, 62; Raboteau 1995, 55; Harvey 2003, 39–40; Fletcher 1852). The myth legitimizes racial violence and separation by arguing that Blackness is evil, uncivilized, and barbaric and, in a broader context, validates racial violence at the religious level by giving divine authority to slaveowners. Anti-Blackness is sanctioned in the West's religious and philosophical heritage and extends back to the Hebrew and Christian Bibles and classical literature of the Greco-Roman era.

These religious myths are used by Christian identity groups to provide a justification for white supremacist groups. White Aryan Nations, the Church of Jesus Christ Christian, the Order, the Posse Comitatus, Patriot Front, Right Brand Clothing (a fascist online clothing store), and Proud Boys are white supremacist groups that adhere to the "Christian identity myth" connecting race purity with Christianity that has its roots in nineteenth-century Britain (British Israelism) (Cowan 2003, 164, 166–167; Barkun 1997, 4–5; Aho 1990, 52–53). The myth establishes the difference between pre-Adamic "mud peoples" (people of color) who were closer to animals (incomplete humans) and Adamic peoples (descendants of Adam). Cain, after murdering Abel, joins the pre-Adamics and racial impurity begins (Cowan 2003, 172). It is this mixing that ultimately leads to the destruction of the world by God through rain (Zack 1993, 118). Thus, modern white supremacists like James Combs argue that the mixing of the races leads to the destruction of the white race (Combs n.d.). Kimmel and Ferber found that most white militias in the United States adhere to this Christian identity mythology believing that the descendants of whites come from Adam via the Lost Tribes of Israel (Barkun 1997, 58–59; Cowan 2003, 164; Aho 1990, 52).

Hate groups circulate self-published manifestos and traffic in violent conspiracy theories. The 1978 publication of William Pierce's *The Turner Diaries* depicted a violent revolution in America and race war, which exterminates Jews, Blacks, and other ethnic groups. The influence of *The Turner Diaries* inspired the emergence of white supremacist organizations and individuals to commit acts of murder under the guise of white supremacy, like the Order founded by Robert Jay Mathews in Metaline, Washington, in 1983. Based in Indiana, the White Aryan Resistance, founded by former Ku Klux Klan grand wizard Tom Metzger, published a racist newspaper, *The Insurgent*, and engaged in anti-immigrant violence in Oceanside California in the Spring of 1980. Metzger joined David Duke's Knights of the Ku Klux Klan in 1965 and became Grand Dragon of the Ku Klux Klan in California, which harassed Latinos and Vietnamese refugees. Metzger founded the White American Political Association in 1982, a group dedicated to promoting pro-white candidates for office. Founded on October 20, 1994, Volksfront organized as an American white separatist group in Portland, Oregon as an international fraternal organization for people of European descent. Volksfront used common neo-Nazi symbols, such as the Algiz rune, and the Nazi flag with the slogan "Race Over All." Turner's legacy is evident in current white supremacist ideology circulating on online message boards, such as the "great replacement theory" and criticism of "antiwhite" rhetoric.

White supremacist groups at home and abroad have connected through the Internet to form communities of hate under a shared vision of segregation, racial violence, and Christianity. Online discussion boards such as a 4chan regurgitate racial ideologies and create memes to harass antiracists. One of the coauthors of this essay drew the recent ire of white supremacists, who made online death threats in four separate 4chan threads. Kevin C. Thompson states that white nationalists have a "history of employing violence in the pursuit of their goals, along with their tendency to espouse religious views that are radically removed from the conventional Christian orthodoxy" (Thompson 2001, 32). Throughout the current presidency, white supremacists launched a series of attacks against political correctness and increased online harassment and attacks during marches and protests. Western cities such as Portland, Oregon, Seattle, and Washington contribute to this racial violence as Patriot Prayer and the Proud Boys disrupt peaceful protests, create racist memes, and engage in anti-Muslim, anti-immigrant, and misogynistic rhetoric. Dog-whistle politics using Christianity as a backdrop for a racial war is an effective method for galvanizing a base of supporters. During recent civil unrest in the capital, President Trump took a picture holding a Christian Bible at St. John's Church that drew criticism of being a tone-deaf photo opportunity. However, to others, like white supremacists, it was a call to arms.

References

Aho, James Alfred. 1990. *The Politics of Righteousness: Idaho Christian Patriotism*. Seattle: University of Washington Press.

Barkun, M. 1997. *Religion and the Racist Right: The Origins of the Christian Identity Movement*. Chapel Hill: University of North Carolina Press.

Combs, James. n.d. "Tolerance." http://www.jrbooksonline.com/PDF_Books_added2009-3/Tolerance.pdf.

Cowan, Douglas. 2003. "Theologizing Race: The Construction of Christian Identity." In Craig R. Prentiss, ed. *Religion and the Creation of Race and Ethnicity*, 112–123. New York: New York University Press.

Fletcher, John. 1852. *Studies on Slavery in Easy Lessons: Compiled into Eight Studies and Subdivided into Short Lessons for the Convenience of Readers*. Natchez, MS: J. Warner.

Glaude, Eddie S., Jr. 2003. "Myth and African American Self-Identity." In Craig R. Prentiss, ed. *Religion and the Creation of Race and Ethnicity*, 28–42. New York: New York University Press.

Harvey, Paul. 2003. "A Servant of Servants Shall He Be: The Construction of Race in American Religious Mythologies." In Craig R. Prentiss, ed. *Religion and the Creation of Race and Ethnicity*, 13–27. New York: New York University Press.

Lincoln, B. 1992. *Discourse and the Construction of Society: Comparative Studies of Myth, Ritual, and Classification*. New York: Oxford University Press.

Prentiss, Craig, ed. 2003. *Religion and the Creation of Race and Ethnicity*. New York: New York University Press.

Raboteau, Albert. 1995. *A Fire in my Bones: Reflections on African-American Religious History*. Boston: Beacon Press.

Thompson, Kevin C. 2001. "Watching the Stormfront: White Nationalists and the Building of Community in Cyberspace." *Social Analysis: The International Journal of Social and Cultural Practice* 45 (1): 32–52.

Zack, N. 1993. *Race and Mixed Race*. Philadelphia, PA: Temple University Press.

Dawn A. Dennis, PhD, is a public historian and educator at Cal State University, Los Angeles, and focuses on race and ethnicity in the United States and archival studies.

Jorge A. Munoz, PhD, is an educator in Religious Studies at Cal State University, Los Angeles, focusing on race and ethnicity in the United States, as well as political theory and religion.

Anti-LGBTQ Hate Groups in the United States
Ellen Faulkner

Anti-LGBTQ white Nationalist hate groups in the United States promote the view that LGBTQs are a danger to society, are depraved, sick, dangerous, and conspire to undermine society. An underlying theme is that LGBTQs are responsible for the demise of the heterosexual nuclear family. One prominent U.S. example that gained extensive media coverage is the Westboro Baptist Church's response to the murder of Matthew Shepard. In 1998 Matthew Shepard was murdered in a brutal hate crime in Laramie, Wyoming (Marsden 2014). The Westboro Baptist Church, run by then patriarch, Fred Phelps, showed up to protest at his funeral, carrying signs that read "God Hates Fags" and "AIDS Kills Fags Dead" (Morton 2011). Their "God Hates Fags" website promotes antigay beliefs. According to the Southern Poverty Law Center (SPLC) the "group's website maintains a virtual 'memorial' to Matthew Shepard, which depicts him burning in hell" (SPLC 2020j, 2). The public outcry and response to the crime motivated the family to set up the Matthew Shepard Foundation and in 2019 the Matthew Shepard and James Byrd Jr. Hate Crimes Prevention Act was signed (Sheerin 2018). Shepard's death became the topic of the play *The Laramie Project*, which has toured the United States and many other countries. The Westboro Baptist Church and its ideology is the most virulent example of online anti-LGBTQ hate group advocacy in the United States. Protected by their First Amendment rights and the Internet's cultural philosophy that all ideas should be allowed to proliferate, U.S. hate extremist groups have the freedom to create poisonous virtual communities of intolerance. Many other Christian right groups in the United States promote such anti-LGTBQ ideology.

The SPLC tracked 940 hate groups across the United States in 2019. Of these 940 hate groups, 70 targeted LGBTQs (SPLC 2020l, 12). According to the SPLC, a hate group is "an organization that—based on its official statements or principles, the statements of its leaders, or its activities—has beliefs or practices that attack or malign an entire class of people, typically for their immutable characteristics" (SPLC 2020l, 23; Olvera 2019). The SPLC continues, "We define a 'group' as an entity that has a process through which followers identify themselves as being part of the group, such as donating, paying membership dues or participating in activities like meetings and rallies" (SPLC 2020l, 23).

The SPLC finds that anti-LGBTQ hate groups are primarily Christian right groups, promoting a traditional view of the white heterosexual family unit including one male and one female with children. The SPLC reports that "groups that vilify the LGBTQ community represented the fastest growing sector among hate groups in 2019, expanding from 40 in 2018 to 70 in 2019, a nearly 43% increase" (SPLC 2020l, 12). The rise in anti-LGBTQ hate groups aligns with their attempt to influence Trump administration policies at the federal and state level to reduce LGBTQ rights, suggesting a concern with increased challenges to white heterosexual hegemony (SPLC 2020i, 2020l, 33; Sarrubba 2020, 1; NCAVP 2017, 10).

Anti-LGBTQ views are promoted by U.S. and Canadian hate groups by making the following claims: (1) LGBTQs are linked to pedophilia, (2) marriage equality is a danger to children, (3) LGBTQs are a danger to society, (4) LBTQs are criminals, and (5) there is a conspiracy of a "homosexual agenda" that works to destroy Christianity and the whole of society (SPLC 2020l; Faulkner 2006/2007). Research by the SPLC finds that the following anti-LGBTQ groups actively promote hate in the United States. For example, the Family Research Council promotes the view that gay men are pedophiles and claims that the LGBTQ community indoctrinates children (SPLC 2020d). The Alliance Defending Freedom (ADF) pushes an antitransgender agenda and supports the criminalization of LGBTQ people (SPLC 2020a). Liberty Counsel, an evangelical litigation group, opposes including sexual orientation in the 2019 antilynching bill (SPLC 2020f). The group advocates for "anti-LGBTQ discrimination under the guise of religious liberty" (SPLC, 2020f, 1). They battle hate crimes legislation and link gay people to pedophilia via their Internet site Barbwire.com. The group is prolife, proconversion therapy, and anti-same-sex marriage and uses courts to oppose radical sex-education curriculum. The American Family Association attempts to combat the "homosexual agenda" through organizing boycotts against companies that have progay policies (SPLC 2020b). The American College of Pediatricians (ACPeds) promotes anti-LGBTQ pseudoscience via far-right conservative media, files amicus briefs in cases involving gay adoption and marriage equality, and links homosexuals to pedophilia (SPLC 2020c). They endorse conversion therapy for gay youth and believe that transgender people are mentally ill. Family Watch International promotes the view that homosexuality is a "mental disorder derived from childhood trauma, and that so-called 'conversion therapy' can effectively eliminate same-sex attraction" (SPLC 2020e, 1). The group further alleges that LGBTQs are promiscuous, promote diseases, and engage in pedophilia. The Pacific Justice Institute is a legal organization that specializes in the defense of religious freedom, parental rights, and other civil liberties. They work to ban "sexualized" sex-education curriculum in schools and promote anti-LGBTQ falsehoods (SPLC 2020g). The Ruth Institute (RI) is a Catholic organization aimed at halting the "sexual revolution" and believe that homosexuals undermine the traditional heterosexual family (SPLC 2020h). The RI claims that homosexuals are sexual abusers and transgenderism is a psychological condition. The RI also claims that children raised by same-sex parents are likely to suffer emotional problems later in life. The Westboro Baptist Church is an extremist group known for its slogan "God Hates Fags," and their website promotes the view that gays are dirty and sodomites (SPLC 2020j). The group has been banned from picketing in Canada and Britain (CBC News 2008). The World Congress of Families is a massive network of interconnected organizations that push for restrictions to LGBTQ rights (SPLC 2020k). They resist same-sex marriage and promote the "natural family"—heterosexual married couples and biological children. The preceding quotes are just a sample of the hate promoted by anti-LGBTQ groups in the United States.

Despite the marketplace of ideas approach in the United States and the limited ability to challenge anti-LGBTQ hate speech, critical race theorists choose to challenge hate through education, critical reflection, political activism, examination of incidents and legal cases, and exploration of the impact of hate speech on communities (Matsuda 1993). Community-based responses show how ordinary citizens can stand up to hate (Not in Our Town 1995). Advocacy groups such as the National Coalition of Anti-Violence Programs, The Human Rights Campaign, the Anti-Defamation League, the National LGBTQ

Task Force, and Lambda Legal document anti-LGBTQ hate and lobby for change (McBride 2019; National Coalition of Anti-Violence Programs 2017; Anti-Defamation League 2020; National LGBTQ Task Force 2020; Lambda Legal 2020).

References

Anti-Defamation League ADL. 2020. "LGBTQ Rights." https://www.adl.org/what-we-do/discrimination/lgbtq-rights.

CBC News. 2008. "Church Members Enter Canada, Aiming to Picket Bus Victim's Funeral." *CBC News Manitoba*. https://www.cbc.ca/news/canada/manitoba/church-members-enter-canada-aiming-to-picket-bus-victim-s-funeral-1.703285.

Faulkner, E. 2006/2007. "Homophobic Hate Propaganda in Canada." *Journal of Hate Studies, Special Issue on "Hate and Communication"* 5 (1): 63–98.

Lambda Legal. 2020. "Transgender." Lambda Legal Rights. https://www.splcenter.org/fighting-hate/extremist-files/group/westboro-baptist-church.

Marsden, Jason. 2014. "The Murder of Matthew Shepard." WYOHistory.org. A Project of the Wyoming State Historical Society, November 8, 2014. https://www.wyohistory.org/encyclopedia/murder-matthew-shepard.

Matsuda, M. J., ed. 1993. *Words that Wound: Critical Race Theory, Assaultive Speech and the First Amendment*. Boulder, CO, San Francisco, CA, and Oxford: Westview Press.

McBride, Sarah. 2019. "HRC Releases Annual Report on Epidemic of Anti-Transgender Violence." Human Rights Campaign, November 18, 2019. https://www.hrc.org/blog/hrc-releases-annual-report-on-epidemic-of-anti-transgender-violence-2019.

Morton, Tom. 2011. "Matthew Shepard Funeral Put Westboro Baptist Church on the Map." *Billings Gazette*,

March 2, 2011. https://billingsgazette.com/news/state-and-regional/wyoming/matthew-shepard-funeral-put-westboro-baptist-church-on-the-map/article_fa10936e-cb5b-5170-afd8-e7eaa0a43aa8.html.

National Coalition of Anti-Violence Programs. 2017. *LGBTQ and HIV-Affected Hate and Intimate Partner Violence in 2017*. New York: National Coalition of Anti-Violence Programs. http://avp.org/wp-content/uploads/2019/01/NCAVP-HV-IPV-2017-report.pdf.

National LGBTQ Task Force. 2020. *National LGBTQ Task Force Statement: Stonewall Was a Riot #BlackLivesMatter*. Washington, DC, New York, and Miami, FL: National LGBTQ Task Force. https://www.thetaskforce.org/national-lgbtq-task-force-statement-stonewall-was-a-riot-blacklivesmatter/.

Not in Our Town: Billings Montana. 1995. "Not in Our Town: A Film that Launched the Anti-Hate Movement." The Working Group/Not in Our Town. Oakland, CA. https://www.niot.org/niot-video/not-our-town-billings-montana-0.

Olvera, Erik. 2019. "Yes, the FRC and ADF are Hate Groups. Here's Why!" Southern Poverty Law Centre, August 19, 2019. https://www.splcenter.org/news/2019/08/19/yes-frc-and-adf-are-hate-groups-heres-why.

Sarrubba, Stefania. 2020. "Anti-LGBTQ Groups in the U.S. are on the Rise and they're Targeting Trans Rights." International Observatory of Human Rights, April 17, 2020. https://observatoryihr.org/blog/anti-lgbtq-groups-in-the-us-are-on-the-rise-and-theyre-targeting-trans-rights/.

Sheerin, Jude. 2018. "Matthew Shepard: The Murder that Changed America." *BBC News: US & Canada*, October 26, 2018. https://www.bbc.com/news/world-us-canada-45968606.

SPLC (Southern Poverty Law Center). 2020a. "Alliance Defending Freedom ADF." https://www.splcenter.org/fighting-hate/extremist-files/group/alliance-defending-freedom.

SPLC. 2020b. "American Family Association." https://www.splcenter.org/fighting-hate/extremist-files/group/american-family-association.

SPLC. 2020c. "American Family of Pediatricians ACPeds." https://www.splcenter.org/fighting-hate/extremist-files/group/american-college-pediatricians.

SPLC. 2020d. "Family Research Council." https://www.splcenter.org/fighting-hate/extremist-files/group/family-research-council.

SPLC. 2020e. "Family Watch International." https://www.splcenter.org/fighting-hate/extremist-files/group/family-watch-international.

SPLC. 2020f. "Liberty Counsel." https://www.splcenter.org/fighting-hate/extremist-files/group/liberty-counsel.

SPLC. 2020g. "Pacific Justice Institute." https://www.splcenter.org/fighting-hate/extremist-files/group/pacific-justice-institute.

SPLC. 2020h. "Ruth Institute." https://www.splcenter.org/fighting-hate/extremist-files/group/ruth-institute

SPLC. 2020i. "SPCL Report a Wake-up Call for LGBTQ People." April 1, 2020. https://www.splcenter.org/news/2020/04/01/splc-report-wake-call-lgbtq-people.

SPLC. 2020j. "Westboro Baptist Church." https://www.splcenter.org/fighting-hate/extremist-files/group/westboro-baptist-church.

SPLC. 2020k. "World Congress of Families." https://www.splcenter.org/fighting-hate/extremist-files/group/world-congress-families.

SPLC. 2020l. *The Year in Hate Extremism 2019* Montgomery, AL: SPLChttps://www.splcenter.org/sites/default/files/yih_2020_final.pdf.

Dr. Ellen Faulkner has researched anti-LGBTQ hate crime for the past twenty years. She teaches for the Institute of Criminology and Criminal Justice at Carleton University, Ottawa, Ontario, Canada.

Making a World of Difference
Phil Fogelman

"Kids want to be called names. That's how they get attention." As I waited for someone in the auditorium to respond, I wondered how the students whose faces I could see felt to hear those words come from one of their teachers, especially any "kids" who'd been targeted with bullying and harassment. Research has shown that, according to students, interventions by adults that seek to place blame back on the students for what has been done are the most likely to lead to things getting worse (Davis and Nixon 2013).

Unfortunately, about 20 percent of students in the United States between the ages of twelve and eighteen report experiencing bullying and harassment (National Center for Education Statistics 2017), which means that in that auditorium alone, there could have been two hundred students in that high school assembly who had been targeted with name calling, threats, assault, vandalism, humiliation, and social exclusion. Some of them might have been targeted, as I had been at their age, because of an aspect of their identity such as race, religion, ability, gender, sexual orientation, ethnicity, or national origin.

While all forms of bullying and harassment are harmful, those that are motivated by hate toward a person's identity can have an even greater impact on the targeted individual's social, emotional, and physical health (Russell et al. 2012), with targeted students 2.6 times more likely to attempt suicide than students who are not targeted (Gini and Espelage 2014). Also concerning is the growing association between student perpetrators of identity-based bullying and harassment and organized hate groups. The editor of the neo-Nazi website Daily

Stormer, Andrew Anglin, has stated the "site is mainly designed to target children. . . . Our target audience is white males between the ages of 10 and 30. I include children as young as ten, because an element of this is that we want to look like superheroes" (Southern Poverty Law Center 2018).

One of the last things I wanted when I was in high school was to be repeatedly called anti-Semitic names. I just wanted it to stop. Instead, it escalated when the perpetrator persuaded other students to join him after school to "wrap a bagel around my Jewish nose." If it hadn't been for my older brother, who blocked them on the bus long enough for me to run home safely, and for the law enforcement investigation that followed, the trauma would have been significantly worse.

In an effort to address student-perpetrated bias and hate incidents, schools have historically held assembly presentations like the one where the teacher said kids wanted to be called names. I had been invited there to speak about the Anti-Defamation League's (ADL) A World of Difference Institute®. Founded in Boston in 1985, A World of Difference began as a grassroots campaign to mobilize people across Massachusetts to recognize and address all forms of prejudice and discrimination in their homes, schools, communities, and workplaces. The campaign later became a comprehensive antibias education and training program that ADL's twenty-five regional offices now operate nationally. In addition to providing schools with professional development of antibias training for staff, A World of Difference sponsors peer-to-peer antibias training for diverse groups of students who cofacilitate activities and discussions for other students. Both staff and student training programs are designed to increase participants' awareness of bias and prejudice in themselves and others; develop safe and practical bias intervention and prevention strategies, including allyship and advocacy; and actively foster inclusive and equitable school communities. As one peer trainer describes, "After the training, I feel like we know exactly what we are talking about, like before, like if somebody were to say the 'R' word, I would be like, yeah that's a bad word, but I wouldn't even say anything 'cause it's like, I'm not going to start an argument where I don't even have a backbone and . . . I don't know exactly what I'm telling you. So like, I wouldn't get into that argument. But now if somebody were to say the 'R' word I'd have the backbone or structure to say like, 'no, don't say that for this and this and this reason'" (Marsico et al. 2019).

What the teacher in the auditorium seemed to be suggesting was that the school didn't need A World of Difference. Nobody there openly disagreed, either—not the Superintendent, the Principal, or the school counselor who had invited me. Not surprisingly, a Southern Poverty Law Center survey of 2,776 educators found that following a bias incident, "nine times out of 10, administrators failed to denounce the bias or reaffirm school values" (Costello and Dillard 2019).

The students in the auditorium needed to hear another adult challenge the teacher's assumption and advocate on behalf of targeted "kids" who would otherwise have even more reason to fear for their safety.

"I don't think it's safe to assume young people want to be called names," I said. "In my experience, they want it to stop, and everyone needs to make sure it does."

No one at the school said a word until after the assembly had ended, when a student in a wheelchair wanted me to know that what the teacher had said wasn't true. The student had been called hurtful names for her first three years of high school. Some of her peers had also picked up garbage cans in the classrooms and dumped the contents on her head. I wondered how many of the silent students and educators in the school-wide assembly had witnessed the harassment. It was now the beginning of her senior year. Her peers hadn't been calling her names and dumping garbage on her head. But she was afraid that if they'd heard her say what she was telling me, they would start again. I asked her how I could help.

"I want to participate in A World of Difference and become a peer leader," she said. And she did.

References

Costello, Maureen, and Coshandra Dillard. 2019. "Hate in Schools." Southern Poverty Law Center. https://www.splcenter.org/sites/default/files/tt_2019_hate_at_school_report_final_0.pdf.

Davis, Stan, and Charisse L. Nixon. 2010. "Youth Voice Project." https://www.fmptic.org/download/the_youth_voice_project.pdf.

Gini, Gianluca, and Dorothy L. Espelage. 2014. "Peer Victimization, Cyberbullying and Suicide Risk in Children and Adults." *JAMA* 312 (5): 545–546.

Marsico, Christine, et al. 2019. "The Anti-Defamation League's Peer Training Program: Findings from Peer Leader Focus Groups." Boston University Wheelock School of Education.

National Center for Education Statistics. 2017. "School Crime Supplement to the National Crime Victimization Survey." U.S. Department of Education. https://nces.ed.gov/pubs2019/2019054.pdf.

Russell, S. T., et al. 2012. "Adolescent Health and Harassment Based on Discriminatory Bias." *American Journal of Public Health* 102 (3): 493. https://www.ncbi.nlm.nih.gov/pmc/articles/PMC3487669/.

Southern Poverty Law Center. 2018. "Andrew Anglin Brags about 'Indoctrinating' Children into Nazi Ideology." https://www.splcenter.org/hatewatch/2018/01/18/andrew-anglin-brags-about-indoctrinating-children-nazi-ideology.

Phil Fogelman is a former teacher and administrator. As ADL New England's education director for more than twenty years, he has been working with hundreds of schools to facilitate safe, equitable, and inclusive learning communities.

Some Medical Aspects of Hate
Joel Grossman

When chronic or overly prolonged, negative emotions like hate, anger, and blame can create excess "physiological arousal," the classic "flight-or-fight" survival and stress response, this can tip the bodily balance from health toward disease. The interconnectedness of mind, emotions, brain, and body is physically measurable as elevated hormones, blood pressure, heart rate, and blood plasma glucose levels, which prepare the body to fight enemies and flee danger. Chronic consequences via the immune, nervous, endocrine, and other bodily systems include promotion of cancerous cell growth and an array of chronic inflammatory and cardiovascular diseases such as sudden death, arrhythmias, and myocardial infarctions (Ter Horst 2000).

"Most alarmingly, hatred involves the dehumanisation of the other, which serves as a gateway through which moral barriers can be removed and violence can be perpetrated," write Abuelaish and Arya (2017) in the journal *Medicine, Conflict and Survival*. Memory allows hatred to self-perpetuate "through cycles of hatred and counter-hatred, violence and counter-violence (sometimes as revenge). Hatred thus, can affect the hater and the hated."

"Most neuroscientists ignore hate because it is too vague a term to work with," as "the word seems to cover the range from a mildly negative opinion to a powerful negative emotion that can indicate the speaker's disposition to commit violence," writes Edmund Glaser (2009) in the *Journal of Hate Studies*. The scientific search for "a brain hatred center" leads to the amygdala and primal limbic system areas controlled by the hormone-secreting hypothalamus, which has "strong connections" with the brain's fear and aggression centers and memory, "the latter because memory seems to be a vital component of human actions that are identified with hatred."

Emotional memories, a necessity for long-term or chronic hate, feuds, and grudges, are malleable and subject to biological modification (e.g., by stress-induced brain theta rhythms) rather than being permanently fixed, though court prosecutors with witnesses might wish to argue otherwise. A brain region intimately involved in hate, "the amygdala has been implicated in numerous aspects of emotional processing including the possible impairment of memory for emotional events," write Morgane et al. (2005). "The amygdala as a whole is extraordinarily complex in terms of its internuclear and input-output wiring," connecting to almost every other brain region, including the hypothalamus and the primitive brainstem "to regulate behavioral, autonomic, arousal and neuroendocrine responses," which makes sense if hate and anger mobilize the body for fight or flight.

From a medical or physiological perspective, everything is so interwoven and interconnected in various ways that no brain or body region really stands alone. Psychological functions like memory and cognition and emotions like hatred seem only partially localized in particular brain structures, and may instead be emergent properties of a complex interacting system. The hypothalamic–pituitary–adrenal (HPA) axis, the main physiological system modulating the fight-or-flight stress response, is a useful simplification. The underlying reality is more complicated than the innards of a supercomputer with parallel and overlapping neural circuitry networks and a mind-boggling plethora of peptides, hormones, neurotransmitter chemicals, and electrical communications with feedback loops circulating within brain and body and affecting the balance between health and disease.

Stressors like chronic hate may deleteriously impact organs like the immune system, and the resulting "dysregulation" is the subject matter of psychoneuroimmunology, psychoneuroendocrinology, and immunopsychology. "Irrespective of the term used, these all highlight the complex interplay of various body systems like nervous system, endocrine system, emotions and behaviours and immune response towards genesis and defense against the diseases," write Khurana et al.

(2009). "The immune response, i.e. the processes involved in body's fight against disease, is governed by a complex organ system in the body called immune system which bidirectionally communicates with other body systems and environment too."

"Biochemical individuality" helps explain why some people are sickened and others seem immune or resilient when facing hate, anger, and other stressors. Variables include genes, nutrition, and environment. "Each of us has innate biochemical factors which influence personality, behavior, mental health, immune function, allergic tendencies, etc.," writes Walsh (2018). Since every child inherits forty-two million genetic combinations from the two biological parents, "individual genetic variation" is large. Environmental factors influence which genes are turned on or off, further boosting individual biochemical diversity. Thus, writes Robert Eckhardt (2001), we are all biochemical "deviates," which also helps explain "many baffling health problems," such as why pharmaceutical efficacy and side effects can vary so greatly from individual to individual.

Also keep in mind that hate and anger are not all bad, as they have survival value. "Anger, rage, and hatred of the enemy is one way our minds might try to help our bodies prepare for a frightening survival situation," writes Freyd (2002). However, the "flight-or-fight" physiological response likely evolved for "one-on-one threat situations" ending relatively quickly and allowing bodily recovery. When chronic or cumulative, the survival response can become toxic or dysfunctional, fostering diseases and fueling an "us/them" mentality supportive of hatred, anger, and violence. Like a match awaiting tinder, anger finds a reason or pretext to burst into flame against a convenient target or hated enemy *de jour*.

Hate and anger are too primal and hardwired in the human brain to completely vanish. Nonviolent antidotes must be learned to minimize disease and foster personal and societal health. To avoid endless cycles of hatred and counterhatred,

Freyd (2002) recommends physiological alternatives such as "tend-and-befriend" or "acts of caring and compassion and unity." "Compassion by no means implies surrender in the face of wrongdoing or injustice," writes the Dalai Lama. "Maintaining an attitude of calmness and nonviolence is actually an indication of strength, as it shows the confidence that comes from having truth and justice on one's side. . . . The only way to change a person's mind is with concern, not with anger or hatred." Plus it is sound medicine.

References

Abuelaish, Izzeldin, and Neil Arya. 2017. "Hatred—a Public Health Issue." *Medicine, Conflict and Survival* 33 (2): 125–130. https://www.researchgate.net/publication/317208293_Hatred-a_public_health_issue.

Eckhardt, Robert B. 2001. "Genetic Research and Nutritional Individuality." *The Journal of Nutrition* 131 (2): 336S–339S. https://academic.oup.com/jn/article-abstract/131/2/336S/4686972.

Freyd, Jennifer J. 2002. "In the Wake of Terrorist Attack, Hatred May Mask Fear." *Analyses of Social Issues and Public Policy* 2 (1): 5–8. https://scholarsbank.uoregon.edu/xmlui/bitstream/handle/1794/61/asap018.pdf.

Glaser, Edmund M. 2009. "Is There a Neurobiology of Hate." *Journal of Hate Studies* 7 (7): 7–19. https://jhs.press.gonzaga.edu/issue/8/file/16/#page=14.

Khurana, Hitesh, Paramjeet Singh Gill, and Reenu Bathls. 2009. "Physiology and Psychoimmunology." In Rajbir Singh, et al. eds. *Psychoneuroimmunology: A Behavioural Approach*, 39–80. New Delhi, India: Global Vision Publishing House. http://globalvisionpub.com/globaljournalmanager/pdf/1391073275.pdf.

Morgane, Peter J., Janina R. Galler, and David J. Mokler. 2005. "A Review of Systems and Networks of the Limbic

Forebrain/limbic Midbrain." *Progress in Neurobiology* 75 (2): 143–160. http://users.phhp.ufl.edu/rbauer/cognitive/articles/Morgane-05-ProgNeurobiol.pdf.

Ter Horst, Gert J. 2000. "Emotions and Heart-Activity Control." In Gert J. Ter Horst, ed. *The Nervous System and the Heart*, 55–115 Totowa, NJ: Humana Press. https://link.springer.com/chapter/10.1007/978-1-59259-713-0_2.

Walsh, William J. 2018. *Biochemical Individuality and Nutrition*. Naperville, IL: Walsh Research Institute. https://www.academia.edu/download/54333148/biochemical_individuality_and_nutrition.pdf.

Joel Grossman's interests include the intersection of biology and sociology. He writes the Biocontrol Beat *blog.*

Punish Crime, Not Thought Crime
Jeff Jacoby

When President Barack Obama signed the Matthew Shepard and James Byrd Jr. Hate Crimes Prevention Act in October 2009, he hailed it as "another step forward" on America's "journey towards a more perfect union" (Obama 2009). In reality, it was just the opposite. Like all such laws, the measure signed by the President prevents not hatred, but fairness. Every criminal code punishes bad deeds; hate crime statutes punish bad opinions. However well-intentioned, that is something no liberal democracy should tolerate.

The law was named for the victims in two of the most notorious murders of the 1990s. Matthew Shepard was a gay student at the University of Wyoming who was lured from a bar in Laramie by two acquaintances on the night of October 6, 1998 (Gumbel 2013). They drove him to a remote spot out of town, pistol-whipped him to a bloody pulp, then tied him to a fence, and left him to die.

Four months earlier, three white supremacists in Jasper, Texas, had lynched James Byrd Jr., a middle-aged black man. It was a ghastly killing: The victim was stripped, chained by his ankles to the back of a pickup truck, and dragged along an asphalt road until he was decapitated. Byrd's shredded body parts stretched along a grisly, miles-long trail ("3 whites . . ." 1998).

The atrocities in Jasper and Laramie set off a vehement national outcry for the passage of stronger legislation to deter "hate crimes"—acts of violence motivated by bigotry, racism, or intolerance. Hate crime laws, which increase the punishment for offenses fueled by bias, were already on the books in forty-one states by 1998. But because Texas and Wyoming were among the few holdouts, Democrats (and a few Republicans) in Congress and the White House insisted it was imperative to enact a federal law.

"Crimes that are motivated by hate really are fundamentally different and I believe should be treated differently under the law," contended the then president Bill Clinton after meeting with members of Byrd's family ("Senate passes . . ." 2000). Massachusetts Senator Ted Kennedy, the chief sponsor of a measure that would add new categories of hate crimes to the federal code, declared that if the bill were passed, "we'd have fewer hate crimes in all the days that follow" ("Mother of . . ." 1999).

The punishment meted out to Shepard's and Byrd's murderers could hardly have been stronger: Two received the death penalty, and the others were sentenced to life imprisonment with no possibility of parole. In any event, hate crime laws were being widely enforced by the late 1990s. Not only had the great majority of states adopted such measures but the federal government had as well. In 1988, Congress had passed the Hate Crimes Statistics Act. That was followed in 1994 by the Hate Crimes Sentencing Enhancement Act and the Violence Against Women Act, and then by the Church Arson Prevention Act in 1996. The measure named for Shepard and Byrd, eventually passed during the Obama administration, broadened the federal government's reach still further, enlarging the power of U.S. attorneys to prosecute attacks based on race, religion, national origin, gender, sexual orientation, or disability.

For all their popularity, though, hate crime statutes advance no legitimate criminal justice end. The laws serve a symbolic function, not a practical one—they proclaim that crimes inspired by certain types of bigotry are particularly wicked, and deserve to be punished with particular harshness. But that is tantamount to proclaiming that the exact same crimes, if spurred by bigotry against other groups, or by motives having nothing to do with bias at all, wouldn't be so terrible. Is that a message any decent society should wish to promote?

Bias crimes are said to be uniquely toxic because they target and terrorize both individuals and groups. "Hate violence is very personal," writes Wade Henderson, the president of the Leadership Conference on Civil and Human Rights, "with an especially emotional and psychological impact on the victim and the victim's community" (Henderson 2012). The Anti-Defamation League argues that a "priority response" is justified for hate crimes because they "may effectively intimidate other members of the victim's community, leaving them feeling isolated, vulnerable, and unprotected by the law. . . . These incidents can damage the fabric of our society and fragment communities" (Anti-Defamation League 2019).

But isn't that true of all violent crime? Doesn't every murder, every rape, every armed robbery, every bombing intimidate or frighten more people than just the immediate victim?

When a child is abducted and killed, or a jogger is gang raped by "wilding" predators, or elderly bank customers are mugged outside an automated teller machine (ATM), entire neighborhoods or groups are apt to be rocked by panic and dread. It is hard to see the logic of demanding harsher penalties for crimes that inflict "an especially emotional and psychological impact" on, say, African Americans, gays, or Muslims, while refusing to demand the same penalties for attacks that have the same effect on senior citizens, or joggers, or young parents.

There is no evading the double standard: By definition, a law that cracks down harder on offenses that hurt members of certain groups signals simultaneously that hurting members of other groups isn't as bad. That is immoral and indefensible.

The lynching of James Byrd by three white bigots was unspeakable. Wouldn't it have been just as unspeakable had the killers been black? It should have made no difference to the law—or to the media, or to the political class—whether the monsters who murdered Byrd were motivated by racism, by a personal grudge, or by greed for his money. The blood of a man assaulted by bigots is no redder than that of a man attacked by ruthless thieves or thrill-seeking sadists. The grief of his loved ones is the same either way. So is the threat to society. A legal system that upholds the principle of "equal justice under law"—the very words are engraved over the door to the U.S. Supreme Court—must not have rules that make some victims of hatred more equal than others.

In fact, the law has no business intensifying the punishment for violent crimes motivated by bigotry at all. Murderers or arsonists or terrorists should be prosecuted and punished with equal vehemence regardless of their agenda. It is not a criminal's evil thoughts that society has a right to avenge, only his evil acts. Advocates of hate crime laws maintain that what is being punished isn't the ugly state of mind, but the crime it led to. But that argument doesn't wash. When the judge has you thrown in prison for an extra ten years because the crime you committed was influenced by your opinion of the victim, the inescapable conclusion is that your opinion has been criminalized.

That is "thought crime," in George Orwell's chilling phrase. And if Big Brother can penalize you today for your inappropriate thoughts about Jews, Asians, or lesbians, it is only a matter of time until you can be penalized for having impermissible thoughts about anything else.

The best hate crimes law is none at all. But if we are going to have such laws, let's not restrict them to only six or eight categories of victims. Lawmakers should expand their scope to cover every crime of violence—regardless of the attacker's motive, or of the group to which the victim(s) belong. Let us learn to treat every murder, rape, and brutal assault as a crime of "hate"—not the criminal's hate for his victim, but society's hate for the crime.

References

Anti-Defamation League. 2019. "Hate Crimes Law: The ADL Approach." https://www.adl.org/media/2143/download.

Gumbel, Andrew. 2013. "Matthew Shepard's Murder: 'What It Came Down to Is Drugs and Money.'" *The Guardian.* http://www.theguardian.com/world/2013/oct/14/matthew-shepard-murder-wyoming-book.

Henderson, Wade. 2012. "Bias Laws Ensure Action against Hate." *The New York Times.* http://www.nytimes.com/roomfordebate/2012/03/07/are-hate-crime-laws-necessary/bias-laws-ensure-action-against-hate.

"Mother of Slain Student Pleads for Hate Crime Bill." 1999. *CNN.* http://edition.cnn.com/US/9905/11/hate.crimes/.

Obama, Barack. 2009. "Remarks by the President at Reception Commemorating the Enactment of the Matthew Shephard and James Byrd Hate Crimes Prevention Act." https://obamawhitehouse.archives.gov/the-press-office/remarks-president-reception-commemorating-enactment-matthew-shepard-and-james-byrd-.

"Senate Passes Hate Crimes Legislation; Prosecutors Revisiting Murders of Chaney, Goodman, and Schwerner." 2000. *CNN.* http://transcripts.cnn.com/TRANSCRIPTS/0006/20/wt.07.html.

"3 Whites Indicted in Dragging Death of Black Man in Texas." 1998. *CNN.* http://edition.cnn.com/US/9807/06/dragging.death.02/.

Jeff Jacoby is a columnist for The Boston Globe.

A Century of Resilience: The History of Anti-Sikh Hate in America
Aasees Kaur and Nikki Singh

At the start of the twentieth century, Davinder Singh and his family moved to the United States from Punjab, India in search of the American dream. Davinder started work at a lumber mill in Bellingham, Washington, but shortly after immigrating, his family experienced the first wave of violence due to their identity. In 1907, a mob of five hundred white workers brutally attacked Davinder and his colleagues. They blamed Sikhs for "taking their jobs." The mob saw a tide of turbans and attacked the mills and bunkhouses, pulling these migrant workers from their homes, beating them senselessly, and demanding they leave. The white mob terrorized this community and within days the entire South Asian population departed.

This was not the last time Davinder and his community would experience hate. Sikhs, who represent the fifth largest organized religion in the world, with approximately 500,000 followers currently in the United States, continue to experience anti-immigrant sentiments, violence, and backlash as a result of white supremacist ideology. Relative to other minorities, Sikhs disproportionately face hate and discrimination because of their religious articles of faith, including turbans and unshorn hair.

Wanting to move somewhere safer after the Bellingham Riots, many Sikhs migrated up and down the Pacific Coast. Davinder and his family moved to Oregon. A few years later, similar attacks occurred. On the night of March 21, 1910, St. Johns erupted in anti-South Asian violence perpetrated once again by a mob of white laborers. This mob of 200 local residents included the town's mayor, the police chief, and many police officers. Sikhs and other South Asians were taken out of their homes, violently beaten in the streets, and many were forcibly placed on streetcars and sent to Portland.

Over the next seventy years, Davinder and his wife Tejinder Kaur worked hard to build a life for their children. Davinder became a taxi driver and saved up enough money to open a small convenience store, which Tejinder and their kids ran. Due to the varying immigration requirements, including the Immigration Act of 1917, Davinder's family was separated from their relatives for decades. The civil rights movement brought attention to the racially motivated immigration policies and the passing of the Immigration and Nationality Act of 1965 led to the reunification of their family.

Davinder was thrilled to be reunited with his younger brother Mangal, whose family settled in New Jersey in the early 1980s. His family had just begun to adjust to life in the United States when Mangal, also a turbaned Sikh, was called "Ayatollah" and told to "Go back to Iran" by a group of white people on the street. Sikhs maintain unshorn hair because it is regarded as living in harmony with the will of God. Wearing a turban is a spiritual discipline signifying sovereignty, commitment, morality, and courage. Due to the increase in anti-immigrant sentiments during the Iran Hostage Crisis, Mangal Singh and many Sikhs felt so unsafe that they resorted to cutting their hair and removing their turbans.

Throughout the 1980s and 1990s, Davinder and Mangal worked and raised their families. While they both experienced bigotry, discrimination, and even violence, nothing compared to the fear and backlash that came immediately after September 11, 2001. On September 15, 2001, the murder of Sikh American Balbir Singh Sodhi was the first deadly hate crime reported after 9/11. It shook the Sikh community across the country. Mr. Sodhi started his day by donating the contents of his wallet to victims of 9/11. He then went to his gas station and began to plant a garden. A white man who sought retaliation for 9/11 told his friends that he planned to "shoot some towel-heads." He drove by, shot, and killed Balbir. Within a month, the Sikh Coalition documented more than 300 cases of violence and discrimination targeting Sikhs.

Davinder Singh and his family represent the numerous Sikh families who have experienced hate violence over the past century. Although Sikhs have been an integral part of the American fabric for over 125 years, they remain disproportionately targeted in cases of bigotry, bias, and bullying. According to the FBI's 2018 Hate Crime Report, between 2017 and 2018, while hate crimes nationally remained relatively the same, hate crimes against Sikhs increased by 200 percent, making Sikhs the third most targeted faith group.

On August 5, 2012, a neo-Nazi gunman walked into a gurdwara in Oak Creek, Wisconsin and opened fire, killing six worshippers and injuring several more. At the time, it was the most violent attack inside an American house of worship since the 1963 16th Street Baptist Church bombing. These cases of hate violence continue across the United States.

In 2013, eighty-two-year-old Piara Singh was brutally attacked while leaving a gurdwara. In 2015, Inderjit Singh Mukker was attacked while driving to the grocery store in Chicago. The assailant cut him off with his car and repeatedly punched him in the face, causing him to lose consciousness. In 2016, a group of men severely beat Mann Singh Khalsa and forcefully cut his hair in California. In 2017, in Washington, Sikh taxi driver Swarn Singh was attacked by a man with a hammer who persistently targeted his turban and another Sikh was shot in his driveway by a man who shouted: "Go back to your own country!" In 2018, two teenagers mercilessly attacked an elderly Sikh man taking a neighborhood walk in California. In December 2019 in Bellingham, 112 years after Davinder and his colleagues were attacked and forced to leave town, a Sikh Uber driver was verbally and physically attacked by a passenger. More than a century later, the similarities of events are striking and the lack of change is tragic.

Despite the challenges the Sikh community has faced, Sikhs firmly believe in living in *chardi kala* or eternal optimism. While optimism is grounding, it is essential to implement actionable solutions to address hate. Change starts at home with families embracing and celebrating the ethnic mosaics of their neighborhoods. Sikh stories and the Sikh experience need to be taught in history, civics, and religion classes. Exposure to multiculturalism results in increased understanding and compassion for one another, which in turn reduces incidents of hate and bias. On the policy side, states need to have inclusive and effective legislation surrounding hate crime, employment discrimination, and school bullying. This helps to ensure a bias-based crime can be identified, reported, and charged accurately. By understanding the sources of these incidents, one can develop more precise solutions to address the issue. Our communities need legislative and social change to safeguard our liberties and lives. To do anything less would be a disservice to the thousands of other Sikhs, like Davinder Singh, who endured unjust violence in the name of white supremacy. We owe future generations the freedom to live and practice their faith fearlessly.

Aasees Kaur serves as the first line of defense in anti-Sikh hate crime cases in her role as legal client and community services manager at the Sikh Coalition. As a community organizer, she has built grassroots support for hate prevention for nearly a decade. She lives in Cincinnati, Ohio, with her husband.

Nikki Singh is a policy and advocacy manager at the Sikh Coalition, where she supports the organization's advocacy to combat and prevent hate crime by improving legislation and Sikh civic engagement at the state and federal level. She lives in New York City and holds an MPA. in public policy and non-profit management from New York University.

Descent, Dissent, and Rising Out: The Narrative Arc of the Ex-Hate Group Leader
Jesse Kavadlo

First, he ascends the hierarchy of the hate group. And then, through friends or family, he turns against it: the redemptive arc of the ex-hate group leader has generated a number of significant stories, both fictional and nonfictional. And yet, while these narratives deserve praise for renouncing hate groups, they also raise questions: are they bringing conversations about hate groups to the forefront of the culture, or merely rehabilitating their protagonists? Do they make hate seem too much like an individual or family choice, while obscuring larger history of systemic racism? And do they rely on their readers' presumption of white innocence while obscuring the real harm that they have inflicted on minorities?

The prototype for the modern version of this story is the film *American History X* (1998). Actor Edward Norton depicts the reform of skinhead Derek Vineyard, whose prison friendship with an African American, Lamont, and mentoring from his former principal, Dr. Sweeney, also African American, coupled with fear of his younger brother's descent into hatred, turns him against the Aryan Brotherhood. Screenwriter David McKenna said that his "premise was that hate starts in the family." This is certainly true in the film, but hatred flourishes in a political system that does not explicitly disavow it, something the film, in its violence and tensions, doesn't explore. It provides a cautionary tale about racists, as people, but not, exactly, about racism, which is, despite the film's title, historical. While Lamont and Dr. Sweeney are developed African American characters, the others serve only as foils and violent antagonists for our ostensible white heroes, Derek and his brother Danny, who is murdered by an African American classmate at the end.

Two decades after that film's acclaim, life imitated art: two nonfiction successes, *Rising Out of Hatred: The Awakening of a Former White Nationalist* (Saslow 2018) and *White American Youth: My Descent into America's Most Violent Hate Movement—and How I Got Out* (Picciolini 2017), seemingly borrow from the film's playbook. They share its excitement, but its limitations: by focusing on the lives of particular individuals, most of the stories' power lies in depictions of violence and hatred, not reform.

In *Rising Out of Hatred*, journalist Eli Saslow chronicles the true story of Derek Black, whose father was a former Alabama KKK leader and founder of Stormfront, the largest racist website. In his early twenties, he began leading a double life: an ordinary college student, and Stormfront contributor. As Saslow writes, Derek began "cultivating separate personalities since he was about ten, when he built two websites in the same week. On one, derekblack.com, he shared Spider-Man, Alan Jackson, and his baby niece. . . . The other, kids.stormfront.org, was aimed at white people across the globe, and it had links to racist songs and (former KKK leader David) Duke's website." Like Derek in *American History X*, Derek Black becomes friends with students of color, immigrants, and Jews, so that after his white supremacist identity is exposed, like Dr. Sweeney in *American History X*, his friends ask questions, listen, and never give up on the possibly of reform. By the end of his college years, he not only turns against white nationalism, but also, by extension, his family:

"More immigration, more diversity—I think those are very good things," he said.

"That's the opposite of what you always believed."

"I was wrong." Derek stopped to correct himself. "We were wrong."

Meanwhile, rock star and LGBTQ icon Joan Jett provides the foreword to *White American Youth*: "Hating the LGBTQ community, non-white minorities, Jews, and others when he was involved with the white-power skinhead movement is tantamount to a disgusting and immoral blind allegiance to hatred. And yet, [author] Christian [Picciolini] managed to do the one great thing that anyone who has ever been in his position . . . could do: he learned to recognize his blindness, to see how violently corrupted he's become" (Picciolini 2017, xvi). Picciolini, in keeping with *American History X*'s Nazi punk rock imagery, finds community through music but becomes the leader of the Hammerskin Nation, a violent white supremacist hate group. Once again, after describing hatred, rallies, and crimes, the narrative concludes with Picciolini's change of heart, like *American History X*, through family: "The birth of our son changed my life. I started to imagine the world through his eyes, still unsullied by any prejudice. . . . The only thing that seemed to matter to Devin was love" (Picciolini 2017, 215).

Black's and Picciolini's stories fit a familiar, almost archetypal arc: the story of the fall, and then rise, culminating in the production of the very book that we are now reading. Yet, they must rely on tropes of white privilege, even as they're in the service of antiracism. What is more, they continue to posit racism, and white supremacy, as a series of individual choices rather than a system or movement.

Black and Picciolini grant themselves what legal scholar Thomas Ross termed "white innocence," and their victims, who, like the African Americans killed in *American History X*, are nameless and undeveloped, what Ross calls "black abstraction." White innocence and black abstraction help historians to understand the racist legal decisions of the nineteenth century, including the infamous Dred Scott case, which denied the citizenship and right of anyone of African descent, free or slave, to sue in federal court. As Ross explains, these decisions rely on "the innocence or absence of responsibility of the contemporary white person" (Ross 1990, 3) while at the same time featuring "the rhetorical depiction of the black person in an abstract context, outside of any real and rich social context" (Ross 1990, 6).

Ironically, in order to be persuasive, the narrative of the ex-hate group leader unknowingly relies on these same tropes: by consistently framing these stories around white individuals, families, and choices, they ignore the larger systems of white supremacy that provide Black and Picciolini with the very possibility of redemption. Unlike *American History X*, the books were published in 2018 and 2017, respectively, at precisely the time that, as they were rising out of hate, their fringe hate groups' ideas were entering the mainstream. To rile skinheads into attacking immigrants, *American History X*'s white supremacist Derek gives xenophobic speeches that in retrospect mirror the rhetoric then-candidate Donald Trump used to announce his campaign: "This is about your life and mine; it's about decent, hardworking Americans falling through the cracks and getting the shaft because their government cares more about the constitutional rights of a bunch of people who aren't even citizens of this country!" After Unite the Right, the neo-Nazi march in Charlottesville, Virginia, in August 2017, which resulted in the murder of counterprotester Heather Heyer, President Donald Trump declared, "You also had some very fine people on both sides," a powerful iteration of white innocence and black abstraction that ex-hate narratives ultimately rely upon—that is, that they too are fine people who simply needed understanding and education—even if they seek to work against hate.

As Chanequa Walker-Barnes writes, "Because the term White supremacy has become identified with terrorists and hate groups, people rarely use it in discussing racism and reconciliation" (Walker-Barnes 2019). For all of its power, the narrative of the ex-hate group member ultimately allows a white readership to see white supremacy as something outside of their own range of experience or thought, when history insists on telling us otherwise.

References

Picciolini, Christian. 2017. *White American Youth: My Descent into America's Most Violent Hate Movement—and How I Got Out*. New York: Hachette Books.

Ross, Thomas. 1990. "The Rhetorical Tapestry of Race: White Innocence and Black Abstraction." *William and Mary Law Review* 32 (1): 1–40

Saslow, Eli. 2018. *Rising Out of Hatred: The Awakening of a Former White Nationalist*. New York: Anchor Books.

Walker-Barnes, Chanequa. 2019. *I Bring the Voices of My People: A Womanist Vision for Racial Reconciliation*. Grand Rapids, MI: Eerdmans.

Jesse Kavadlo, PhD, is a professor of English at the Maryville University in St Louis. He has published three books, including American Popular Culture in the Era of Terror: Falling Skies, Dark Knights Rising, *and* Collapsing Cultures.

Contemporary Anti-Semitism in American Higher Education
Kenneth L. Marcus

Although Jewish Americans today enjoy unprecedented tolerance, some American universities have maintained atmospheres that are hostile toward Jewish students. Research suggests that faculty and student attitudes toward Jewish students are generally favorable. Nevertheless, anti-Semitic incidents have worsened on several campuses since roughly the turn of this century, including assault, battery, vandalism, and hate speech. In 2006, the U.S. Commission on Civil Rights concluded that "many college campuses throughout the United States continue to experience incidents of antisemitism" and that "this is a serious problem which warrants further attention" (U.S. Commission on Civil Rights 2006).

Prior to 2004, the U.S. Department of Education's Office for Civil Rights had refused to investigate anti-Semitism cases because it lacks jurisdiction over religion. Ten years ago, the U.S. Department of Education's Office for Civil Rights (OCR), under my direction, issued policy guidance to protect the rights of students who are members of groups that exhibit ethnic as well as religious characteristics. The 2004 policy, which clarified provisions of Title VI of the Civil Rights Act of 1964, applied to Jewish and Sikh students, among others. Over the ensuing years, OCR's enforcement of this policy has been unsteady, as agency leaders initially resisted it, then officially embraced it, while often appearing to misunderstand it. In some cases, they balked at the idea of extending Title VI to Jewish students; in others, they have had difficulty distinguishing between anti-Semitism and hostility to Israel; and in still others, they have interpreted challenged conduct as being protected by the First Amendment to the U.S. Constitution.

In 2004, the Zionist Organization of America (ZOA) filed an OCR complaint alleging a hostile environment for Jewish students at the University of California at Irvine. ZOA described rock-throwing, epithets, threats, among others. At my direction, OCR investigated. After my departure, regional officials proposed finding that a hostile environment had existed for Jewish students but that Irvine had responded adequately. OCR headquarters reversed this proposed determination. OCR then issued a decision closing the case. Specifically, OCR dismissed some allegations as untimely filed, including claims that anti-Israel activists destroyed a Holocaust memorial and called Jewish students "dirty Jew," telling at least one to "go back to Russia," and proposing to "slaughter the Jews." OCR conceded that other allegations were timely filed, including intimidation of Jewish students, defacement of an Israel flag on a student's dormitory room door, and allegations of anti-Semitic activities at anti-Israel protests. OCR found that some of these statements were offensive to Jewish students but nevertheless dismissed them on the questionable grounds that they were based on the Jewish students' political views rather than their ethnic identity.

While OCR was investigating Irvine I, ZOA provided investigators evidence of more recent incidents. OCR investigated these allegations in a separate case, Irvine II. Irvine II involved claims that Jewish students were targeted for adverse treatment, or otherwise subjected to a hostile environment, based on their Jewish identity in nine separate incidents of varying severity. For example, Jewish students argued that a campus event comparing Israel with apartheid South Africa worsened the campus's anti-Jewish atmosphere. OCR countered that such matters are constitutionally protected free speech. A rabbi who attended the event was loudly taunted, "Don't you have somebody's money to steal?" OCR found this statement to be "offensive" but found that it was not, standing on its own, sufficiently serious to constitute a legal violation. This finding was odd since the allegation was not "standing on its own." Rather, it was included with a myriad of other troubling allegations not only in Irvine II but also in the Irvine I complaint from which it had been separated. On August 19, 2013, OCR dismissed this case as well.

In 2009, University of California at Santa Cruz (UCSC) lecturer Tammi Rossman-Benjamin complained to OCR that UCSC had created a hostile environment for Jewish students at university-sponsored public events featuring strongly anti-Israel rhetoric. OCR dismissed this case on August 19, 2013, finding that the facts did not warrant finding a violation. OCR held that all of the events amounted to "expression on matters of public concern directed to the University community." He added that "exposure to such rough and discordant expressions, even when personally offensive and hurtful, is a circumstance that a reasonable student in higher education may experience" (UC Berkeley News Center 2013).

In March 2010, during the so-called Israel Apartheid Week, Jewish undergraduate student Jessica Felber stood in Sproul Plaza at the University of California at Berkeley holding a sign that read, "Israel wants peace." In response, another student allegedly rammed a shopping cart into Felber, causing her physical injuries that required medical attention. Activists conducting a mock checkpoint protest during the so-called Israel Apartheid Week blocked Brian Maissy, a disabled Jewish student, from passage through the Berkeley campus. Felber and Maissy sued in federal court, arguing that Berkeley had tolerated a hostile environment for Jewish students. The court partially dismissed Felber and Maissey's complaint with leave to amend, holding that much of the protesters' activity was protected under the First Amendment. The students later settled their case with Berkeley. The students' lawyers then filed a similar complaint before OCR, repeating their hostile environment allegations. OCR dismissed this case.

In the wake of these cases, it is fair to ask whether OCR remains committed to its 2004 Title VI policy. Meanwhile, incidents are frequently reported at other campuses, such as the recent assault on a Jewish student at Temple University and the taunting of University of Michigan students as "kike" and "dirty Jew." These cases point to three problems. First, OCR needs further guidelines clarifying what constitutes anti-Semitism under its 2004 policy and what does not. Second, OCR should better clarify the relationship between the First Amendment freedom of speech protections and its antiharassment regulations. Third, Congress should prohibit religious harassment at federally funded institutions in order to close a glaring loophole that continues to exist in American civil rights law. Until these changes are made, Jewish students will face legal uncertainty amidst worsening campus climates.

References

UC Berkeley News Center. 2013. "Department of Education Dismisses Complaint Alleging Anti-Semitism at Berkeley." http://newscenter.berkeley.edu/2013/08/27/doe-dismisses-anti-semitism-complaint/.

U.S. Commission on Civil Rights. 2006. "Findings and Recommendations of the United States Commission on Civil Rights Regarding Campus Anti-Semitism." https://www.usccr.gov/pubs/docs/050306FRUSCCRRCAS.pdf.

Kenneth L. Marcus is currently assistant secretary for education for civil rights in the U.S. Department of Education. He was previously president and general counsel of the Louis D. Brandeis Center for Human Rights Under the Law. He is author of Jewish Identity and Civil Rights in America *(New York: Cambridge University Press: 2010). Marcus founded the Brandeis Center in 2011 to combat the resurgence of anti-Semitism in American higher education.*

Perpetuating Historical Genocide: Anti-Indian Groups Deserve Hate Group Designation
Travis McAdam

In 2000, the Montana Human Rights Network (MHRN) published the first extensive report about Montana's anti-Indian movement. In "Drumming Up Resentment," we declared the anti-Indian movement is "a systematic effort to deny legally-established rights to a group of people who are identified on the basis of their shared culture, history, religion, and tradition. This makes it racist by definition" (MHRN 2000, 6).

The movement's ideological foundation makes MHRN's determination regarding its racism readily apparent. First and foremost, the anti-Indian movement wants to eradicate tribal sovereignty and Indian Nations. This is generally done through a combination of ignoring, mocking, and undermining legally established treaty rights. Activists deride treaties as ancient documents that are no longer legitimate, so they show up and oppose Tribes whenever Indian Nations attempt to exert their treaty rights.

The second core of the movement's ideology is erasing Indigenous culture, history, and heritage. The movement euphemistically says American Indians need to "assimilate." While that sounds like a synonym for "adapt," an Indigenous lawmaker in Montana explained what American Indians hear when "assimilate" is used: genocide (MHRN 2017). Of course, anti-Indian activists avoid using the word *genocide*, instead insisting that American Indians are U.S. citizens and should be treated "equally." This obscures the right to self-determination contained in treaties. It also implies that Indigenous folks are conquered nations that must adopt white culture and leave their culture in the past.

Ever since "Drumming," people have asked MHRN if the groups comprising the anti-Indian movement should be categorized as hate groups. We always answered in the affirmative, and, in 2018, MHRN published a report making our case. It examines how the movement's groups match the hate-group criteria used by national organizations (MHRN 2018a). These criteria focus on groups that malign entire constituencies of people based on immutable characteristics like race and ethnicity. The anti-Indian movement's focus on eliminating both Indian Nations and Indigenous culture clearly fits the bill. Additionally, movement activists frequently crossover into the areas of white nationalism and antigovernment beliefs.

Examining CERA and Elaine Willman

With this quick overview, let's look at the activity of the Citizens Equal Rights Alliance (CERA) and one of its longtime board members, Elaine Willman. Since its founding in the late 1980s, CERA has served as the movement's main national organization. In many ways, CERA is a standard advocacy group, lobbying for and against government policy, filing lawsuits and briefs in litigation cases, sponsoring events, and more.

Early on, CERA made its purpose clear, stating in 1989, "We want legislation to stop tribal government jurisdiction—all forms" (MHRN 2018a, 11). A 1998 newsletter directed everyone to "get over this Indian sovereignty myth" (MHRN 2018a, 11). CERA's legal counsel has declared tribal sovereignty is "legal fiction" (IREHR 2013). In addition to opposing tribal sovereignty, CERA frequently invokes the notion that Indigenous people should be glad America's white Founding Fathers conquered them, instead of totally exterminating them (MHRN 2018a, 5–6).

The anti-Indian movement frequently teams up with other right-wing entities. In October 2018, CERA helped sponsor an event featuring prominent antigovernment activists. The keynote speaker was Ammon Bundy, the militia hero whose family led armed standoffs against federal agencies in both Nevada and Oregon (MHRN 2018b). Another speaker was Matt Shea, a Washington state legislator who, according to his fellow lawmakers, engaged in domestic terrorism (MHRN 2019). The speakers' list also included two former CERA board members, one of which proudly had Bundy write the forward for his new book (MHRN 2018b).

Longtime CERA board member Elaine Willman epitomizes the anti-Indian movement's ideology. For years, she worked for the Village of Hobart in Wisconsin, which, not coincidentally, was involved in numerous lawsuits seeking to undermine the tribal sovereignty of the Oneida Nation (MHRN 2015, 17). She moved to Montana's Flathead Indian Reservation in 2015 specifically to fight against the Confederated Salish and Kootenai Tribes' Water Compact, which she hyperbolically claimed could spawn a second American Revolution (MHRN 2018b, 4).

Willman frequently displays the anti-Indian movement's white nationalist leanings. On Facebook, she shared a meme asking, "When is White History Month?" featuring a white nationalist logo reading "100% White" and "100% Proud" (MHRN 2018a, 4). Various white power record companies sell merchandise featuring the same logo. Willman has also combined bigotry directed toward American Indians and Muslims into one narrative. During many of her stump speeches, Willman promotes a conspiracy involving Middle Eastern countries using reservations as staging grounds for Muslim extremists (MHRN 2018b). This links two favorite targets of right-wing vitriol—American Indians and Muslims—into one conspiratorial narrative.

With six years as CERA's chairperson, it's not surprising that Willman aggressively advocates ending tribal sovereignty (MHRN 2018b, 4). She devotes lot of time to calling treaty rights "invalid," unconstitutional, "dead language," and fairy tales (MHRN 2015, 2018b). She's even written to President Trump and asked him to "terminate tribal governments and reservations" (Willman 2019).

Willman pushes the movement's efforts to erase Indigenous culture. She says American Indians should be thankful they exist, commenting the country's white settlers could have exterminated them. "We could be studying you like dinosaurs," she told a 2017 crowd (MHRN 2018a, 6). Willman also represents how movement activists like to, when possible, tout their own American Indian heritage, only to downplay its importance. She claims to be part Cherokee and says she "treasures" that heritage. However, she then asserts the superiority of her American citizenship (MHRN 2018a, 9). On social media, Willman posted a meme reinforcing this idea of European superiority: "You are WHITE. Your ancestors did not steal this country; . . . they BUILT this country" (MHRN 2018a, 4).

Part of the reason Willman is sought after as a speaker is that she blends various right-wing conspiracy theories with her anti-Indian focus. This allows her to radicalize and recruit from a broader audience. Willman has claimed American Indians work with "environmental extremists" and the United Nations because both are "adversarial to the United States" (MHRN 2018b, 5). She also said the UN is using Tribes to "facilitate the dismantling of our country" (MHRN 2018b, 5). She helped organize the 2018 conference featuring Bundy and Shea (MHRN 2018c). In addition to her planned remarks bashing Tribes at the event, she discussed her support for various antigovernment doctrines (MHRN 2018c).

It's important to understand that, like most anti-Indian activists, Willman's crossover into white nationalism and antigovernment ideas isn't an accident. That's where anti-Indian ideology and the movement's activists exist—clustered on the fringe. Willman and the anti-Indian movement are comfortable in far-eight circles because that's their ideological home.

Conclusion

Applying the label of "hate group" isn't something MHRN takes lightly. For guidance, MHRN turned to the Southern Poverty Law Center (SPLC), which is considered the leading national authority when it comes to mapping and determining hate groups across the country. SPLC defines a hate group as "an organization that—based on its official statements or principles, the statements of its leaders, or its activities—has beliefs or practices that attack or malign an entire class of people, typically for their immutable characteristics" (SPLC 2020).

Since race and ethnicity are considered immutable (unchangeable) characteristics, we found that SPLC's definition of a hate group matched the ideology and actions of Montana's anti-Indian groups. MHRN believes that anti-Indian groups deserve the hate group designation.

It's clear the anti-Indian movement and its activists are dedicated to the idea that American Indian rights should be eliminated through assimilation and subordination to white culture, which is another point on the path toward genocide. MHRN rejects the agenda of these groups and emphatically supports the sovereignty of Indian Nations, Indigenous culture, and people.

References

IREHR. 2013. "Take These Tribes Down." 2013. https://www.irehr.org/2013/04/26/take-these-tribes-down/.

MHRN (Montana Human Rights Network). 2000. "Drumming Up Resentment." 2000. https://www.mhrn.org/publications/specialresearchreports/DrummingUp.pdf.

MHRN. 2015. "Racism Mars Opposition to CSKT Water Compact." https://www.mhrn.org/publications/specialresearchreports/Right-Wing%20Conspiracies%20and%20Racism%20Mar%20Opposition%20to%20Confederated%20Salish%20and%20Kootenai%20Tribes%20and%20State%20of%20Montana%20Water%20Compact.pdf.

MHRN. 2017. "Notes from House Judiciary Committee Hearing on SB 97." MHRN Archives.

MHRN. 2018a. "The Case for Categorizing Anti-Indian Groups as Hate Groups." https://mhrn.org/wp-content/uploads/2018/07/FINALAntiIndianGroups.pdf.

MHRN. 2018b. "The 'New' Code of the West." https://mhrn.org/2018/09/25/codeofwest/.

MHRN. 2018c. "Notes from The New Code of the West." MHRN Archives.

MHRN. 2019. "Montanans Hobnobbed with Matt Shea at 2018 Whitefish Event." 2019. https://mhrn.org/2019/12/21/sheareport/.

SPLC. 2020. "What Is a Hate Group?" https://www.splcenter.org/20200318/frequently-asked-questions-about-hate-groups.

Willman, Elaine. 2019. "Federal Indian Policy is Destroying America: Open Letter to President Trump." *The Liberty Sentinel.* https://libertysentinel.org/federal-indian-policy-is-destroying-america-open-letter-to-president-trump.

Travis McAdam is a nationally recognized expert on right-wing social movements. He has worked for the MHRN for more than fifteen years.

Anti-Hispanic Immigrant Hate Crimes
Michele Stacey, Kristin Carbone-Lopez, and Richard Rosenfeld

Over the course of the past century, immigration patterns in the United States have changed. Prior to the 1970s, the majority of immigrants came from Western European countries; by 2007, 80 percent of the foreign-born population in the United States originated in Latin American and Asian countries (Grieco 2010). Along with these changing immigration patterns, there has been an increased concern both in public and political spheres over U.S. immigration policy, and a number of recent changes to those policies have been enacted (e.g., SB 1070 in Arizona in 2010). Many of these policies are born out of and act to perpetuate an immigrant-as-threat narrative (Ibrahim 2005), which portrays immigrants as threatening national security, economic security, and cultural security. To what extent these concerns have filtered down to the individual level remains uncertain. It is possible that the anti-immigrant sentiment that follows increased immigration may contribute to increased intolerance and subsequent violence against immigrant groups, including in the form of hate crime.

In this paper we examine the question of whether recent population changes in immigration patterns are associated with hate crimes against Hispanics. Specifically, we ask: To what extent is anti-Hispanic hate crime related to patterns of Hispanic immigration to the United States? While research on hate crimes has been increasing over the past decade, most studies focus on hate crimes against racial and sexual minorities. Less attention is paid to the role of ethnicity, specifically with regard to Hispanics, many of whom are immigrants. Immigrants, however, are not a protected category in hate crimes, and as such crimes against them are not considered "hate crimes." Therefore, we focus on bias crimes against Hispanics, who are often assumed to be immigrants, and hypothesize that Hispanics may be targeted in response to fear over changing patterns of immigration.

Blalock (1967) proposed a thesis on minority threat, which argues that minority groups pose a threat to the majority group when resources are limited. As the minority population grows in numbers, they compete with the majority for scarce economic and political capital. Group conflict increases as a result, and the majority group will seek to discriminate against the minority in both formal and informal ways. Research examining minority group threat has found evidence of these processes in studies of formal social control (Eitle, D'Alessio, and Stolzenberg 2002), and recently research on hate crime (a form of informal social control) has shown evidence of similar processes (King, Messner, and Baller 2009; Perry 2001). Most of this research has focused on racially motivated hate crime, however, and where ethnic hate crime is considered, prior research does not address the role that immigration patterns and anti-immigrant sentiment may play.

To address this limitation in prior research, we use data from the Uniform Crime Reports (2000–2004), Department of

Homeland Security (DHS), and the Census to examine Hispanic hate crimes. We hypothesize that an increase in Hispanic immigration will result in an increase in anti-Hispanic hate crime. We also expect, consistent with the traditional minority threat theory, that the relative size of the Hispanic population in the state will be positively related to anti-Hispanic hate crime. The threat framework also suggests that there may be a nonlinear effect of minority group size on social control, such that when the minority group grows large enough to exert political power, it may be able to limit the majority group's social control efforts. The minority threat framework also predicts that economic competition will result in increased social control from the majority group. To test this hypothesis we examine the effect of the ratio of white-to-Hispanic unemployment on anti-Hispanic hate crime, as well as the effect of general economic conditions on hate crime.

The results of the study reveal a positive relationship between state-level variation in anti-Hispanic hate crime and recent Hispanic immigration, consistent with our expectations and the minority threat framework. The relative size of the Hispanic population is negatively related to anti-Hispanic hate crime, however, suggesting that where Hispanics are more numerous, hate crimes against them are less frequent. Taken together, these results suggest that anti-Hispanic hate crime is a consequence of Hispanic immigration, and arguably the fear and anger it produces in segments of the majority population, rather than the relative size or economic position of the Hispanic minority, which if anything may serve as protective factors.

Our analysis is limited to the relationship between hate crime and legal immigration, despite the fact that the primary concerns of policymakers and public sentiment focus on the control of undocumented immigrants. The validity of our analysis rests heavily on two assumptions about the connection between legal and illegal immigration. The first is that the settlement patterns of both legal and illegal immigrants are largely the same. The second is that, as a practical matter, potential hate crime offenders are unable to distinguish readily between legal and illegal immigrants or, for that matter, between immigrants and the longstanding residents who resemble them. Although we believe both assumptions appear reasonable, more research is needed to validate them. The current estimates of illegal immigration are imperfect and vary considerably depending on the source (Bialik 2010).

Likewise, while the measurement of hate crime has improved since the FBI first started collecting data, many agencies consistently fail to report any hate crime in their jurisdiction. Research shows that many police officers do not take victim reports of hate crime seriously or do not understand how to identify a hate crime (McDevitt et al., 2003; Nolan and Akiyama 2003). The abundance of zeroes in the hate crime data indicates a need to improve hate crime reporting by both victims and law enforcement. Immigrant victims may be especially likely to forgo reporting an incident because they fear deportation. Although Congress has attempted to encourage and facilitate reporting of particular crimes by undocumented immigrants by creating special visa categories (the S, T, and U visas), it is unclear whether these alleviate the underreporting problem (Kittrie 2006). There are limits on the number of such visas that can be extended, and only victims of certain crimes are eligible. An alternative approach may be the implementation of "sanctuary policies" with law enforcement agencies to ensure undocumented immigrant crime victims are not reported to federal immigration authorities (Kittrie 2006). Additionally, specialized training of police officers is needed regarding hate crime identification. Formal policies on how to handle hate crime within police agencies could also improve the accuracy and integrity of hate crime statistics. In addition, greater attention to crimes experienced by immigrants that go unreported to police is needed to assess victimization risk more accurately and strengthen policies to reduce the risk of hate crime.

References

Bialik, Carl. 2010. "The Pitfalls of Counting Illegal Immigrants." *Wall Street Journal.* http://blogs.wsj.com/numbersguy/the-pitfalls-of-counting-illegal-immigrants-937/.

Blalock, Hubert M., Jr. 1967. *Toward a Theory of Minority-group Relations.* New York: John Wiley and Sons.

Eitle, David, Stewart J. D'Alessio, and Lisa Stolzenberg. 2002. "Racial Threat and Social Control: A Test of the Political, Economic, and Threat of Black Crime Hypotheses." *Social Forces* 81: 557–576.

Grieco, Elizabeth M. 2010. "Race and Hispanic Origin of the Foreign-Born Population in the United States: 2007, American Community Survey Reports, ACS-11. U.S. Census Bureau, Washington, DC. https://www.census.gov/library/publications/2010/acs/acs-11.html.

Ibrahim, Maggie. 2005. "The Securitization of Migration: A Racial Discourse." *International Migration* 43: 163–187.

King, Ryan D., Steven F. Messner, and Robert D. Baller. 2009. "Contemporary Hate Crimes, Law Enforcement, and the Legacy of Racial Violence." *American Sociological Review* 74: 291–315.

Kittrie, Orde F. 2006. "Federalism, Deportation, and Crime Victims Afraid to Call the Police." *Iowa Law Review* 91: 1449–1508.

McDevitt, Jack, et al. 2003. "Improving the Quality and Accuracy of Bias Crime Statistics Nationally: An Assessment of the First Ten Years of Bias Crime Data Collection." In Barbara Perry, ed. *Hate and Bias Crime: A Reader.* New York: Routledge.

Nolan, James J., and Yoshio Akiyama. 2004. "Assessing the Factors that Affect Law Enforcement Participation, in Hate Crime Reporting." In Diana R. Grant and Phyllis

B. Gerstenfeld, eds. *Crimes of Hate: Selected Readings.* Thousand Oaks, CA: Sage Publications.

Perry, Barbara. 2001. *In the Name of Hate: Understanding Hate Crimes.* New York: Routledge.

Michele Stacey is assistant professor in the Department of Criminal Justice at East Carolina University. Kristin Carbone-Lopez was formerly associate professor in the Department of Criminology and Criminal Justice at the University of Missouri-St. Louis.

Richard Rosenfeld is professor emeritus in the Department of Criminology and Criminal Justice at the University of Missouri-St. Louis.

Unmasking "Antifa": More than Black Bloc
Kitty Stryker

My name is Kitty Stryker. I'm queer, I'm a writer, and I'm a mom to two adorable cats. I'm teaching myself to cook through a mixture of peer support and personal pressure. I play Dungeons and Dragons every Sunday, I know how to knit, and I'm a bit of a doomsday prepping nerd. I'm a consent activist. I sleep with a stuffed raccoon.

I'm also that "antifa" the media has been warning you about.

Yep, the kind who goes to protests masked. I was there when Milo got shut down by student protesters, who fought back when they had pepper rounds shot at them by the police. I was at the various Battles for Berkeley offering medic care to people who were injured even while being shoved and swung at. What I saw and see out there on the ground was (and is) very different from what gets reported. I wore a mask and covered my tattoos to protect myself from being doxxed again, further harassed by white supremacists, misogynists, and police who are too often showing up in the news as one, the other, or both. I also wore a mask to protect myself from pepper spray and tear gas so I could care for people who were struggling to see and breathe.

But we've all had that back and forth already. I want to talk about what I do when the cameras aren't there.

See, antifascism isn't just a catchphrase for me. It's a way of life. I spend a lot of time figuring out how to disentangle myself from the whims of a government I see increasingly (and boldly) influenced by white supremacy and big money. Antifascism isn't a movement—there's no membership card, however much we joke about it—it's an ideology. If you believe that far-right, authoritarian ultranationalism is Bad, then you're "antifa." I didn't "join" so much as "started acknowledging my politics more clearly in public."

When I'm not at a protest, I'm still hard at work for the movement. It just may not look like that's what I'm doing if you listen to Fox or CNN. On any given day, I work on my urban garden. I teach my neighbors how to prepare for a natural disaster. I cook meals and deliver extra to folks sleeping rough on the streets. I trade resources—clothes, food, appliances—with friends and friends of friends. I constantly try to learn new skills, whether that means fixing the shifter, bushing on my car, or mending socks, and when I feel I know them enough, I pass those skills along to others.

How is that "antifa"? Well, to me, antifascism isn't just about physical direct action pushing back against racist police or inflammatory Proud Boys. It's also antifascist to provide mutual aid to your community so they have the strength to keep fighting. It also reminds us all that there's something worth fighting for, not just something worth fighting against. In a world that feels increasingly hopeless with climate change and a president that seems hellbent on destroying this country, hope is a precious resource.

Who protects us? We protect us.

This holds true even at a protest, where emotions are heightened. While the media reports on what seems "exciting" for them—fires in trash cans, moments of violence—most of the time I spend at protests as "antifa" is spent listening to music, chanting, passing out snacks, and smoking cigarettes. It's pretty much what I do at a music festival too. We don't have shadowy meetings where we all wear balaclavas and talk about destruction. Instead, we gather with our similarly minded friends and discuss what community aid we can be focused on when we're not pushed into protesting honest-to-god Nazis in our neighborhood. We discuss what roles we feel best equipped for, maybe train each other for new roles—I'm a medic, for example, and I help others learn basic skills for being a medic at a protest too. Friends of mine are best at de-escalation, or talking to cops, or childcare, or aftercare. It takes a village.

That's why it's so frustrating to hear people equate "antifa" with fascists. So often, white supremacists are bussing into our towns from right-wing strongholds to hold purposefully inflammatory events. They're blatantly buddying up with people who talk about white genocide and how Jewish people control the media and the money. Meanwhile, the "antifa" you see? Those are your neighbors, standing up against hate speech and talk of genocide. The people we're protesting? Consistently getting charged with felonies, usually for assault with weapons, usually not at the protests themselves. Antifascists? We're getting arrested for wearing masks, often by officers who are, themselves, Proud Boys and white supremacists. We're not exactly on the same playing field. Do we have some people (usually, let's be honest, white twenty- to thirty-something-year-old men) who come to a protest to black bloc up and fight? Absolutely. But there's fewer on our side than on the side we're protesting, and sometimes, those fighters are a godsend to peaceful protesters when police refuse to step in. As a medic, I have relied on black bloc more than once to protect me and my patient from the crowd and the cameras.

Meanwhile, every day, I get messages on Twitter and Facebook threatening me. Sometimes they're vague threats about how I'll "get what's coming to me." Sometimes they try to scare me with information about who I am or where I live. Sometimes, the threats are graphic and detailed. The oldest person who has ever threatened me was eighty-four; the youngest was sixteen, as far as I'm aware. I messaged his father to tell him his son was encouraging me, a midthirties adult, to fly to his hometown so he could beat me up. I told him to teach his kid about etiquette, and about online safety. I blocked him because

I didn't know if his father would agree with me, apologize, or up the ante. I don't go to the police about these things, because half the time the police are actively supporting (or are) the sort of men harassing me.

I've become pretty desensitized to the constant hum of harassment. Usually, these people say I deserve it because I'm "antifa," therefore (as some right-wing politicians say) a domestic terrorist who deserves to fear for her life. The facts of what I do in my day-to-day life—caring for houseless folks, helping addicts, listening to abuse survivors, and connecting them with resources—are irrelevant. The men who I protest when I mask up, the men who scream in my face that I deserve to be murdered for tending to the wounded, the men who over and over again end up arrested for felony violence—they are more believable to the public than I am. It is exhausting, and it's disheartening. But I'm going to keep going, because I must. We all must.

There is an incentive for people in power to want you, the reader, to distrust people like me. The status quo is killing people—directly, through unchecked extremist right-wing violence, and indirectly, through policies that are racist, classist, sexist, transphobic, homophobic, ableist. The status quo needs you to ignore all of the work we do to fill potholes and feed the hungry because we're showing that there's another way that doesn't involve them. The status quo needs you to be afraid of people like me, people who center mutual aid over individualist "success." The status quo, after all, is built on the backs of the marginalized via white supremacist violence. The status quo needs you to desire authoritarianism disguised as "freedom."

And my story gets so many more clicks if I'm a thug.

Kitty Stryker doesn't just play a cleric in D&D. She plays one in real life, with over ten years experience as a street medic. Kitty is a queer, disabled, antifascist journalist, and the cofounder of Strugalo Circus, a group of radical activists and Juggalos.

4 Profiles

No book on hate groups is complete without some mention of the individuals and organizations who have been involved in the history of this topic. This chapter provides brief summaries of a few of the most important individuals and organizations that had played a role in this story.

Anti-Defamation League (ADL)

ADL is the name by which the Anti-Defamation League is most commonly known today. The organization was founded in 1913 by attorney and activist Sigmund Livingston. Livingston was concerned about the social, cultural, political, and other ways in which Jews were subject to discrimination at the time. He was convinced that these problems were a consequence of emotional feelings held by perpetrators of hate crimes, not on their rational thoughts about the Jewish culture. He founded ADL for providing better information to the general public about Judaism, hoping thereby to decrease the discrimination and terror to which Jews were historically subjected.

ADL was originally created as an arm of the Independent Order of B'nai B'rith, itself founded on October 13, 1843, in New York City. The name *B'nai B'rith* means "children of the

---

A supporter of the Human Rights Campaign hands out flags in Des Moines, Iowa, 2015. HRC is one of the most active organizations against hate crimes committed against LGBTQ people. (Jill Lehmann/Dreamstime.com)

convent," a reflection of the belief that Jews are God's chosen people. B'nai B'rith was founded by a group of twelve German Jews in response to "the deplorable condition of Jews in this, our newly adopted country" (*https://www.bnaibrith.org/about-us.html*). The purpose of the organization was to provide the material and other resources needed by American Jews to attain some level of safety and comfort in the United States.

ADL first appeared as a part of the Bloomington, Indiana chapter of B'nai B'rith. Among the organization's earliest targets were the Ku Klux Klan (KKK) and industrialist Henry Ford. Jews were among the groups especially targeted by the Klan, and ADL sought to publicize and bring action against some of the most heinous of the Klan's crimes. Ford was one of the most successful capitalists of his day, but one with very strong anti-Semitic feelings. He is best known in this regard for his series of four books that originally appeared in his newspaper, *The Dearborn Independent*. Ford blamed every manner of problem and defect in the world on Jews in volumes entitled *The International Jew: The World's Foremost Problem* (1920); *Jewish Activities in the United States* (1921); *Jewish Influence in American Life* (1921); and *Aspects of Jewish Power in the United States* (1922). The information in these books supposedly came, to a large extent, from a fictitious historical work, *The Protocols of the Learned Elders of Zion*. The series became widely popular, especially in Germany in the early days of National Socialism. In response to Ford's works, the ADL published a pair of pamphlets responding to the charges made in *The Dearborn Independent*, "The Poison Pen" and "The Protocols—A Spurious Document." The ADL claims success for these efforts because of a letter Ford wrote much later (January 1942) to Livingston, expressing the view that "the hate-mongering prevalent for some time in this country against the Jews, is a distinct disservice to our country, and to the peace and welfare of humanity" (https://www.adl.org/who-we-are/history#in-the-1940s).

The 1930s were a period of special concern to the ADL as it attempted to respond to a "perfect storm" of criticism against

Jews. They were both criticized for the worst of these events, such as the strongly anti-Semitic campaign of Roman Catholic priest Father Charles Coughlin and the development of the Great Depression, and punished for their very existence by the German Holocaust of the late 1930s and early 1940s. It was during this time that the ADL created the first program for identifying and describing anti-Semitic hate groups and individuals, a program that has existed to the present day.

The 1940s and 1950s were a period in which the ADL became even more active in fighting against hate groups and hate crimes, often turning to the courts for actions in this area. In the earliest of these actions, the ADL filed an *amicus curiae* brief with the Supreme Court in the case of *Shelley v. Kraemer*. That case resulted in a revolutionary decision that individuals could not be denied housing because of their race (thus providing proof that ADL was concerned with more than strictly anti-Semitic incidents). (For a detailed history of the ADL from the 1910s to the present day, see https://www.adl.org/who-we-are/history.)

Throughout the twenty-first century, the ADL has greatly expanded its range of activities in the fight against hate crimes and hate groups. One of its best known activities is the organization's "Hate on Display™ Hate Symbols Database." This database lists more than two hundred logos, banners, styles of clothing, tattoos, hand signals, slang terms, and other symbols used by hate groups of all kinds (*https://www.adl.org/hate-symbols*). The group also provides an annual "Audit of Anti-Semitic Incidents," a report roughly similar to the Southern Poverty Law Center's (SPLC) annual review of hate groups in the United States. Other areas in which the ADL is active include anti-Semitism in the United States; anti-Semitism globally; combating hate and protecting communities; extremism, terrorism, and bigotry; cyberhate; hate crimes; community security; confronting discrimination and securing justice; religious freedom; free speech; racial justice; criminal justice reform; education equity; women's equity; voting rights;

LGBTQ rights; immigrant and refugee rights; Israel advocacy and education; anti-Israel activity and boycott, divestment, and sanctions movement; domestic Israeli issues; antibias education; bullying and cyberbullying prevention; and interfaith and intergroup relations.

The league has also developed and published a wide range of documents dealing with all aspects of these areas. Some of these include a hate crime statute map and table of state laws; an extensive document on the nature, goals, and results of hate crime laws in the United States; a report on anti-Asian hate crimes; the organization's position on the coronavirus pandemic and its relationship to hate crimes; and reports on specific examples of hate crimes and hate groups. ADL also publishes several educational documents for use in schools and for public programs, such as two curriculum programs for schools, A World of Difference® Institute and No Place for Hate®. Other educational tools available from ADL include sample lesson plans; books matter: children's literature, including the book of the month program; antibias tools and strategies; bullying/cyberbullying resources; table talk: family conversations; Rosalind's classroom conversations; early childhood FAQs; and education blog, as well as a list of webinars and podcasts.

Zainab Al-Suwaij (1971–)

Zainab Al-Suwaij is the cofounder and executive director of the American Islamic Congress (AIC). She was born in Basra, Iraq, and raised by her grandfather, the Ayatollah of Basra. When she was still in elementary school, one of her best friends suddenly disappeared, along with her family, after making a negative comment about the ruling Baath Party. The lesson taught her, she later wrote, "was to remain silent, and not to challenge the regime" (https://news.harvard.edu/gazette/story/2004/11/dispatches-from-iraqs-feminist-front/). Al-Suwaij later had a somewhat similar experience during her high school days. She was told that she could take her final exams only if she became a member of Saddam Hussein's Baath Party. When she refused, she was allowed to go ahead with her exams only if she signed an agreement promising that she would not join any opposition party. She did so, she later said, as it was the only way she could complete her high school studies.

In 1990, while visiting family in Kuwait, she heard of the uprising against Hussein. She returned to Iraq immediately and became involved in that movement. When the revolution failed in 1991, she went into hiding, escaped to Italy, and eventually was able to get to the United States. After completing her college degree in the United States, she accepted an appointment as refuge case manager in New Haven, Connecticut, at the Interfaith Refugee Ministry. She also began to work as a teacher of Arabic at Yale University. She held those positions until 2001, when she cofounded the AIC. The purpose of this action, she later said, was "to represent those American Muslims who cherished the freedoms of the US after living under repressive regimes" (https://pakistanlink.org/Community/2012/Nov12/23/04.HTM).

Al-Suwaij has continued to work both within the AIC and other settings on women's issues and challenges facing moderate Muslim citizens. For example, she has cofounded several organizations designed to help Iraqi women develop and exercise their own political rights in their native land. Among these organizations are the Iraqi Women Higher Counsel, the Iraqi-American Freedom Alliance, the Revitalization of Iraqi Schools and Stabilization of Education program, and Hands Across the Mideast Support Alliance (HAMSA). It was through the first of these organizations that Al-Suwaij was able to convince the Iraqi parliament to establish a policy of having women make up at least 25 percent of its membership.

Al-Suwaij was named an "Ambassador of Peace" by the Interreligious and International Peace Council in 2005 and was awarded a Dialogue on Diversity's Liberty Award in 2006. Also in 2006, she was recognized as "2006 International Person of the Year" by the National Liberty Museum. In 2012, Al-Suwaij received the East West Vision of Peace Award from the Levantine Cultural Center in recognition of her work to bridge political and religious divides between the United States and the Middle East and North Africa.

Heidi L. Beirich (1967–)

Beirich was employed at the Southern Poverty Law Center for nearly two decades from 2000 to 2019. During that time, she served on the organization's Intelligence Project, as senior writer (2000–2004), deputy director (2004–2009), codirector (2009–2012), and director (2012–2019). In 2019, she left the organization as part of a wholesale "housecleaning" of the organization resulting from issues relating to possible misconduct on the part of cofounder Morris Dees.

Following her departure from SPLC, Beirich was involved in the founding of a new antihate organization, the Global Project against Hate and Extremism. This organization focuses on an international, rather than strictly American, analysis of hate groups. Its goal is to learn more about the activities of hate groups around the world, provide that information to the general public, and, in particular, analyze the ways in which such hate groups use social media and other aspects of the Internet to achieve their objectives.

Heidi L. Beirich's parents were Russell and Evelyn (née Paschmann) Beirich. They reportedly met in Germany during World War II, when her father was serving in the U.S. Army, and her mother was a resident of Kaldenhausen in the Ruhr District of West Germany. The couple made their home in Palm Springs, California, where Heidi was born in 1967. Heidi attended elementary and high school in Palm Springs before the family moved to Vista in San Diego County, California, in 1983. She then entered Vista High School, from which she graduated in June 1985.

Beirich has spoken at some length about her early years in Southern California. It was a time when right-wing hate groups were ascendant and present in many aspects of most people's lives. She reports, for example, that one of her best friends in high school was the son of the head of the White Aryan Resistance. She also described her high school history teacher as "like somebody out of Dr. Strangelove . . . a rabid anti-communist" (https://abcnews.go.com/US/video/country-founded-white-supremacy-47425451).

After completing her high school studies, Beirich enrolled at the University of California at Berkeley and received her BA degree in international developmental studies in 1989. She then continued her studies at the University of California at Riverside, where she earned her MA in economics in 1990. She later earned a second MA in political science at San Diego State University in 1993 and a PhD in political science at Purdue University in West Lafayette, Indiana, in 1998. The following year, Beirich began her career as an intern at SPLC, working on the Intelligence Report, a connection she retained until 2019.

Beirich has specialized in the study of neo-Confederate hate groups and written several articles on the topic. She was also coeditor of and contributor to the anthology *Neo-Confederacy: A Critical Introduction*, published in 2008 (University of Texas Press). She has also contributed articles to several other books, including *The Confederate Flag: Current Issues, Countering the Islamophobia Industry: Toward More Effective Strategies, Rightwing Populism across Europe: Politics and Discourse*, and *Barack Obama and the Vision of Post-Racial America*.

In addition to her many writing projects, she has been a guest speaker at various events and meetings, such as "Hate and Extremism Today" (University of Alabama, 2015), "The Rising Tide of Hate in America" (New College of Florida, 2015), "What is Violent Extremism: A Global and US Perspective" (Cleveland State University, 2016), "Life After Hate: Defeating White Supremacy" (Women in the World, 2017 Summit), "Hate Groups and Extremism" (San Mateo Bar Association, 2018), "Hate in America" (Shepard Symposium, University of Wyoming, 2019), and RightCon Tunis (2019).

Center for the Study of Hate and Extremism, California State University, San Bernardino. *See* Brian Levin

Morris Dees (1936–)

Dees is the cofounder and longtime president and CEO of the SPLC. He was fired from these positions in March 2019 following a spate of accusations that he had acted in sexist, racist, and gender discrimination ways that brought discredit to the organization that he had founded and led for nearly fifty years.

Morris Seligman Dees Jr. was born on December 16, 1936, in Shorter, Macon County, Alabama. His parents were Morris Seligman Dees and Annie Ruth Dees, tenant cotton farmers in the thinly populated rural county. Although poor, the Dees held high moral standards that they imparted to their son. Morris Jr.'s first introduction to racism came when he was still a teenager. His father sent him to represent a local Black farmer, Clarence Williams, who had been arrested by a state trooper for drunken driving and resisting arrest. The judge in the case paid little or no attention to the defendant's case, whom he found guilty and fined (see Bill Blum. 1991. "Public Defender." *ABA Journal* 77 (6): 104 for the full story of this episode).

Dees' next involvement with legal racism came in 1962 when, as a naive young attorney, he volunteered to defend KKK member Claude Henley for attacking Freedom Riders protesting in Alabama. Dees won an acquittal for its client, but later realized that he had been on the wrong side of a hate crime in this instance. He never made that mistake again.

After graduating from Sidney Lanier High School in Montgomery, Alabama, in 1955, Dees matriculated at the University of Alabama, where he earned his bachelor's degree and his law degree in 1960. He then returned to Montgomery, where he began practicing law part-time, while also opening a publishing business with fellow attorney, Millard Fuller (Fuller went on to earn his own degree of fame as the founded of Habitat for Humanity). After five years, Dees bought out his partner's share of the company, which had by then become very successful. Two years later, Dees sold the company to the Times Mirror Company, largely securing his financial status for some years to come. He later wrote that the decision to sell the publishing company was inspired largely by his reading of *The Story of My Life* by the famous attorney, Clarence Darrow. Dees became convinced that he could make a greater contribution to society working as an attorney for the abused and dispossessed than continuing in the publishing business. At the time, he was involved in a law firm with fellow Alabaman, Joseph Levin. Over the years, that partnership evolved into a more formal civil rights–oriented business that became the basis of the Southern Poverty Law Center in 1971.

Dees decided at an early stage of his civil rights career that legal action against hate groups and hate acts was perhaps the most powerful way of dealing with hate crimes. In one of his earliest actions, he sued the Young Men's Christian Association of Montgomery for discrimination on the basis of race, on behalf of two seven-year-old African American cousins who had been banned from using the YMCA's community pool. The court ruled that the ban was unconstitutional and required that the City of Montgomery and the YMCA remove all barriers to the use of their facilities on the basis of race.

Dees developed an enviable string of legal successes of this type over the next forty years. In 1981, he filed and won a lawsuit against the United Klans of America (UKA) for their use of lynching, a decision resulting in a $7 million judgment against the UKA. A decade later he won a similar case against the White Aryan Resistance that resulted in a fine of $12 million against the hate group. Ten years later, in 2001, he won yet another judgment against a large hate group, the Aryan Nation, in the amount of $6.5 million (largely putting the group out of business in the process). Many of SPLC's accomplishments against hate groups into the late 2010s can be credited at least in some part to the work of Dees as president and CEO of the organization.

In addition to his autobiography, *A Season of Justice: The Life and Times of Civil Rights Lawyer Morris Dees* (Charles Scribners and Sons, 1991), Dees has written three other books, *Hate on Trial: The Case Against America's Most Dangerous Neo-Nazi* (Villard Books, 1993), *Gathering Storm: America's Militia Threat* (Harper Perennial, 1997), and (with Steve Fiffer) *A Lawyer's Journey: The Morris Dees Story* (Chicago: American Bar Association, 2003). Dees was awarded an honorary Doctor of Laws degree by Whittier College, the ABA Medal of the American Bar Association, and the Martin Luther King Nonviolent Peace Prize. The University of Alabama has also established the Morris Dees Justice Award in his honor.

Gonzaga Institute for Hate Studies

The founding of the Gonzaga University Institute for Hate Studies (GIHS) dates to the mid-1990s. Over a period of three years, African American students at the university's School of Law had been subjected to various racist actions, including hate mail and phone calls. In response to this problem, members of the university joined together in 1997 to create the GIHS. The purpose of the institute was to develop a program of research on hate topics, to take a stand against hate crimes, and to educate the general public about the problems posed by hate actions and crimes. The institute's first formal meeting was held in the fall of 1998. Two years later, trustees of the university approved a name change for the institute to its current Gonzaga Institute for Hate Studies.

The primary function of the Institute is to provide a setting in which scholars from various fields can "expand theoretical and applied knowledge, personal and social awareness, and values-based research-supported methods in our areas of humanitarian engagement" (https://www.gonzaga.edu/academics/centers-institutes/institute-for-hate-studies/about). Among the specific research topics included in this general outline include understanding the sources, manifestations, and consequences of indignity, intolerance, and inequality; addressing hate, violent conflict, and oppression; working for universal freedom from fear, indignity, and want; supporting nonviolent systems, strategies, and solutions; and catalyzing and creating stable communities.

Possibly the best known component of the institute's activities is the publication of the *Journal of Hate Studies*. The journal has been published on (usually) an annual basis and is recognized as one of the major repositories of research on all aspects of hate crimes, hate groups, and related topics. A second major component of the institute's activities is its biennial International Conference on Hate Studies. The sixth conference in this series is scheduled for February 2021.

Among the Institute's other activities are the following (from its website at https://www.gonzaga.edu/academics/centers-institutes/institute-for-hate-studies/about):

- Special workshops, symposia, lectures, and mini-conferences
- Hosting of distinguished visiting fellows
- Organizing interdisciplinary research teams
- Support for interdisciplinary courses in hate studies and the production of promising model projects and student research
- Presentation of the Eva Lassman Memorial Student Research Award and Take Action Against Hate Awards
- Advocating for the field of hate studies and encouraging increased discussion about hate across disciplines
- Integration of theory and practice through an active International Council of Experts and roster of Gonzaga affiliates
- Fortifying connections of knowledge, skills, and service via student employment and internships

Human Rights Campaign

The Human Rights Campaign (HRC) was founded in 1980 by gay rights activist Steve Endean. Endean was one of the major figures in the early history of the gay rights movement. At the age of twenty-five, he was instrumental in convincing the Minneapolis City Council to adopt a gay rights ordinance, the first of its kind in the nation. He later became director of the Gay Rights National Lobby (1978) and later served as cochair of the National Gay Task Force (now the National LGBTQ Task Force). In 1980, he became executive director of the organization he founded, HRC. Endean died in 1993 of AIDS-related causes.

HRC has a long and honorable career fighting for the rights of lesbians, gay men, bisexuals, transgenders, queers, and related groups. Its history is studded with several political successes, including a 1992 meeting between President Bill Clinton and representatives from HRC in the Oval Office, the first such event of its kind in American history; the first appearance of a gay and lesbian rights spokesperson before a Congressional committee reviewing the Defense of Marriage Act in 1996; campaigns against the Federal [Constitutional] Marriage Amendment in 2004 and 2006; active involvement in the campaign to elect Barack Obama as president of the United States in 2008 and 2012; a multimillion dollar campaign to elect lesbian and gay candidates to office in the 2008 campaign; efforts to defeat anti-same-sex marriage laws in several states and to win approval of same-sex legislation in even more states; more than a decade of work to gain Congressional approval for the Matthew Shepard and James Byrd Jr. Hate Crimes Prevention Act in 2009; copartnership with the Courage Campaign in 2010 against the anti-LGBTQ propaganda of the National Organization for Marriage; and an aggressive #LoveConquersHate effort to offer support for LGBTQ Russian athletes in the Olympic Games of 2014.

HRC conducts a vigorous, ongoing campaign monitoring the activities of hate groups that target LGBTQ people in particular. These efforts result in the annual publication of two reports on the topic, the most recent of which are "Research Overview: Hate Crimes and Violence Against

Lesbian, Gay, Bisexual and Transgender People" (https://assets2.hrc.org/files/assets/resources/Hatecrimesandviolenceagainstlgbtpeople_2009.pdf) and "A National Epidemic: Fatal Anti-transgender Violence in the United States in 2019" (https://assets2.hrc.org/files/assets/resources/Anti-TransViolenceReport2019.pdf). The first of these reports includes sections on federal legislative efforts, anatomy of violence, predictors of bias and sexual prejudice, hate crime responders and reporting, bias crime reporting and best practices for hate crime reporting, and future research and advocacy efforts. The second report consists primarily of chapters on demographics of hate crimes against transgenders, law and policy data, safety data, reporting and enforcement data, and a closing section on "What We Can Do."

Brian Levin

Levin is currently director of the Center for the Study of Hate and Extremism at California State University, San Bernardino (CSU-SB), a program that he founded at CSU-SB in 1999. Levin has a long and distinguished history of dealing with problems relating to hate groups and other forms of extremism. He was born in Long Island, New York to a New York City policewoman and veterinarian, Howard Levin. Levin credits much of his moral development to principles laid out by his father, who often treated less fortunate individuals and families with pets, often at little or no charge.

Levin attended the University of Pennsylvania and earned his bachelor's degree in history in 1989. He was also employed from 1985 to 1989 as a police officer in New York City, where he was assigned to the Harlem and Washington Heights service areas. During his time with the NYPD, he was awarded an Excellent Police Duty Medal and Academic Excellence Award. In 1989, Levin entered Stanford Law School, where he received his JD degree in 1992. While at Stanford, he was honored with the Block Civil Liberties Award for his research on hate crimes.

After earning his law degree, Levin joined the law firm of Irell and Manela in Newport Beach, California, where he specialized in corporate litigation cases. In 1995, he took a position as associate director for legal affairs in the Klanwatch/Militia Task Force (now the Intelligence Project) at the SPLC. A year later, Levin left SPLC to become associate professor of criminal justice at Richard Stockton College (now, Stockton University) in Stockton, California. He served simultaneously as the director of the Center on Hate and Extremism (CHE) at Stockton. In 1999, CHE, along with Levin, was transferred to the University of California at San Bernardino, with Levin retaining his position of the center. The center was also renamed the Center for the Study of Hate and Extremism. He is now full-tenured professor at CSU-SB, specializing in criminal law and procedure, national security, terrorism, extremism, and hate crime. In 2020, Levin was awarded the Wang Family Excellence Award from the California State University. This award is given annually to "the university system's outstanding faculty members and one outstanding staff member who, through extraordinary commitment and dedication, have distinguished themselves by exemplary contributions and achievements" (https://www.recordgazette.net/news/schools/csusb-professor-brian-levin-to-be-honored-with-the-wang-family-excellence-award-for-outstanding/article_9fb03674-4858-11ea-bb46-57c6fa747513.html).

The Center for the Study of Hate and Extremism is a rich repository of resources on the study of hate groups. Its contributions fall into two general categories: (1) a set of about four dozen videos on specific topics in the fields of hate and extremism and terrorism, and (2) reports on specific topics in the field of hate crime. Some examples of the videos available deal with topics such as hate offenders, anti-Semitism and prejudice, protecting immigrants, anti-Sikh crimes, transgender equality, hate crimes in the UK, and hate crime law in Europe. Among reports available from the center are "Hate Crime Analysis and Forecast for 2016/2017," "Hate Crime In California,"

"Organizations who Focus on Terrorism-related Issues," Reports and Data on Terrorism in Europe," "Reports and Data on Terrorism in the United States," "Reports and Data on Recruitment Efforts by Terrorist Organizations," and "Reports and Data on Counter-Radicalization Efforts." Special reports on hate-related topics are also available, such as "Illustrated Almanac, Decade Summary: Hate & Extremism," "Illustrated Almanac (November 2019)," "Factbook on Hate and Extremism in the U.S. and Internationally (July 2019)," "Hate Crimes in Los Angeles and Other Major U.S. Cities, 2017–2018," and Hate Crime Rise in U.S. Cities and U.S. Counties in Time of Division and Foreign Interference."

Sigmund Livingston (1872–1946)

Livingston was the founder and first president of the Anti-Defamation League of B'nai B'rith in 1913. The purpose of the organization was "to stop, by appeals to reason and conscience and, if necessary, by appeals to law, the defamation of the Jewish people. Its ultimate purpose is to secure justice and fair treatment to all citizens alike and to put an end forever to unjust and unfair discrimination against and ridicule of any sect or body of citizens" (https://www.adl.org/who-we-are/excerpt-of-the-anti-defamation-league-founding-charter). The organization later changed its name to just the Anti-Defamation League, and today it is generally known simply as ADL.

Sigmund G. Livingston was born in Giessen, Germany, on December 27, 1872. His parents were Dora and Mayer Livingston, who emigrated to the United States in 1881, settling in Bloomington, Indiana. Mayer and his brother Samuel opened a dry goods store in Bloomington, where three of Mayer's sons were also later employed. Two other sons, Sigmund and Irvin, took a different route, choosing to earn law degrees. Sigmund received his degree from Illinois Wesleyan University Law School in 1894, after which he opened an office with a Wesleyan classmate, William Bach, in Bloomington.

Soon after returning to Bloomington, Livingston became active in various Jewish organizations, in particular, the Independent Order of B'nai B'rith (also known as the Sons of Israel, and more commonly, as Binai Brith). By 1908, he had been appointed chairman of the organization's committee on combating anti-Semitism. One of his achievements is said to have been his success in convincing an important travel book publisher to delete the phrase "No Jews Wanted" from its listings.

An important factor in the founding of the ADL was the trial of one Leo Frank, convicted in Atlanta, Georgia, in 19313 of the murder of a thirteen-year-old coworker. Circumstances surrounding the case were strongly in doubt, and the governor of the state commuted Frank's death sentence to life in prison. Two years later, an angry mob stormed the prison where Frank was being held and lynched him. The complete story of the Frank case aroused worry and anger among Jewish citizens in all parts of the country, possibly most strongly in Sigmund Livingston in Bloomington. He proposed to the local B'nai B'rith chapter that they create a new organization to work toward a better understanding of the Jewish tradition among the general public and to work to combat anti-Semitism by whatever legal means necessary. The modern version of that organization, ADL, is today one of the two strongest forces (along with SPLC) studying and reporting on the existence and actions of hate groups in the United States.

In 1927, Livingston moved to Chicago, where he formed a new law firm, Lederer, Livingston, Kahn and Adler, with which he was associated for the rest of his active life. He died at his home in Highland Park on June 13, 1946. In 1944, Livingston had published the work for which he is almost certainly best known, *Must Men Hate?* In the book, he attempts to explain the origin of anti-Semitism, concluding that the concept is formed not through rational thinking but as the result of emotional forces. He suggests some of the actions that both Christians and Jews must take to overcome these feelings of hatred.

Not in Our Town

Not in Our Town (NIOT) is a project created in 1995 by a film production organization in Oakland, California, founded in 1988. Today, NIOT is the main program making up The Working Group's activities.

The NIOT project got under way with the production of a film *Not in Our Town: Billings, Montana*, produced by PBS as a documentary motion picture. The film told the story of the ways in which the citizens of Billings came together to combat a growing problem of hate crimes in their city. The film is available in full on YouTube at https://www.youtube.com/watch?v=Z5yaMhcTCdw. It has become a model for the way in which citizens of a town of all races, colors, creeds, sexual orientation, nationalities, and other characteristics can band together and develop a program for resisting the efforts of hate groups to begin operations in their communities. Over the years, NIOT has produced various other films and videos telling similar stories in other locations, such as *Waking in Oak Creek*, based on the mass murder of six Sikhs in the town of Oak Creek, Wisconsin; *Not in Our Town: Class Actions*, telling the stories of ways in which students at the secondary and college level have found ways to counteract the activities and influence of hate groups on campus; *Not in Our Town: Light in the Darkness*, explaining how the residents of Patchogue, New York, came together to deal with the murder of a local immigrant resident; *Not in Our Town: Northern California: When Hate Happens Here*, reviewing the actions taken by five towns in Northern California in response to an five-year epidemic of hate crimes in the area; *What about Walter?*, a film inspired by the burning murder of a fifteen-year-old boy in Poplar Bluff, Missouri; and *Instruments of Peace: Anniversary of Hate Attack on Unitarians*, describing reactions to a church shooting at the Tennessee Valley Unitarian Universalist Church in 2008. Trailers or complete films of some of these titles are available on the NIOT website at https://www.niot.org/category/niot-videos/dvds-sale.

Over the past twenty-five years, NIOT has expanded its program for combating hate groups. Films and videos are still a fundamental part of its program, resources that can be purchased or borrowed from the organization. The group has also developed a kit for helping communities develop their own NIOT committees. Its "Quick Start Guide" includes ideas for dealing with specific problems relating to hate groups, fighting back against bullying of school children and others, and, in general, building safe and inclusive communities. NIOT also sponsors a program called Gold Star Cities that invites communities to join with the organization to work toward safer towns. NIOT provides help to these cities through training programs, mentorships, and peer-to-peer exchanges.

NIOT has also created a specialized program for dealing with hate issues in schools, called Not in Our School (NIOS). The program is designed to adapt the fundamental principles and practices on which NIOT is based to specific problems of schools at all age levels. The organization provides materials for forming NIOS clubs in schools, with more than five videos and films especially designed for such settings. It also supplies targeted materials for students at specific age groups, such as middle schools and high schools. Materials are also available for teachers and other educators, as well as parents.

Another area of special interest is NIOT's program Not in Our Town + Cops, developed and operated in cooperation with the U.S. Department of Justice COPS Office. Among the resources available in this program are course materials on "Transgender Issues and Awareness for Law Enforcement;" a "Hate Crime Reporting" article; a podcast on the Not in Our Town + Cops program stories and materials on hate crimes and law enforcement in specific communities, such as Seattle and St. Paul; a description of a program on engagement strategy with the Muslim community in Las Vegas; and guides on several topics, such as *How to Support Trust Building in Your Agency*, *How to Increase Cultural Understanding*, *How to Serve Diverse Communities*, *Enhancing Community Relations*, and *Responding to Hate and Bias*. The law enforcement arm of NIOT also provides an inspiring collection of biographical sketches of individual officers who have been active in anti–hate crime activities.

NIOT has maintained its working relationship with PBS, as well as adding connections with the radio station KQED in San Francisco and the Golden State Warriors basketball team.

Southern Poverty Law Center

The Southern Poverty Law Center (SPLC) is almost certainly the most important organization in the United States dealing with hate groups. While other organizations focus on hate *crimes* (which SPLC also studies), none devotes as much effort as SPLC does to hate *groups*. The single aspect of its work that is likely best known and most useful to professionals in the field and the general public is its annual "Intelligence Report." This report lists organizations that SPLC has identified as hate groups for the preceding year, with a detailed analysis of the overall problem of hate groups in the country. Much of the information presented in the report is summarized in the center's annual *Hate Map*. This resource is an interactive map of the United States, showing the location of many of the hate groups identified for the year, along with the classification of each such group. Detailed data about the groups can also be accessed from the map itself.

SPLC was founded in 1971 by civil rights lawyers Morris Dees and Joe Levin. The two were responding to a time in American history during which the civil rights of minorities were receiving more attention than at almost any other time in history. The Civil Rights Act of 1960 (CRA) had codified many of these rights that had long been available to white citizens, but not necessarily to African Americans, Latinx, Asian Americans, and other people of color. Passage of the act did not necessarily ensure, however, that these groups would suddenly and totally receive the guarantees of equality ensconced in the Civil Rights Act. Dees and Levin realized that many poor people and people of color would not have the experience, financial resources, or information needed to use the opportunities provided by the CRA. Dees sold his profitable book publishing company to found a law office willing and able to take on specific civil rights cases for needy clients on a pro bono basis.

The first case in which SPLC was involved was *Smith v. YMCA*. That case was brought by the center when two Black children were denied entry to a summer camp program operated by the YMCA in South Montgomery, Alabama. During the discovery phase of the case, Dees and Levin found that a secret agreement existed between the city and the YMCA, under which the former turned over operation of many recreational activities to the latter. A district court found the practice to be unconstitutional and awarded judgment to the plaintiffs.

During its first decade of existence, SPLC attorneys filed (and usually won) several cases like that of *Smith v. YMCA*. They pursued cases involving, for example, equal public improvement projects for African Americans in Dallas County, Alabama; fairness in reapportionment decisions in the state of Alabama; provision of equal work benefits for men and women in the military; freeing of three Black men because of an erroneous finding of guilt in a murder case; adequacy of prison facilities in the state of Alabama; and action against the illegal use of sterilization of women in the South.

The center's campaign against hate groups began in 1981 with the creation of a program known as Klanwatch. The Klan was, of course, the oldest and often the most effective hate group in the history of the United States. While often subject to legal actions by state and federal government, no long-term, consistent effort had been developed to track and monitor the group's activities. Klanwatch was designed to be such an organization, not only keeping an eye on Klan groups but also working against their activities through legal actions and educational programs. The program was later to become a model for the more general hate-watch activities that constituted the

Intelligence Project, created in 1998. Under that program today, the center classifies hate groups into one of eleven categories: Ku Klux Klan, Neo-Nazi, White Nationalist, Racist Skinhead, Neo-Confederate, Black Separatist, Christian Identity, Anti-LGBTQ, Anti-Immigrant, Anti-Muslim, and General Hate. The specific titles of each category and the number of categories may change from year to year.

One of the center's most significant legal triumphs came in 2000 when it won a case against the hate group, Aryan Nations. The fine assessed by the court, $6.3 million, was so large that it forced the group to sell its valuable property in Idaho and essentially go out of business. This method of dealing with hate groups has had similar success over the years. Its greatest success came in the case of *Macedonia v. Christian Knights of the Ku Klux Klan*. The center filed the suit on behalf of the Macedonia Baptist Church, whose building was burned to the ground by members of the Klan on June 21, 1995. The jury in the case awarded the church $37.8 million in damages, later reduced by the court to $21.5 million, still the largest penalty of its kind in U.S. history.

In addition to its legal program, SPLC has developed robust educational programs for children, young adults, and adults. Perhaps the best known of these is a program called Teaching Tolerance, first released in 1991. The goal of the program is to attack hate groups at their base by teaching about hate at an earlier age. The program publishes a print magazine, *Teacher Tolerance*, twice a year and an electronic version of the publication three times a year. It has also produced several publications on specific topics, such as "A K-5 Framework for Teaching American Slavery," "Hate at School Report," "Best Practices for Serving LGBTQ Students," "Teaching Tolerance in Higher Education," "Teaching Hard History: American Slavery," "After Election Day: The Trump Effect," and "Civil Rights Done Right."

Several new programs have originated from the Teaching Tolerance model and program. For example, the center created Mix

It Up at Lunch Day in 2002, an activity in which students are encouraged to find new lunch mates for at least one day. It not only outlines the principle behind the program but also provides materials through which it can be carried out more effectively. Other offshoots include programs focusing on race and ethnicity, religion, class, diversity of abilities, immigration, gender and sexual identity, bullying and bias, and rights and activism.

As might be expected, SPLC has been criticized about its activities. Most often, this criticism comes from groups that have been defined as hate groups by the center, but who call that classification unfair or unjustified. In a handful of cases, such groups have even filed suit against the center for its classification methodology. Thus far, no such suit has been successful. Complaints about the center's work still arise, however, for a variety of other reasons (see, as an example, Marc Thiessen. 2018. "The Southern Poverty Law Center Has Lost Credibility." *Twin Cities Pioneer Press*. https://www.twincities.com/2018/06/25/marc-thiessen-the-southern-poverty-law-center-has-lost-credibility/).

Stop AAPI Hate

Stop AAPI Hate is a website for monitoring and reporting on hate crimes committed against Asian Americans and Pacific Islanders. It is sponsored by A3PCON (Asian Pacific Policy and Planning Council), located in Los Angeles (https://www.asianpacificpolicyandplanningcouncil.org/stop-aapi-hate/). The website was created in response to the significant rise in hate crimes against Asian Americans and Pacific Islanders and growing concerns about the continuation of such trends in the future. Its founders had been receiving anecdotal information about such crimes, but no organized system existed for measuring the intensity of such crimes or their general nature. The website provides reports of hate crimes in twelve languages, including two forms of Chinese, Korean, Thai, Japanese, Vietnamese, Khmer, Punjabi, Tagalog, Hmong, and Hindi, as well as English.

In its first eight weeks of operation, the website received 1,843 reports of harassment, from forty-five states and the District of Columbia. The most common forms of hate were verbal harassment (69.3 percent of all cases) and shunning (22.4 percent), followed by workplace discrimination (4.8 percent), being barred from establishments (2.9 percent), and being barred from transportation (1.1 percent). A total of 8.1 percent of all incidents involved physical assaults, and the majority occurred in business settings compared to public places. Women were confronted about two and a half times as often as men, and the elderly made up 7.8 percent of all complaints.

In addition to the regular statistical reports issued by Stop AAPI Hate, the organization provides separate reports on specific topics of special interest, such as President Trump's decision to cancel student visas for Chinese students.

Ida B. Wells (1862–1931)

In a much-belated obituary in *The New York Times*, published in 2018, Wells was called "the most famous black woman in the United States during her lifetime" (https://www.nytimes.com /interactive/2018/obituaries/overlooked-ida-b-wells.html). Her fame was, to a large extent, the result of her research and writings about the practice of lynching, widely popular by whites in the South following the end of the Civil War. In her earliest work on the topic, an 1892 pamphlet called "Southern Horrors: Lynch Law in all its Phases," Wells reviewed several instances of lynching that she had observed or learned about in various parts of the South. She was outraged by her findings and described ways in which African Americans could help eliminate the practice. In particular, she wrote that her pamphlet had shown how "he [the Afro-American'] may employ the boycott, emigration, and the press, and I feel that by a combination of all these agencies can be effectually stamped out lynch law, that last relic of barbarism and slavery" (the pamphlet in its entirety is available online at https://www.gutenberg.org/files/14975/14975-h/14975-h.htm).

Ida B. Wells (later, Ida Bell Wells-Barnett) was born on July 16, 1862, into slavery at a plantation in Holly Springs, Mississippi. Her mother, Elizabeth ("Lizzie") Warrenton Wells, was one of ten children who was sold away from her family to an architect in Holly Springs. Her father, James Wells, was the son of a white slaveowner and Black slave, raised under more comfortable conditions to be a carpenter. After slaves were freed by the Emancipation Proclamation in 1863, James Wells became active in Reconstruction politics designed to help African Americans achieve equality under the law. He was one of the founders of one of the first educational institutions for freed slaves, Shaw University, in Holly Springs. Ida began her early educational career at Shaw, since having been renamed Rust College.

Disaster struck the Wells family in 1878, when Ida's father, mother, and one sibling died during an epidemic of yellow fever. Rejecting a proposal that the remaining seven children be sent to separate foster homes, Ida left Shaw and assumed responsibility for the raising of her siblings. In order to finance that challenge, she took a position as an elementary school teacher in a nearby county. She was eighteen years old at the time. In 1881, Wells and her two youngest sisters left Holly Springs to live with an aunt in Memphis, Tennessee. There she was able to find another teaching job in the nearby town of Woodstock. During her summer vacations, she also continued her own education at Fisk University in Nashville.

In 1883, Wells had a formative experience in her life. She normally traveled from her home in Memphis to Woodstock by train. On one such trip that year, she was seated in a first-class cabin when she was asked to move to a car reserved for "Coloreds." When she refused to do so, two employees of the railroad forcibly removed her to the "proper" car. They were cheered along by white passengers during the episode. Wells was outraged by the experience and hired an attorney to sue the railway for its actions (a copy of the suit can be found online at https://dp.la/primary-source-sets/ida-b-wells-and-anti-lynching-activism/sources/1113). The Circuit Court of Shelby County ruled in Wells's favor and awarded her $500 in damages. That decision was later overruled, however, by the Tennessee Supreme Court. The court decided that Wells had caused the incident on the train herself as a means of filing a case against the railway. Wells was ordered to return the $500 and to pay an additional $200 in fees to the railway.

The railway case marked a turning point in Wells life. She wrote in her diary about the incident: "O God, is there no redress, no peace, no justice in this land for us?" (https://www.crf-usa.org/images/pdf/Ida-B-Wells.pdf). She decided to begin a crusade to do what she could to achieve the "peace and justice" for Blacks in America. She traveled across the South collecting data and information about atrocities against African Americans, most dramatic of which was the widespread use of lynching. She reported on her experiences in numerous newspaper articles, pamphlets, and books. One of the most famous of these works was a one-hundred-page pamphlet recording the history of lynching in the South, *The Red Record: Tabulated Statistics and Alleged Causes of Lynching in the United States*, published in 1895. The work included a list of specific examples of lynchings that had occurred since the end of the Civil War, along with more general statistics on the practice. In 1900, Wells followed up with an even more ambitious book, *Mob Rule in New Orleans: Robert Charles and His Fight to Death, the Story of His Life, Burning Human Beings Alive, Other Lynching Statistics*. The book contains many horrifying stories of the brutal treatment and murders of African Americans throughout the South. Wells concludes her investigation with a plea to citizens everywhere: "We do not believe that the moral conscience of the nation—that which is highest and best among us—will always remain silent in face of such outrages, for God is not dead, and His Spirit is not entirely driven from men's hearts (find the book in its entirety at https://www.gutenberg.org/files

/14976/14976-h/14976-h.htm). Wells's final book was an autobiography, *Crusade for Justice*. She died before completing the work, a task that was taken on by her daughter Alfreda Barnett Duster, and published posthumously in 1970.

As part of her crusade against lynching, Wells traveled to Great Britain in 1893 and 1894 to lecture on her experiences in the American South. Her talks were well received and raised the awareness of the British of a problem about which they previously knew very little. When Wells returned to the United States, however, her efforts received little attention and most of it negative. The *New York Times*, for example, called Wells "a slanderous and dirty-minded mulatress," and most African American critics offered similar assessments. One H. C. C. Ashwood, then a consul to the Dominican Republic, claimed that no "respectable negro" had ever been lynched.

Concerned about her safety from both whites and Blacks in Memphis, Wells moved to Chicago in 1893, not to return to Tennessee for another thirty years. In Chicago, she remained politically active, speaking and writing widely on a number of topics, moving her home into a white segregated neighborhood, and founding the first kindergarten for Black children in the city. In 1896, Wells was also one of the founding members of the National Association for the Advancement of Colored People (NAAC). Wells died in Chicago of kidney failure on March 25, 1931.

5 Data and Documents

Insights into the nature of hate groups are often available from sources such as documents on the topic as well as statistical information about trends in the area. This chapter presents selected data and statistics on hate groups in the United States. It also provides relevant historical documents, such as laws, courts cases, and presidential statements.

Data

In the tables presented here, values for variables may vary significantly dependent on the definition used for "hate crime." In many cases, for example, victims report hateful language as their main complaint. Other surveys include only physical attacks under the term *hate crime*.

Table 5.1. Trends in Hate Crimes by Various Characteristics, 1996–2018

This table provides data on hate crime rates for various personal characteristics, such as race, ethnicity, and religion.

A Black Lives Matter protest in Atlanta, Georgia, on May 29, 2020, following the murder of George Floyd. The murder was one of the most recent prominent examples of hate crimes against individuals because of the color of their skin. (Lance Lowrie/Dreamstime.com)

Table 5.1 Trends in Hate Crimes by Various Characteristics, 1996–2018

Year	Race	Religion	Sexual Orientation	Ethnicity/Ancestry	Disability	Gender	Gender Identity	Total
1995	6,438	1,617	1,347	1,044	n/d	n/d	n/d	10,469
1996	6,994	1,535	1,281	1,207	n/d	n/d	n/d	11,039
1997	6,084	1,586	1,401	1,132	12	n/d	n/d	10,255
1998	5,514	1,720	1,488	956	27	n/d	n/d	9,722
1999	5,485	1,686	1,558	1,040	23	n/d	n/d	9,802
2000	5,397	1,699	1,558	1,216	36	n/d	n/d	9,924
2001	5,545	2,118	1,664	2,634	37	n/d	n/d	12,020
2002	4,580	1,659	1,513	1,409	50	n/d	n/d	9,222
2003	4,754	1,489	1,479	1,326	43	n/d	n/d	9,100
2004	5,119	1,586	1,482	1,254	73	n/d	n/d	9,528
2005	4,895	1,405	1,213	1,228	54	n/d	n/d	8,804
2006	5,020	1,750	1,472	1,305	95	n/d	n/d	9,652
2007	4,956	1,628	1,512	1,347	84	n/d	n/d	9,535
2008	4,934	1,732	1,706	1,226	85	n/d	n/d	9,691
2009	4,057	1,575	1,482	1,109	99	n/d	n/d	8,336
2010	3,949	1,552	1,528	1,122	48	n/d	n/d	8,208
2011	3,645	1,480	1,572	939	61	n/d	n/d	7,713
2012	3,467	1,340	1,376	866	102	n/d	n/d	7,164
2013	3,563	1,223	1,461	821	99	30	33	7,242
2014	3,227	1,140	1,248	821	96	40	109	6,727
2015	#	1,402	1,263	#	88	30	122	7,173
2016	#	1,584	1,255	#	77	36	131	7,615
2017	#	1,749	1,338	#	160	54	132	8,828
2018	#	1,617	1,445	#	179	61	189	8,819

\# Categories changed to Race/Ethnicity/Ancestry:

2015 = 4,216
2016 = 4,426
2017 = 5,060
2018 = 5,155
n/d: No data collected for this year

Source: Compiled from hate crime data, 1995–2018 at "Hate Crime" [2019]. Federal Bureau of Investigation. Criminal Justice Information Services Division. https://ucr.fbi.gov/hate-crime.

Table 5.2. Trends in Hate Crimes, 2004–2015

Detailed statistics on hate crimes rate have been collected at least since 2004. This table shows trends in those data from 2004 to 2015.

Table 5.2 Trends in Hate Crimes, 2004–2015

Year	Total	Violent Crime		Property Crime	
	Number	Number	Rate*	Number	Rate*
2004	281,670	220,060	0.9	61,610	0.5
2005	223,060	198,400	0.8	21,740	0.2
2006	230,490	211,730	0.9	15,830	0.1
2007	263,440	236,860	1.0	24,640	0.2
2008	266,640	241,800	1.0	22,890	0.2
2009	284,620	267,170	1.1	17,450	0.1
2010	273,100	255,810	1.0	17,290	0.1
2011	218,010	195,880	0.8	22,130	0.2
2012	293,790	263,540	1.0	30,250	0.2
2013	272,420	242,190	0.9	30,230	0.2
2014	215,010	194,310	0.7	19,000	0.1
2015	207,880	192,020	0.7	14,160	0.1

*Events per 1,000 persons, age 12 and over.

Source: "Hate Crime Victimization, 2004–2015." 2017. U.S. Department of Justice. Bureau of Justice Statistics, Table 1. https://www.bjs.gov/content/pub/pdf/hcv0415.pdf.

Table 5.3. Hate Crime Data by Group and Type, 2018

Among the most detailed data on hate crimes collected by the FBI are those committed against very specific groups, such as males, females, transgenders, gender nonconforming, and various specific religions. This table summarizes some of those data.

Table 5.3 Hate Crime Data by Group and Type, 2018

Bias Motivation	Incidents	Offenses	Victims	Offenders
Total	7,120	8,496	8,819	6,266
Single-Bias Incidents	7,036	8,327	8,646	6,188
Race/Ethnicity/Ancestry	4,047	4,954	5,155	3,634
Anti-White	762	1,001	1,038	754
Anti-Black or African American	1,943	2,325	2,426	1,707
Anti-American Indian or Alaska Native	194	204	209	163
Anti-Asian	148	171	177	125
Anti-Native Hawaiian or Other Pacific Islander	20	26	26	15
Anti-Multiple Races, Group	137	166	174	91
Anti-Arab	82	100	100	80
Anti-Hispanic or Latino	485	644	671	495
Anti-Other Race/Ethnicity/Ancestry	276	317	334	204
Religion	1,419	1,550	1,617	917
Anti-Jewish	835	896	920	484
Anti-Catholic	53	59	63	36
Anti-Protestant	34	38	39	22
Anti-Islamic (Muslim)	188	225	236	153
Anti-Other Religion	91	96	109	60
Anti-Multiple Religions, Group	46	50	52	18
Anti-Mormon	9	9	11	8
Anti-Jehovah's Witness	9	9	9	4
Anti-Eastern Orthodox (Russian, Greek, Other)	31	32	33	26
Anti-Other Christian	35	42	43	25
Anti-Buddhist	10	10	11	9
Anti-Hindu	12	14	14	10
Anti-Sikh	60	64	69	49
Anti-Atheism/Agnosticism/etc.	6	6	8	13

(*continued*)

Table 5.3 (continued)

Bias Motivation	Incidents	Offenses	Victims	Offenders
Sexual Orientation	1,196	1,404	1,445	1,268
Anti-Gay (Male)	726	839	863	841
Anti-Lesbian	129	171	177	105
Anti-Lesbian, Gay, Bisexual, or Transgender (Mixed Group)	303	353	360	294
Anti-Heterosexual	17	20	24	13
Anti-Bisexual	21	21	21	15
Disability	159	177	179	151
Anti-Physical	60	67	68	52
Anti-Mental	99	110	111	99
Gender	47	58	61	38
Anti-Male	22	26	28	21
Anti-Female	25	32	33	17
Gender Identity	168	184	189	180
Anti-Transgender	142	157	160	156
Anti-Gender Non-Conforming	26	27	29	24
Multiple-Bias Incidents	84	169	173	78

Source: "2018 Hate Crime Statistics." 2019. Federal Bureau of Investigation. U.S. Department of Justice, Table 1. https://ucr.fbi.gov/hate-crime/2018/topic-pages/tables/table-1.xls.

Table 5.4. Hate Crimes by Known Offender's Race and Ethnicity and by Bias Motivation, 2018

Data for hate crimes committed against specific groups (see table 5.3) is also available for character traits of offenders. Those data are summarized here for a single year, 2018.

Table 5.4 Hate Crimes by Known Offender's Race and Ethnicity and by Bias Motivation, 2018

Bias motivation	Total offenses	Known offender's race							Known offender's ethnicity[1]				Unknown offender
		White	Black or African American	American Indian or Alaska Native	Asian	Native Hawaiian or Other Pacific Islander	Group of multiple races	Unknown race	Hispanic or Latino	Not Hispanic or Latino	Group of multiple ethnicities	Unknown ethnicity	
Total	8,496	3,511	1,605	64	95	19	285	718	412	1,847	51	3,065	2,199
Single-Bias Incidents	8,327	3,462	1,536	64	93	19	282	714	402	1,765	49	3,032	2,157
Race/Ethnicity/Ancestry:	4,954	2,309	907	46	62	9	185	276	218	1,180	27	1,939	1,160
Anti-White	1,001	252	492	20	6	1	23	36	40	287	12	431	171
Anti-Black or African American	2,325	1,330	115	16	34	3	100	149	106	491	7	918	578
Anti-American Indian or Alaska Native	204	106	27	1	2	0	7	2	8	39	0	97	59
Anti-Asian	171	70	33	0	14	2	4	6	8	42	0	59	42
Anti-Native Hawaiian or Other Pacific Islander	26	8	11	0	0	2	0	0	0	13	0	7	5

Anti-Multiple Races, Group	166	45	8	0	2	0	15	11	2	22	3	42	85
Anti-Arab	100	62	17	0	1	0	1	4	3	29	0	40	15
Anti-Hispanic or Latino	644	322	152	8	2	1	24	47	41	212	1	240	88
Anti-Other Race/ Ethnicity/ Ancestry	317	114	52	1	1	0	11	21	10	45	4	105	117
Religion:	1,550	439	122	6	16	6	30	306	28	193	10	360	625
Anti-Jewish	896	179	41	1	7	0	14	258	7	82	3	143	396
Anti-Catholic	59	26	3	1	1	0	0	5	3	10	0	16	23
Anti-Protestant	38	13	3	0	0	0	2	1	2	3	0	14	19
Anti-Islamic (Muslim)	225	98	32	0	5	0	6	22	7	31	4	88	62
Anti-Other Religion	96	31	12	0	1	5	2	8	2	11	0	33	37
Anti-Multiple Religions, Group	50	12	6	0	0	0	0	3	0	2	0	15	29
Anti-Mormon	9	4	0	0	0	1	0	0	0	1	0	2	4
Anti-Jehovah's Witness	9	3	0	1	0	0	0	0	1	2	0	1	5

(continued)

Table 5.4 (continued)

Bias motivation	Total offenses	Known offender's race							Known offender's ethnicity[1]				Unknown offender
		White	Black or African American	American Indian or Alaska Native	Asian	Native Hawaiian or Other Pacific Islander	Group of multiple races	Unknown race	Hispanic or Latino	Not Hispanic or Latino	Group of multiple ethnicities	Unknown ethnicity	
Anti-Eastern Orthodox (Russian, Greek, Other)	32	19	4	1	0	0	0	1	1	12	0	12	7
Anti-Other Christian	42	11	5	0	1	0	5	5	2	8	0	8	15
Anti-Buddhist	10	4	3	0	1	0	0	0	0	7	0	1	2
Anti-Hindu	14	8	1	0	0	0	0	3	1	2	0	8	2
Anti-Sikh	64	30	10	2	0	0	1	0	2	21	3	17	21
Anti-Atheism/ Agnosticism/ etc.	6	1	2	0	0	0	0	0	0	1	0	2	3
Sexual Orientation:	1,404	535	380	11	12	4	56	110	130	299	11	531	296
Anti-Gay (Male)	839	307	245	6	6	3	39	83	94	205	9	284	150
Anti-Lesbian	171	80	36	0	2	0	5	7	18	35	1	60	41

Bias motivation	353	128	92	5	4	1	12	19	18	53	1	167	92
Anti-Lesbian, Gay, Bisexual, or Transgender (Mixed Group)													
Anti-Heterosexual	20	14	1	0	0	0	0	0	0	2	0	12	5
Anti-Bisexual	21	6	6	0	0	0	0	1	0	4	0	8	8
Disability:	177	92	37	1	3	0	3	4	8	37	1	92	37
Anti-Physical	67	30	15	0	2	0	1	1	4	9	1	33	18
Anti-Mental	110	62	22	1	1	0	2	3	4	28	0	59	19
Gender:	58	30	14	0	0	0	1	0	1	9	0	32	13
Anti-Male	26	13	8	0	0	0	1	0	1	8	0	13	4
Anti-Female	32	17	6	0	0	0	0	0	0	1	0	19	9
Gender Identity:	184	57	76	0	0	0	7	18	17	47	0	78	26
Anti-Transgender	157	50	65	0	0	0	7	16	17	36	0	72	19
Anti-Gender Non-Conforming	27	7	11	0	0	0	0	2	0	11	0	6	7
Multiple-Bias Incidents[2]	169	49	69	0	2	0	3	4	10	82	2	33	42

[1]The aggregate of offenses by the known offender's ethnicity does not equal the aggregate of offenses by the known offender's race because not all law enforcement agencies that report offender race data also report offender ethnicity data.

[2]A *multiple-bias incident* is an incident in which one or more offense types are motivated by two or more biases.

Source: "Offenses: Known Offender's Race and Ethnicity by Bias Motivation, 2018." 2019. Federal Bureau of Investigation. U.S. Department of Justice, Table 5. https://ucr.fbi.gov/hate-crime/2018/tables/table-5.xls.

Table 5.5. Major Attacks on Aid Workers, 2008–2018

One type of activity committed by hate groups perhaps less well known involves acts against members of various international nongovernmental agencies trying to provide services to less developed countries. These data reflect the information available about such events.

Table 5.5 Major Attacks on Aid Workers, 2008–2018

Type	2008	2009	2010	2011	2012	2013	2014	2015	2016	2017	2018
Number of incidents	165	155	130	152	170	265	192	148	162	158	226
Total aid worker victims	278	295	249	309	277	475	332	287	294	313	405
Total killed	128	108	72	86	70	156	122	109	107	139	131
Total injured	91	94	84	126	115	179	88	109	98	102	144
Total kidnapped	59	93	93	97	92	140	122	69	89	72	130
International victims	51	74	41	29	49	59	32	28	43	28	29
National victims	227	221	208	280	228	416	300	259	251	285	376
International NGO staff	157	128	148	135	94	136	152	176	157	98	180
LNGO and RCS staff	46	55	47	77	116	207	98	62	51	154	146
ICRC staff	5	9	10	5	3	14	16	3	12	13	10

Key for organization type
UN: United Nations
INGO: International nongovernmental organization
LNGO and NRCS: Local nongovernmental organisation or National Red Cross/Red Crescent Society
ICRC: International Committee of the Red Cross
IFRC: International Federation of Red Cross and Red Crescent Societies

Source: Major Attacks on Aid Workers: Summary Statistics (2008–2018). 2020. Humanitarian Outcomes and the Aid Worker Security Database. https://aidworkersecurity.org/incidents/report/summary. Used by kind permission of the publishers.

Documents

Presidential Statements on Hate Violence (1868–2017)

Individuals in position of authority often have the opportunity, and sometimes the obligation, to express publicly their views on hate crime issues. American presidents are among the authorities whose views are most significant in such cases. History records many occasions on which a president has spoken out about hate crimes against African Americans, members of religions other than Christianity, Native Americans, Jews, and other minority groups. Two examples of such instances are presented here, events separated by about 150 years. The first incident followed a riot in New Orleans in 1866, when a group of former Confederate soldiers stormed a state Constitutional Convention and slaughtered nearly fifty individuals, the majority of whom were African American Union veterans. President Johnson expressed the view that white attackers really had no choice in carrying out the attack because their rights were being threatened. The second incident occurred in August 2017, when a group of white supremacists and neo-Nazis held a "Unite the Right" rally in Charlottesville, Virginia. The group was met and opposed by several individuals opposed to the principles and practices of these groups. That rally resulted in thirty-three injuries and one death on both sides of the field. President Donald Trump commented on the event in remarks that were later interpreted in quite different ways by various individuals.

Andrew Johnson (1868)

If you will take up the riot at New Orleans and trace it back to its source or its immediate cause, you will find out who was responsible for the blood that was shed there. If you will take up the riot at New Orleans and trace it back to the Radical Congress, you will find that the riot at New Orleans was substantially planned. If you will take up the proceedings in their caucuses, you will understand that they there knew that a convention was to be called which was extinct by its power having expired; that it was said that the intention was that a new government was to be organized, and on the organization of that government the intention was to enfranchise one portion of the population, called the colored population, who had just been emancipated, and at the same time disfranchise white men. When you design to talk about New Orleans you ought to understand what you are talking about. When you read the speeches that were made, and take up the facts on the Friday and Saturday before that convention sat, you will there find that speeches were made incendiary in their character, exciting that portion of the population, the black population, to arm themselves and prepare for the shedding of blood. You will also find that that convention did assemble in violation of law, and the intention of that convention was to supersede the reorganized authorities in the State government of Louisiana, which had been recognized by the Government of the United States; and every man engaged in that rebellion in that convention, with the intention of superseding and upturning the civil government which had been recognized by the Government of the United States, I say that he was a traitor to the Constitution of the United States, and hence you find that another rebellion was commenced having its origin in the Radical Congress.

Source: "The Impeachment and Trial of the President." 1868. https://www.govinfo.gov/content/pkg/GPO-HPREC-HINDS-V3/pdf/GPO-HPREC-HINDS-V3-25.pdf. Also see Adam Sewer. 2019. "The President's Pursuit of White Power." *The Atlantic.* https://www.theatlantic.com/politics/archive/2019/01/trump-embraces-white-supremacy/579745 and Joe Gray Taylor. 1968. "New Orleans and Reconstruction." *Louisiana History* 9 (3): 189–208. https://www.jstor.org/stable/4231016?seq=1.

Donald Trump (2017)

Q (Inaudible) both sides, sir. You said there was hatred, there was violence on both sides. Are the—

THE PRESIDENT: Yes, I think there's blame on both sides. If you look at both sides—I think there's blame on both sides. And I have no doubt about it, and you don't have any doubt about it either.

And if you reported it accurately, you would say.

Q The neo-Nazis started this. They showed up in Charlottesville to protest—

THE PRESIDENT: Excuse me, excuse me. They didn't put themselves—and you had some very bad people in that group, but you also had people that were very fine people, on both sides. You had people in that group.

. . .

So you know what, it's fine. You're changing history. You're changing culture. And you had people—and I'm not talking about the neo-Nazis and the white nationalists—because they should be condemned totally. But you had many people in that group other than neo-Nazis and white nationalists. Okay? And the press has treated them absolutely unfairly.

Now, in the other group also, you had some fine people. But you also had troublemakers, and you see them come with the black outfits and with the helmets, and with the baseball bats. You had a lot of bad people in the other group.

Q Who are the good people?

Q Sir, I just didn't understand what you were saying. You were saying the press has treated white nationalists unfairly? I just don't understand what you were saying.

THE PRESIDENT: No, no. There were people in that rally—and I looked the night before—if you look, there were people protesting very quietly the taking down of the statue of Robert E. Lee. I'm sure in that group there were some bad ones. The following day it looked like they had some rough, bad people—neo-Nazis, white nationalists, whatever you want to call them.

But you had a lot of people in that group that were there to innocently protest, and very legally protest—because I don't know if you know, they had a permit. The other group didn't have a permit. So I only tell you this: There are two sides to a story. I thought what took place was a horrible moment for our country—a horrible moment. But there are two sides to the country.

Source: "Remarks by President Trump on Infrastructure." 2017. The White House. https://www.whitehouse.gov/briefings-statements/remarks-president-trump-infrastructure/.

Third Enforcement Act (1871)

As the Civil War came to an end in 1865, the federal government began to make plans for integrating former slaves into the everyday life of American citizenship, providing them with all the rights and privileges appertaining thereto. At the same time, former governmental officials and military officers of the former Confederate States, along with many ordinary citizens of those states, were determined to maintain the status quo for African Americans, "no matter what." Out of these efforts arose several anti-African American hate groups, the most famous of which was the Ku Klux Klan (KKK). Throughout the end of the 1860s, the Klan created a reign of terror whose goal it was to discourage Blacks from becoming integrated into white society. In response to this campaign by the Klan, the federal government, under the newly created Republican Party, passed a series of laws to give the President and the federal government the right to use whatever measures might be necessary to put down the Klan's rebellion. Among the three of these acts, the third is also known as the Ku Klux Klan Act of 1871 because of its goal of providing President Grant with the tools needed to bring the Klan under control. Perhaps the single most important section of the act gave President Ulysses Grant the right to suspend the right of habeas corpus, a pillar of the American judicial system since the nation's origins. The act is also known as the Enforcement Act of 1871, the Force Act of 1871, the Civil Rights Act of 1871, and the Third Ku Klux Klan Act of 1871. The following selection includes some of the most important provisions of the act.

Be it enacted by the Senate and House of Representatives of the United States of America in Congress assembled, That any person who, under color of any law, statute, ordinance, regulation, custom, or usage of any State, shall subject, or cause to be subjected, any person within the jurisdiction of the United States to the deprivation of any rights, privileges, or immunities secured by the Constitution of the United States, shall, any such law, statute, ordinance, regulation, custom, or usage of the State to the contrary notwithstanding, be liable to the party injured in, any action at law, suit in equity, or other proper proceeding for redress; such proceeding to be prosecuted in the several district or circuit courts of the United States, with and subject to the same rights of appeal, review upon error, and other remedies provided in like cases in such courts, under the provisions of the act of the ninth of April, eighteen hundred and sixty-six, entitled "An act to protect all persons in the United States in their civil rights, and to furnish the means of their vindication;" and the other remedial laws of the United States which are in their nature applicable in such cases.

Sec. 2. That if two or more persons within any State or Territory of the United States shall conspire together to overthrow, or to put down, or to destroy by force the government of the United States, or to levy war against the United States, or to oppose by force the authority of the government of the United States, or by force, intimidation, or threat to prevent, hinder, or delay the execution of any law of the United States, or by force to seize, take, or possess any property of the United States contrary to the authority thereof, or by force, intimidation, or threat to prevent any person from accepting or holding any office or trust or place of confidence under the United States, or from discharging the duties thereof, or by force, intimidation, or threat to induce any officer of the United States to leave any State, district, or place where his duties as such officer might lawfully be performed, or to injure him in his person or property on account of his lawful discharge of the duties of his office, or to injure his person while engaged in the lawful discharge of the duties of his office, or to injure his property so as to molest, interrupt, hinder, or impede him in the discharge of his official duty, or by force, intimidation, or threat to deter any party or witness in any court of the United States from attending such court, or from testifying in any matter pending in such court fully, freely, and truthfully, or to injure any such party or witness in his person or property on account of his having so attended or testified, or by force, intimidation, or threat to influence the verdict, presentment, or indictment, of any juror or grand juror in any court of the United States, or to injure such juror in his person or property on account of any verdict, presentment, or indictment lawfully assented to by him, or on account of his being or having been such juror, or shall conspire together, or go in disguise upon the public highway or upon the premises of another for the purpose, either directly or indirectly, of depriving any person or any class of persons of the equal protection of the laws, or of equal privileges or immunities under the laws, or for the purpose of preventing or hindering the constituted authorities of any State from giving or securing to all persons within such State the equal protection of the laws, or shall conspire together for the purpose of in any manner impeding, hindering, obstructing, or defeating the due course of justice in any State or Territory, with intent to deny to any citizen of the United States the due and equal protection of the laws, or to injure any person in his person or his property for lawfully enforcing the right of any person or class of persons to the equal protection of the laws, or by force, intimidation, or threat to prevent any citizen of the United States lawfully entitled to vote from giving his support or advocacy in a lawful manner towards or in favor of the election of any lawfully qualified person as an elector of President or Vice-President of the United States, or as a member of the Congress of the United States, or to injure any such citizen in his person or property on account of such support or advocacy, each and every person so offending shall be deemed guilty of a high crime, and, upon conviction thereof in any district or circuit court of the United States or district or supreme court of any Territory of the United States having jurisdiction of similar offences, shall be punished by a fine not less than five hundred nor more than five thousand dollars, or by imprisonment, with or without hard labor, as the court may determine, for a period of not less than six months nor more than six years, as the court may determine, or by both such fine and imprisonment as the court shall determine. And if any one or more persons engaged in any such conspiracy shall do, or cause to be done, any act in furtherance of the object of such conspiracy, whereby any person shall be injured in his person or property, or deprived of having and exercising any right or privilege of a citizen of the United States, the person so injured or deprived of such rights and privileges may have and maintain an action for the recovery of damages occasioned by such injury or deprivation of rights and privileges against any one or more of the persons engaged in such conspiracy, such action to be prosecuted in the proper district or circuit court of the United States, with and subject to the same rights of appeal, review upon error, and other remedies provided in like cases in such courts under the provisions of the act of April ninth, eighteen hundred and sixty-six, entitled "An act to protect all persons in the United States in their civil rights, and to furnish the means of their vindication."

Sec. 3. That in all cases where insurrection, domestic violence, unlawful combinations, or conspiracies in any State shall so obstruct or hinder the execution of the laws thereof, and of the United States as to deprive any portion or class of the people of such State of any of the rights, privileges, or immunities, or protection, named in the Constitution and secured by this act, and the constituted authorities of such State shall either be unable to protect, or shall, from any cause, fail in or reuse protection of the people in such rights, such facts shall be deemed a denial by such State of the equal protection of the laws to which they are entitled under the Constitution of the United States; and in all such cases, or whenever any such insurrection, violence, unlawful combination, or conspiracy shall oppose or obstruct the laws of the United States or the due course of justice under the same, it shall be lawful for the President, and it shall be his duty to take such measures, by the employment of the militia or the land and naval forces of the United States, or of either, or by other means, as he may deem necessary for the suppression of such insurrection, domestic violence, or combinations; and any person who shall be arrested under the provisions of this and the preceding section shall be delivered to the marshal of the proper district, to be dealt with according to law.

Sec. 4. That whenever in any State or part of a State the unlawful combinations named in the preceding section of this act shall be organized and armed, and so numerous and powerful as to be able, by violence, to either overthrow or set at defiance the constituted authorities of such State, and of the United States within such State, or when the constituted authorities are in complicity with, or shall connive at the unlawful purposes of, such powerful and armed combinations; and whenever, by reason of either or all of the causes aforesaid, the conviction of such offenders and the preservation of the public safety shall become in such district impracticable, in every such case such combinations shall be deemed a rebellion against the government of the United States, and during the continuance of such rebellion, and within the limits of the district which shall be so under the sway thereof, such limits to be prescribed by proclamation, it shall be lawful for the President of the United States, when in his judgment the public safety shall require it, to suspend the privileges of the writ of habeas corpus, to the end that such rebellion may be overthrown: Provided, That all the provisions of the second section of an act entitled "An act relating to habeas corpus, and regulating judicial proceedings in certain cases," approved March third, eighteen hundred and sixty-three, which relate to the discharge of prisoners other than prisoners of war, and to the penalty for refusing to obey the order of the court, shall be in full force so far as the same are applicable to the provisions of this section: Provided further, That the President shall first have made proclamation, as now provided by law, commanding such insurgents to disperse: And provided also, That the provisions of this section shall not be in force after the end of the next regular session of Congress.

Source: CHAP. XXII.—An Act to enforce the Provisions of the Fourteenth Amendment to the April 20, 1871. Constitution of the United States, and for other Purposes. 1871. Forty-second Congress. Sess. I. Cu. 22. 1871.

Knights of the Ku Klux Klan v. Strayer (1928)

Throughout its long history, the Ku Klux Klan has generally been on the receiving end of criminal accusations and legal actions. One major exception to that history occurred in 1928, when the Klan sued five of its former members for their improper actions after leaving the organization. Specifically, the Klan argued that the former members had "conspired to injure it by inducing other members to secede from the organization, thereby depriving it of annual dues and per capita taxes in vast sums; that the banished members clandestinely maintain unlawful Klans, operating as individual units of the parent order under the Klan name; have collected admission fees and annual dues in large amounts; that they are in possession of large numbers of robes, helmets, lodge altars, flags, bibles, books, papers, and so on, all property of the plaintiff, the national order; and are guilty of other doings not necessary here to recite. The plaintiff, therefore, prayed first for a temporary and then a permanent injunction restraining the defendants from in any wise doing the acts complained of, that they be required to account for and deliver to it all its property so improperly acquired and held, and in addition pay it the sum of $100,000" (taken from decision by the Court of Appeals for the Third Circuit on the district court's decision; see https://law.justia.com/cases/federal/appellate-courts/F2/34/432/1481865/). The Klan's decision to *bring this suit was ill-advised, since it brought to light details of its own actions, of far greater import than any actions taken by five former members. Selections from the ruling of the district court judge, W. H. Seward Thomson, are provided here.*

. . . the court has no difficulty in finding, and does now find:

That the plaintiff corporation obtained its charter for charitable, eleemosynary, patriotic, and other purposes, and, being so chartered, was granted by the state of Pennsylvania a right to do business within the commonwealth, presumably for the purposes set forth in its charter; that, acting under the guise of its chartered purposes, it acquired a membership in this state of from 240,000 to 300,000 persons; that in violation of its charter, and in violation of its own constitution, it has established and is maintaining a form of despotic rule, which is being operated in secret, under the direct sanction and authority of the plaintiff's chief officers; that, in violation of the rights and liberties of the people, it has set up tribunals not known to the law, before which citizens of the commonwealth, not members of the Klan, are brought, subjected to some form of trial, and, upon conviction, severe corporal punishments are imposed, painful, humiliating, and often brutal in their character, and in some instances destructive of life itself.

That, under the direct authorization of the principal officers of the Klan in the state, men are designated for punishment, and are punished and maltreated, without any legal charge being preferred against them, and without a hearing or trial, in open and flagrant violation of the Constitution and laws of the land; that the plaintiff organization, through its actual operations and teachings, has stirred up racial and religious prejudices, fomented disorder, and encouraged riots and unlawful assemblies, which have resulted in flagrant breaches of the peace, defiance of law, bloodshed, and loss of life; and that such unlawful assemblies and riots have, in many instances, been brought about for the avowed purpose on the part of the officers in control of increasing the membership of the organization.

That in the secret operation of the corporation's activities, and in hostility to the civil authorities, military organizations are established and maintained, with arms, regalia, and equipment, with officers of varying rank and military titles, these officers being bound to obey without question the commands of the superior officer in authority of the plaintiff corporation.

In addition to this, bands known as "Knight Riders," or the "black-robed gang," armed, equipped, and masked, are formed and operated here and there throughout the country, both organizations being used at times as instruments of terror, oppression, and violence, and being thus a continuing menace to the public peace and destructive of the public order. The evidence in this case established conclusively gross violations of the law committed by the plaintiff within the Western district of Pennsylvania.

. . .

In view of all the facts disclosed by the evidence, the plaintiff corporation, stigmatized as it is by its unlawful acts and conduct, could hardly hope for judicial assistance in a court of the United States, which is highly commissioned to extend to all litigants before it, without distinction of race, creed, color, or condition, those high guarantees of liberty and equality vouchsafed by the Constitution of the United States. A court whose duty it is to recognize and uphold religious freedom as the first fruits of our civilization, to secure to every accused the right to full knowledge of the accusation against him, and a fair and impartial trial of the issue before a jury of his peers; a court which fully recognizes that this is a government of law, and not of men, and that no man shall be deprived of his life, his liberty, or his property without due process of law.

This unlawful organization, so destructive of the rights and liberties of the people, has come in vain asking this court of equity for injunctive or other relief. They come with filthy hands and can get no assistance here. Plaintiff's prayers for relief are denied and the bill is dismissed, at the costs of the plaintiff.

And now, to wit, April 13, 1928, the foregoing action having come on for hearing on bill and answers and testimony taken, and after argument by counsel, on full consideration thereof, the prayers of plaintiff's bill are denied, and the bill is dismissed, at the plaintiff's costs.

[This decision was appealed to the Third Circuit Court of Appeals, whose decision in the case is listed in the citation given in the introductory paragraph of this entry.]

Source: *Knights of the Ku Klux Klan v. Strayer*, 26 F.2d 727 (W.D. Pa. 1928). https://law.justia.com/cases/federal/district-courts/F2/26/727/1471466/.

Federal Hate Crime Law (1968)

The first hate crimes law passed in the United States was part of the Civil Rights Act of 1964. It established the right of an individual not to be persecuted in any way on the basis of his or her race, color, religion, or national origin. The law was limited not only on the basis of these four personal characteristics but also in a restricted number of situations, those in which the person was engaged in so-called federally protected activities. Such activities included voting, public education, employment, jury duty, travel, or the use of public accommodations. The main features of the bill were as follows.

§249. Hate crime acts

(a) In General.—

(1) Offenses involving actual or perceived race, color, religion, or national origin.—Whoever, whether or not acting under color of law, willfully causes bodily injury to any person or, through the use of fire, a firearm, a dangerous weapon, or

an explosive or incendiary device, attempts to cause bodily injury to any person, because of the actual or perceived race, color, religion, or national origin of any person—
(A) shall be imprisoned not more than 10 years, fined in accordance with this title, or both; and
(B) shall be imprisoned for any term of years or for life, fined in accordance with this title, or both, if—
   (i) death results from the offense; or
   (ii) the offense includes kidnapping or an attempt to kidnap, aggravated sexual abuse or an attempt to commit aggravated sexual abuse, or an attempt to kill.

[A new section was added at this point in 2010 as part of the following Matthew Shepard and James Byrd Jr. Hate Crimes Prevention Act. The original law then continues:]
(B) Circumstances described.—For purposes of subparagraph (A), the circumstances described in this subparagraph are that—
   (i) the conduct described in subparagraph (A) occurs during the course of, or as the result of, the travel of the defendant or the victim—
      (I) across a State line or national border; or
      (II) using a channel, facility, or instrumentality of interstate or foreign commerce;
   (ii) the defendant uses a channel, facility, or instrumentality of interstate or foreign commerce in connection with the conduct described in subparagraph (A);
   (iii) in connection with the conduct described in subparagraph (A), the defendant employs a firearm, dangerous weapon, explosive or incendiary device, or other weapon that has traveled in interstate or foreign commerce; or
   (iv) the conduct described in subparagraph (A)—

(I) interferes with commercial or other economic activity in which the victim is engaged at the time of the conduct; or

(II) otherwise affects interstate or foreign commerce.

Source: 18 U.S. Code § 249.Hate Crime Acts. 1968. 18 USC Ch. 13: Civil Rights.

Hate Crime Statistics Act (1990)

One of the earliest pieces of legislation adopted in the United States dealing with hate crimes was the Hate Crime Statistics Act of 1990. The purpose of the act was relatively simple; it required the FBI to begin collecting data on the number and types of hate crimes committed in the United States each year, to analyze the data, and to make it available to the general public. The significance of the act was that very little was known with certainty about the kinds and numbers of hate crimes committed in the nation each year, information needed before any action against hate groups can be initiated. One point of interest about the legislation was that it was the first time specific recognition of gay, lesbian, and bisexual individuals was included in federal legislation.

As Amended, 28 U.S.C. § 534

§ [Sec. 1.] (a) This Act may be cited as the "Hate Crime Statistics Act."

"(1) Under the authority of section 534 of title 28, United States Code, the Attorney General shall acquire data, for each calendar year, about crimes that manifest evidence of prejudice based on race, *gender and gender identity*, [emphasis added by source] religion, disability, sexual orientation, or ethnicity, including where appropriate the crimes of murder, non-negligent manslaughter; forcible rape; aggravated assault, simple assault, intimidation; arson; and destruction, damage or vandalism of property.

(2) The Attorney General shall establish guidelines for the collection of such data including the necessary evidence and

criteria that must be present for a finding of manifest prejudice and procedures for carrying out the purposes of this section.

(3) Nothing in this section creates a cause of action or a right to bring an action, including an action based on discrimination due to sexual orientation. As used in this section, the term 'sexual orientation' means consensual homosexuality or heterosexuality. This subsection does not limit any existing cause of action or right to bring an action, including any action under the Administrative Procedure Act or the All Writs Act [5 U.S.C.S. §§ 551 et seq. or 28 U.S.C.S. § 1651].

(4) Data acquired under this section shall be used only for research or statistical purposes and may not contain any information that may reveal the identity of an individual victim of a crime.

(5) The Attorney General shall publish an annual summary of the data acquired under this section, *including data about crimes committed by, and crimes directed against, juveniles* [emphasis added by source].

(c) There are authorized to be appropriated such sums as may be necessary to carry out the provisions of this section through fiscal year 2002.

. . .

(b) Nothing in this Act shall be construed, nor shall any funds appropriated to carry out the purpose of the Act be used, to promote or encourage homosexuality."

Source: "Hate Crime Statistics." 2010. U.S. Department of Justice. Federal Bureau of Investigation. https://ucr.fbi.gov/hate-crime/2010/resources/hate-crime-2010-hate-crime-statistics-act.

Violent Crime Control and Law Enforcement Act (1994)

One modest step forward in the battle against hate groups and hate crimes came in 1994, when one provision of the Violent Crime Control and Law Enforcement Act included a provision concerning the sentencing of individuals convicted of hate crimes. The part of the bill authorizing the change is shown at (A) here, followed by the specific directive issued by the Sentencing Commission to implement the authorization (B).

(A): SEC. 280003. DIRECTION TO UNITED STATES SENTENCING COMMISSION REGARDING SENTENCING ENHANCEMENTS FOR HATE CRIMES.

(a) Definition.—In this section, "hate crime" means a crime in which the defendant intentionally selects a victim, or in the case of a property crime, the property that is the object of the crime, because of the actual or perceived race, color, religion, national origin, ethnicity, gender, disability, or sexual orientation of any person.

(b) Sentencing Enhancement.—Pursuant to section 994 of title 28, United States Code, the United States Sentencing Commission shall promulgate guidelines or amend existing guidelines to provide sentencing enhancements of not less than 3 offense levels for offenses that the finder of fact at trial determines beyond a reasonable doubt are hate crimes. In carrying out this section, the United States Sentencing Commission shall ensure that there is reasonable consistency with other guidelines, avoid duplicative punishments for substantially the same offense, and take into account any mitigating circumstances that might justify exceptions.

Source: "H.R.3355—Violent Crime Control and Law Enforcement Act of 1994." 1994. Congress.gov. https://www.congress.gov/bill/103rd-congress/house-bill/3355/text.

(B): §3A1.1—HATE CRIME MOTIVATION OR VULNERABLE VICTIM

(a) If the finder of fact at trial or, in the case of a plea of guilty or nolo contendere, the court at sentencing determines beyond a reasonable doubt that the defendant intentionally selected any victim or any property as the object of the offense of conviction because of the actual or perceived race, color, religion, national origin, ethnicity, gender, gender identity, disability, or sexual orientation of any person, increase by 3 levels.

(b) (1) If the defendant knew or should have known that a victim of the offense was a vulnerable victim, increase by 2 levels.

(2) If (A) subdivision (1) applies; and (B) the offense involved a large number of vulnerable victims, increase the offense level determined under subdivision (1) by 2 additional levels.

(c) Special Instruction

(1) Subsection (a) shall not apply if an adjustment from §2H1.1(b)(1) applies.

Commentary

Application Notes:

1. Subsection (a) applies to offenses that are hate crimes. Note that special evidentiary requirements govern the application of this subsection.

Do not apply subsection (a) on the basis of gender in the case of a sexual offense. In such cases, this factor is taken into account by the offense level of the Chapter Two offense guideline. Moreover, do not apply subsection (a) if an adjustment from §2H1.1(b)(1) applies.

2. For purposes of subsection (b), **"vulnerable victim"** means a person (A) who is a victim of the offense of conviction and any conduct for which the defendant is accountable under §1B1.3 (Relevant Conduct); and (B) who is unusually vulnerable due to age, physical or mental condition, or who is otherwise particularly susceptible to the criminal conduct.

Subsection (b) applies to offenses involving an unusually vulnerable victim in which the defendant knows or should have known of the victim's unusual vulnerability. The adjustment would apply, for example, in a fraud case in which the defendant marketed an ineffective cancer cure or in a robbery in which the defendant selected a handicapped victim. But it would not apply in a case in which the defendant sold fraudulent securities by mail to the general public and one of the victims happened to be senile. Similarly, for example, a bank teller is not an unusually vulnerable victim solely by virtue of the teller's position in a bank.

Do not apply subsection (b) if the factor that makes the person a vulnerable victim is incorporated in the offense guideline. For example, if the offense guideline provides an enhancement for the age of the victim, this subsection would not be applied unless the victim was unusually vulnerable for reasons unrelated to age.

3. The adjustments from subsections (a) and (b) are to be applied cumulatively. Do not, however, apply subsection (b) in a case in which subsection (a) applies unless a victim of the offense was unusually vulnerable for reasons unrelated to race, color, religion, national origin, ethnicity, gender, gender identity, disability, or sexual orientation.

4. If an enhancement from subsection (b) applies and the defendant's criminal history includes a prior sentence for an offense that involved the selection of a vulnerable victim, an upward departure may be warranted.

5. For purposes of this guideline, "gender identity" means actual or perceived gender related characteristics. See 18 U.S.C. § 249(c)(4).

Background: Subsection (a) reflects the directive to the Commission, contained in Section 280003 of the Violent Crime Control and Law Enforcement Act of 1994, to provide an enhancement of not less than three levels for an offense when the finder of fact at trial determines beyond a reasonable doubt that the defendant had a hate crime motivation. To avoid unwarranted sentencing disparity based on the method of conviction, the Commission has broadened the application of this enhancement to include offenses that, in the case of a plea of guilty or nolo contendere, the court at sentencing determines are hate crimes. In section 4703(a) of Public Law 111–84, Congress broadened the scope of that directive to include gender identity; to reflect that congressional action, the Commission has broadened the scope of this enhancement to include gender identity.

Subsection (b)(2) implements, in a broader form, the instruction to the Commission in section 6(c)(3) of Public Law 105–184.

Source: "Adjustments." 2018. Guidelines Manual. United States Sentencing Commission. https://guidelines.ussc.gov/gl/%C2%A73A1.1.

Church Arson Prevention Act (1996)

The Church Arson Prevention Act was written and passed largely in response to a series of arson crimes committed against churches with predominantly Black congregations in the early 1990s. The act itself consists of a group of changes and additions to existing legislation and is perhaps best described in the summary provided by the Congress.gov website, as follows:

Church Arson Prevention Act of 1996—Makes Federal criminal code prohibitions against, and penalties for, damaging religious property or obstructing any person's free exercise of religious beliefs applicable where the offense is in, or affects, interstate commerce. (Currently such provisions apply only where: (1) the defendant, in committing the offense, travels in interstate or foreign commerce or uses a facility or instrumentality of interstate or foreign commerce in interstate or foreign commerce; and (2) the loss exceeds $10,000.)

Prohibits intentionally defacing, damaging, or destroying religious real property (or attempting to do so) because of the race, color, or ethnic characteristics of any individual associated with such property.

Increases penalties for violations of such provisions where bodily injury to any person, including a public safety officer, results or where such acts include the use, or attempted or threatened use, of a dangerous weapon, explosives, or fire.

Includes within the definition of "religious real property" fixtures or religious objects contained within a place of religious worship.

Sets a seven-year statute of limitations for the prosecution, trial, or punishment of a person for any noncapital offense under such provisions.

Directs the Secretary of Housing and Urban Development to make guaranteed loans to financial institutions in connection with loans made to assist certain tax exempt religious or other organizations that have been damaged by arson or terrorism. Authorizes the Secretary to use for such loan guarantees up to $5 million of the amounts made available for FY 1996 for the credit subsidy provided under the General Insurance Fund and the Special Risk Insurance Fund.

Amends the Victims of Crime Act of 1984 to include as "compensable crimes" under such Act crimes under this Act where victims suffer death or personal injury.

Authorizes appropriations to the Departments of the Treasury and Justice, including the Community Relations Service, to increase personnel to investigate, prevent, and respond to potential violations of this Act and Federal explosives prohibitions.

Reauthorizes the Hate Crimes Statistics Act.

Commends those individuals and entities that have responded with funds to assist in the rebuilding of places of worship that have been victimized by arson. Encourages the private sector to continue such efforts.

Source: H.R.3525—Church Arson Prevention Act of 1996. 1996. Congress.gov. https://www.congress.gov/bill/104th-congress/house-bill/3525.

The Matthew Shepard and James Byrd Jr. Hate Crimes Prevention Act (2010)

The original U.S. hate crimes bill made no mention of hate crimes against certain groups now understood to be victims of such acts, such as LGBT individuals. In 2009, President Barack Obama signed into law the Matthew Shepard and James Byrd Jr. Hate Crimes Prevention Act, as a rider to the National Defense Authorization Act for 2010. The act added new groups against which hate crimes could be charged. It also made other changes in the 1968 law, as indicated in the following selections. For comparison, see the preceding 1968 law.

[Addition of new groups: Following Sec. 249, (a)(1)(B)(ii) in the original act:]

"(2) OFFENSES INVOLVING ACTUAL OR PERCEIVED RELIGION, NATIONAL ORIGIN, GENDER, SEXUAL ORIENTATION, GENDER IDENTITY, OR DISABILITY.—

"(A) IN GENERAL.—Whoever, whether or not acting under color of law, in any circumstance described in subparagraph (B) or paragraph (3), willfully causes bodily injury to any person or, through the use of fire, a firearm, a dangerous weapon, or an explosive or incendiary device, attempts to cause bodily injury to any person, because of the actual or perceived religion, national origin, gender, sexual orientation, gender identity, or disability of any person—

  (i) shall be imprisoned not more than 10 years, fined in accordance with this title, or both; and
  (ii) shall be imprisoned for any term of years or for life, fined in accordance with this title, or both, if—
    (I) death results from the offense; or
    "(II) the offense includes kidnapping or an attempt to kidnap, aggravated sexual abuse or an attempt to commit aggravated sexual abuse, or an attempt to kill.

(B) CIRCUMSTANCES DESCRIBED.—For purposes of subparagraph (A), the circumstances described in this subparagraph are that—

(i) the conduct described in subparagraph (A) occurs during the course of, or as the result of, the travel of the defendant or the victim—
  (I) across a State line or national border; or
  (II) using a channel, facility, or instrumentality of interstate or foreign commerce;
(ii) the defendant uses a channel, facility, or instrumentality of interstate or foreign commerce in connection with the conduct described in subparagraph (A);
(iii) in connection with the conduct described in subparagraph (A), the defendant employs a firearm, dangerous weapon, explosive or incendiary device, or other weapon that has traveled in interstate or foreign commerce; or
(iv) the conduct described in subparagraph (A)—
  (I) interferes with commercial or other economic activity in which the victim is engaged at the time of the conduct; or
  (II) otherwise affects interstate or foreign commerce."

[Allows federal agencies to assist state and local agencies in the pursuit of hate crimes.]

SEC. 4704. SUPPORT FOR CRIMINAL INVESTIGATIONS AND PROSECUTIONS BY STATE, LOCAL, AND TRIBAL LAW ENFORCEMENT OFFICIALS.

(a) Assistance Other Than Financial Assistance.—
  (1) IN GENERAL.—
    At the request of a State, local, or tribal law enforcement agency, the Attorney General may provide technical, forensic, prosecutorial, or any other form of

assistance in the criminal investigation or prosecution of any crime that—
(A) constitutes a crime of violence;
(B) constitutes a felony under the State, local, or tribal laws; and
(C) is motivated by prejudice based on the actual or perceived race, color, religion, national origin, gender, sexual orientation, gender identity, or disability of the victim, or is a violation of the State, local, or tribal hate crime laws.

(2) PRIORITY.—

In providing assistance under paragraph (1), the Attorney General shall give priority to crimes committed by offenders who have committed crimes in more than one State and to rural jurisdictions that have difficulty covering the extraordinary expenses relating to the investigation or prosecution of the crime.

(b) Grants.—

(1) IN GENERAL.—

The Attorney General may award grants to State, local, and tribal law enforcement agencies for extraordinary expenses associated with the investigation and prosecution of hate crimes.

. . .

[The legislation authorized grants of $5 million per year for 2010, 2011, and 2012 to help state and local agencies investigate and prosecute hate crimes.]

(7) AUTHORIZATION OF APPROPRIATIONS.—

There is authorized to be appropriated to carry out this subsection $5,000,000 for each of fiscal years 2010, 2011, and 2012.

. . .

[The FBI is directed to begin collecting hate crime statistics that are not already part of the agency's purview.]

SEC. 4708. STATISTICS.

(a) In General.—

Subsection (b)(1) of the first section of the Hate Crime Statistics Act (28 U.S.C. 534 note) is amended by inserting "gender and gender identity," after "race."

(b) Data.—

Subsection (b)(5) of the first section of the Hate Crime Statistics Act (28 U.S.C. 534 note) is amended by inserting "including data about crimes committed by, and crimes directed against, juveniles" after "data acquired under this section."

Source: §249. Hate Crime Acts. 2020. Title 18. U.S. Code. https://www.govinfo.gov/content/pkg/USCODE-2011-title18/pdf/USCODE-2011-title18-partI-chap13-sec249.pdf.

Snyder v. Phelps et al. (2011)

In March 2006, a funeral for Lance Corporal Matthew A. Snyder, killed in Iraq, was held in Baltimore, Maryland. Among the attendees at the funeral were members of the Westboro Baptist Church of Topeka, Kansas. Those individuals regularly conducted protests at funerals and other events involving individuals or groups whom they considered to be sinful. In all cases, they carried signs carrying messages such as "Thank God for Dead Soldiers," "Fags Doom Nations," "America is Doomed," "Priests Rape Boys," and "You're Going to Hell." When made aware of these signs and the protest, Snyder's father was outraged and decided to sue the church and its members for intentional infliction of emotional distress, intrusion upon seclusion, and civil conspiracy. The district court held for the petitioners and awarded a very large fine against the church. The court later reduced the award, but kept the finding of guilty in place. The appeals court reversed that finding, arguing that the church members' statements dealt with matters of public concern, were probably not false, and consisted almost entirely of hyperbolic rhetoric. Under those terms, the statements made by the church on their signs fell under the category of protected speech under the First Amendment of the U.S. Constitution. The case was then heard before the U.S. Supreme Court, which affirmed the appeal court's decision by a vote of 8 to 1. The essence of the court's finding was as follows. Certain citations and footnotes are omitted in this selection.

To succeed on a claim for intentional infliction of emotional distress in Maryland, a plaintiff must demonstrate that the defendant intentionally or recklessly engaged in extreme and outrageous conduct that caused the plaintiff to suffer severe emotional distress. The Free Speech Clause of the First Amendment—"Congress shall make no law . . . abridging the freedom of speech"—can serve as a defense in state tort suits, including suits for intentional infliction of emotional distress.

. . .

Whether the First Amendment prohibits holding Westboro liable for its speech in this case turns largely on whether that speech is of public or private concern, as determined by all the circumstances of the case. "[S]peech on 'matters of public concern' . . . is 'at the heart of the First Amendment's protection.'" The First Amendment reflects "a profound national commitment to the principle that debate on public issues should be uninhibited, robust, and wide-open." That is because "speech concerning public affairs is more than self-expression; it is the essence of self-government." Accordingly, "speech on public issues occupies the highest rung of the hierarchy of First Amendment values, and is entitled to special protection."

. . .

Simply put, the church members had the right to be where they were. Westboro alerted local authorities to its funeral protest and fully complied with police guidance on where the picketing could be staged. The picketing was conducted under police supervision some 1,000 feet from the church, out of the sight of those at the church. The protest was not unruly; there was no shouting, profanity, or violence.

The record confirms that any distress occasioned by Westboro's picketing turned on the content and viewpoint of the message conveyed, rather than any interference with the funeral itself. A group of parishioners standing at the very spot where Westboro stood, holding signs that said "God Bless America" and "God Loves You," would not have been subjected to liability. It was what Westboro said that exposed it to tort damages.

Given that Westboro's speech was at a public place on a matter of public concern, that speech is entitled to "special protection" under the First Amendment. Such speech cannot be restricted simply because it is upsetting or arouses contempt. "If there is a bedrock principle underlying the First Amendment, it is that the government may not prohibit the expression of an idea simply because society finds the idea itself offensive or disagreeable." Indeed, "the point of all speech protection . . . is to shield just those choices of content that in someone's eyes are misguided, or even hurtful."

The jury here was instructed that it could hold Westboro liable for intentional infliction of emotional distress based on a finding that Westboro's picketing was "outrageous." "Outrageousness," however, is a highly malleable standard with "an inherent subjectiveness about it which would allow a jury to impose liability on the basis of the jurors' tastes or views, or perhaps on the basis of their dislike of a particular expression." In a case such as this, a jury is "unlikely to be neutral with respect to the content of [the] speech," posing "a real danger of becoming an instrument for the suppression of . . . 'vehement, caustic, and sometimes unpleasan[t]'" expression. Such a risk is unacceptable; "in public debate [we] must tolerate insulting, and even outrageous, speech in order to provide adequate 'breathing space' to the freedoms protected by the First Amendment." What Westboro said, in the whole context of how and where it chose to say it, is entitled to "special protection" under the First Amendment, and that protection cannot be overcome by a jury finding that the picketing was outrageous.

For all these reasons, the jury verdict imposing tort liability on Westboro for intentional infliction of emotional distress must be set aside.

Source: *Snyder v. Phelps*, 562 U.S. 443 (2011).

United States of America v. Paul Beebe, et al. (2011)

The first case prosecuted under the Matthew Shepard and James Byrd Jr. Hate Crimes Prevention Act of 2009 involved an attack by three young white men against a developmentally disabled Navajo man in the state of New Mexico. The three men took the Navajo man to their apartment, which was adorned with various white supremacist and neo-Nazi symbols. They proceeded to deface his body with blue, red, and black markers, ending with the burning of a swastika into his back. The three men were indicted of a hate crime under the provisions of the Shepard–Byrd Act. They responded by arguing at a pretrial meeting before the U.S. District Court for the District of New Mexico that provisions of the act and their indictment were illegal because they were based on an improper reading of the Thirteenth Amendment of the U.S. Constitution. They claimed that the amendment applied only to the economic rights of freed slaves, and not to general hate crimes such as those of which they were accused. Judge Bruce D. Black rejected that argument and allowed the case to go forward. A few days after the judge's decision, two of the defendants pleaded guilty of the crime. The third had pleaded guilty at an earlier date. The kernel of the judge's decision was as follows (citations and notes are omitted from the selection):

Further, every federal circuit actually faced with the issue has upheld under the Thirteenth Amendment the constitutionality of 18 U.S.C. § 245(b)(2)(B) (2006), a statute that criminalizes intentional racially motivated violence against any person because that person is enjoying a public benefit. The weight of this precedent further confirms that it was rational for Congress to conclude that racially motivated violence is a badge or incident of slavery. Defendants urge that the framers of the Thirteenth Amendment would not have identified hate crimes as a badge of slavery because the focus of the Thirteenth Amendment "was on ensuring economic rights to former slaves." Defendants imply that because hate crimes are non-economic in nature, the framers of the Thirteenth Amendment would not have considered them a badge or incident of slavery. However, the Tenth Circuit has rejected the contention that the Thirteenth Amendment is mere economic legislation. Further, as noted above, the Supreme Court has strongly implied that racially motivated assaults constitute a badge of slavery under the Thirteenth Amendment. Thus, Defendants' argument is unavailing.

. . .

The attack at issue here allegedly involved at least one avowed white supremacist and his white friends branding a swastika, a well known symbol of white power, on the arm of a Navajo man in Farmington, New Mexico, an area with a long history of racially motivated violence. Whatever may be said of the limits of Congress' power under Section Two, these facts fall well within the scope of conduct that Section Two of the Thirteenth Amendment empowered Congress to ban. Consequently, this Court easily finds that Congress' determination that racially motivated violence is a badge of slavery is rational.

. . .

This Court concludes that the purpose of section 249 also appears calculated to further the goal of Section One of the Thirteenth Amendment: to eradicate and keep the institution of slavery permanently suppressed. Congress expressly identified racially motivated violence as a badge or incident of slavery. Since, just as in Jones and Griffin, the legislation targets a badge or incident of slavery, it contains a legitimate enforcement purpose under the Thirteenth Amendment. Further, the means used, here criminal prosecution of individuals that intentionally physically attack victims because of their race, is "plainly adapted" to the end of eradicating racially motivated violence, a badge of slavery, by creating a deterrent to committing such violence. Therefore, this legislation meets the McCulloch test and consequently is valid under the Thirteenth Amendment.

Source: *United States of America v. Paul Beebe, et al.* 2011. https://www.justice.gov/sites/default/files/crt/legacy/2011/10/13/beebeop.pdf.

Objective Evidence That the Crime Was Motivated by Bias (2015)

One of the most difficult issues in dealing with hate crimes is determining whether the crime really was a hate crime, or whether it was a crime motivated by some other factor, such as robbery or simple assault. The FBI has developed a manual to aid for law enforcement agencies to decide when a crime can be classified as a hate crime. A critical part of this manual is the discussion of the types of evidence that can be used for making that determination. That section is excerpted here.

An important distinction must be made when reporting a hate crime. The mere fact the offender is biased against the victim's actual or perceived race, religion, disability, sexual orientation, ethnicity, gender, and/or gender identity does not mean that a hate crime was involved. Rather, the offender's criminal act must have been motivated, in whole or in part, by his or her bias.

Motivation is subjective, therefore, it is difficult to know with certainty whether a crime was the result of the offender's bias. For that reason, before an incident can be reported as a hate crime, sufficient objective facts must be present to lead a reasonable and prudent person to conclude that the offender's actions were motivated, in whole or in part, by bias. While no single fact may be conclusive, facts such as the following, particularly when combined, are supportive of a finding of bias:

1. The offender and the victim were of a different race, religion, disability, sexual orientation, ethnicity, gender,

and/or gender identity. For example, the victim was African American and the offender was white.
2. Bias-related oral comments, written statements, or gestures were made by the offender indicating his or her bias. For example, the offender shouted a racial epithet at the victim.
3. Bias-related drawings, markings, symbols, or graffiti were left at the crime scene. For example, a swastika was painted on the door of a synagogue, mosque, or LGBT center.
4. Certain objects, items, or things which indicate bias were used. For example, the offenders wore white sheets with hoods covering their faces or a burning cross was left in front of the victim's residence.
5. The victim is a member of a specific group that is overwhelmingly outnumbered by other residents in the neighborhood where the victim lives and the incident took place.
6. The victim was visiting a neighborhood where previous hate crimes had been committed because of race, religion, disability, sexual orientation, ethnicity, gender, or gender identity and where tensions remained high against the victim's group.
7. Several incidents occurred in the same locality, at or about the same time, and the victims were all of the same race, religion, disability, sexual orientation, ethnicity, gender, or gender identity.
8. A substantial portion of the community where the crime occurred perceived that the incident was motivated by bias.
9. The victim was engaged in activities related to his or her race, religion, disability, sexual orientation, ethnicity, gender, or gender identity. For example, the victim was a member of the National Association for

the Advancement of Colored People (NAACP) or participated in an LGBT pride celebration.
10. The incident coincided with a holiday or a date of significance relating to a particular race, religion, disability, sexual orientation, ethnicity, gender, or gender identity, e.g., Martin Luther King Day, Rosh Hashanah, or the Transgender Day of Remembrance.
11. The offender was previously involved in a similar hate crime or is a hate group member.
12. There were indications that a hate group was involved. For example, a hate group claimed responsibility for the crime or was active in the neighborhood.
13. A historically-established animosity existed between the victim's and the offender's groups.
14. The victim, although not a member of the targeted racial, religious, disability, sexual orientation, ethnicity, gender, or gender identity group, was a member of an advocacy group supporting the victim group.

Source: "Hate Crime Data Collection Guidelines and Training Manual." 2015. Criminal Justice Information Services (CJIS) Division. Uniform Crime Reporting (UCR) Program. https://ucr.fbi.gov/hate-crime-data-collection-guidelines-and-training-manual.pdf.

Public Law 115–58 Joint Resolution (2017)

From time to time, one or both houses of the U.S. Congress decide to adopt resolutions expressing their view on some aspect of hate groups. Often, the motivation for such an action is a specific event that has occurred to which the House or Senate feels it must express itself. Of the two examples cited here, the first condemns "the violence and domestic terrorist attack that took place during events between August 11 and August 12, 2017, in Charlottesville, Virginia." The second was motivated by comments by U.S. Representative Ilhan

Omar (D-MN) over the "undue influence" exerted by the nation of Israel over U.S. policy. It was designed to express opposition to anti-Semitic hate groups, hate speech, and related actions. Both resolutions (as is usually the case) begin with a series of "Whereas" clauses that explain the background of the resolution involved.

Now, therefore, be it
Resolved by the Senate and House of Representatives of the United States of America in Congress assembled, That Congress—
(1) condemns the racist violence and domestic terrorist attack that took place between August 11 and August 12, 2017, in Charlottesville, Virginia;
(2) recognizes—
   (A) Heather Heyer, who was killed, and 19 other individuals who were injured in the reported domestic terrorist attack; and
   (B) several other individuals who were injured in separate attacks while standing up to hate and intolerance;
(3) recognizes the public service and heroism of Virginia State Police officers Lieutenant H. Jay Cullen and Trooper Pilot Berke M.M. Bates, who lost their lives while responding to the events from the air;
(4) offers—
   (A) condolences to the families and friends of Heather Heyer, Lieutenant H. Jay Cullen, and Trooper Pilot Berke M.M. Bates; and
   (B) sympathy and support to those individuals who are recovering from injuries sustained during the attacks;
(5) expresses support for the Charlottesville community as the community heals following this demonstration of violent bigotry;
(6) rejects White nationalism, White supremacy, and neoNazism as hateful expressions of intolerance that are contradictory to the values that define the people of the United States; and
(7) urges—

(A) the President and his administration to—
  (i) speak out against hate groups that espouse racism, extremism, xenophobia, anti-Semitism, and White supremacy; and
  (ii) use all resources available to the President and the President's Cabinet to address the growing prevalence of those hate groups in the United States; and
(B) the Attorney General to work with—
  (i) the Secretary of Homeland Security to investigate thoroughly all acts of violence, intimidation, and domestic terrorism by White supremacists, White nationalists, neo-Nazis, the Ku Klux Klan, and associated groups in order to determine if any criminal laws have been violated and to prevent those groups from fomenting and facilitating additional violence; and
  (ii) the heads of other Federal agencies to improve the reporting of hate crimes and to emphasize the importance of the collection, and the reporting to the Federal Bureau of Investigation, of hate crime data by State and local agencies.

Source: Public Law 115–58 115th Congress. Joint Resolution. 2017. Public Law 115–58. https://www.govinfo.gov/content/pkg/PLAW-115publ58/pdf/PLAW-115publ58.pdf.

Resolved, That the House of Representatives—

(1) rejects the perpetuation of anti-Semitic stereotypes in the United States and around the world, including the pernicious myth of dual loyalty and foreign allegiance, especially in the context of support for the United States-Israel alliance;

(2) condemns anti-Semitic acts and statements as hateful expressions of intolerance that are contradictory to the values that define the people of the United States;

(3) reaffirms its support for the mandate of the United States Special Envoy to Monitor and Combat Anti-Semitism as part

of the broader policy priority of fostering international religious freedom and protecting human rights all over the world;

(4) rejects attempts to justify hatred or violent attacks as an acceptable expression of disapproval or frustration over political events in the Middle East or elsewhere;

(5) acknowledges the harm suffered by Muslims and others from the harassment, discrimination, and violence that result from anti-Muslim bigotry;

(6) condemns anti-Muslim discrimination and bigotry against all minorities as contrary to the values of the United States;

(7) condemns the death threats received by Jewish and Muslim Members of Congress, including in recent weeks;

(8) encourages law enforcement and government officials to avoid conduct that raises the specter of unconstitutional profiling against anyone because of their race, religion, nationality, political, or particular social group, including the assignment of blame or targeting members of an entire religious group for increased suspicion, based on the conduct of a single individual or small group of individuals; and

(9) encourages all public officials to confront the reality of anti-Semitism, Islamophobia, racism, and other forms of bigotry, as well as historical struggles against them, to ensure that the United States will live up to the transcendent principles of tolerance, religious freedom, and equal protection as embodied in the Declaration of Independence and the first and 14th amendments to the Constitution.

Source: "H.Res.183—Condemning Anti-Semitism as Hateful Expressions of Intolerance . . . 2019." Congress.gov. https://www.congress.gov/bill/116th-congress/house-resolution/183/text.

6 Resources

The notion that some category of individuals may be "better" than some other category—or from all other categories—is probably as old as human civilization. The result of such feelings has ranged from distaste and distrust toward "the other" to outright efforts to eliminate those "others" from a culture or country. It is hardly surprising, then, that an endless number of books, articles, and electronic documents have been written on the topic. Only a small sample of those items can be listed in this chapter. They are designed, however, to suggest the range of ideas people have had about hate groups, along with some of the teachings of such groups themselves. In some cases, a document may be available in more than one format, a journal article and web page, for example, a fact that is so indicated in the section where it is to be found in this chapter. Readers should also be aware of the wealth of resources contained in the notes at the end of chapters 1 and 2 of this book.

Books

Balleck, Barry J. 2019. *Hate Groups and Extremist Organizations in America: An Encyclopedia.* Santa Barbara, CA: Praeger.

People display QAnon messages on cardboard placards during a political rally. QAnon is a discredited philosophy claiming that a group of Satan-worshipping pedophiles is running a global child sex-trafficking ring and plotting against former U.S. president Donald Trump. (Cateyeperspective/Dreamstime.com)

This impressive volume provides good descriptions and discussions of more than two hundred hate groups in the United States. The book should be seen as an essential reference on the topic of hate groups for anyone interested in the subject. A good introduction to the subject is also provided.

Bartoletti, Susan Campbell. 2010. *They Called Themselves the K.K.K: The Birth of an American Terrorist Group*. Boston: Houghton Mifflin Harcourt.

This history of the origin and growth of the Ku Klux Klan (KKK) movement depends heavily on stories of specific events that occurred during those years.

Brooks, Michael E. 2014. *The Ku Klux Klan in Wood County, Ohio*. Charleston, SC: The History Press.

This fascinating book tells the detailed story of Klan activities in just one county in Ohio during the 1920s. The organization was so successful as to be said to actually have "taken over the county" in some regards.

Caspi, David J. 2013. *Ideologically Motivated Murder: The Threat Posed by White Supremacist Groups*. El Paso, TX: LFB Scholarly Publishing LLC.

The author argues that domestic terrorism resulting from hate group actions is a more serious problem than international terrorism. He discusses details of murders caused by hate groups and, of special interest, the influence of geographic location in the frequency of such crimes.

Douglas, Karen. 2009. "Psychology, Discrimination and Hate Groups Online." In Adam N. Joinson, et al., eds. *Oxford Handbook of Internet Psychology*. Oxford, UK: Oxford University Press, Chapter 11.

The author explores the question as to why hate groups tend to be so vociferous and aggressive online when they tend to be so much more subdued in their conversations in other formats. She suggests this question is one of considerable importance to psychologists interested in the structure and function of hate groups.

Dyck, Kirsten. 2017. *Reichsrock: The International Web of White-Power and Neo-Nazi Hate Music*. New Brunswick, NJ: Rutgers University Press.

It is probably no surprise that music often has political overtones. In this book, Dyck discusses the connection between certain types of popular music and right-wing hate groups and the messages they are attempting to send out to the world.

Gerstenfeld, Phyllis B. 2018. *Hate Crimes: Causes, Controls, and Controversies*. 4th ed. Thousand Oaks, CA: SAGE Publications, Inc.

This popular book provides an excellent overview to the general problem of hate crimes. Some specific topics covered include hate group typologies, major American hate groups, hate group ideologies, hate group recruitment and defection, and women in organized hate groups.

Goldwag, Arthur. 2012. *The New Hate: A History of the Fear and Loathing on the Populist Right*. New York: Vintage Books.

Violent actions by hate groups have a long history in the United States. Goldwag traces some of the most important elements in that history and shows how the political philosophy known as populism is closely related both to these historical examples and to hate violence today.

Greenfield, Daniel. 2011. *Muslim Hate Groups on Campus*. Sherman Oaks, CA: David Horowitz Freedom Center.

The author argues that Muslim student groups on college and university campuses in the United States play an important role in the support of anti-Semitic ideas and activities among students at those institutions as well as across the general public.

Hawdon, James, ed. *The Causes and Consequences of Group Violence: From Bullies to Terrorists.* Lanham, MD: Lexington Books.

The essays in this book take a broad view of the subject of "hate groups" ranging from small local gangs to nation-state-sponsored hate crimes. Two long sections deal with characterizations of the perpetrators and victims of hate crimes, with additional sections on the consequences of hate crimes and some reflections on the topic.

Hawley, George. 2019. *The Alt-right: What Everyone Needs to Know.* New York: Oxford University Press.

This excellent introduction to the alt-right movement begins with a long section on the historical origins of the movement, with several biographies of important figures in that movement. Later chapters deal with racist movements abroad, the role of the Internet in the alt-right movement, the alt-right and conservatism, Donald Trump's role in the flowering of the alt-right movement, and "lite" forms of the alt-right.

Jackson, Paul, and Anton Shekhovtsov. 2014. *The Post-war Anglo-American Far Right: A Special Relationship of Hate.* Houndmills, Basingstoke, Hampshire: Palgrave Pivot.

This book is of special interest because of its explanation of the connection between hate groups in the United States and Great Britain following, and partly as a result of, World War II.

Johnson, Greg. 2018. *The White Nationalist Manifesto.* San Francisco: Counter-Currents Publishing Ltd.

Johnson is a leading figure in the white American nationalist movement, calling for the right of all white people for their own self-determination. This book lays out the basic principles of the movement.

Keipi, Teo, et al. 2017. *Online Hate and Harmful Content: Cross-national Perspectives*. London; New York: Routledge, Taylor & Francis Group.

The authors explore the use of electronic methods for distributing the basics and methods of various hate groups. They use examples from several countries to illustrate their arguments.

Klein, Adam. 2009. *A Space for Hate: The White Power Movement's Adaptation into Cyberspace*. Duluth, MN: Litwin Books.

The Internet has provided hate groups with a very special and very effective mechanism for getting their messages out, both to their own members and supporters, as well as the general public. This book explores the process by which that change has occurred and what its significance may be for the future of hate group activity.

Kontos, Louis, and David C. Brotherton, eds. 2007. *Encyclopedia of Gangs*. Westport, CT: Greenwood Press.

While the terms "gang" and "hate group" are certainly not identical, the two concepts share many ideas in common. This excellent resource book contains articles not only on individual gangs but also on broader concepts, such as gang theory, gangs in prisons, gangs in the United States, hate groups, gang symbols, organized crime, and transnational gangs.

Levine, Deborah, and Marc Brenman. 2019. *When Hate Groups March down Main Street: Engaging a Community Response*. Lanham, MD: Rowman & Littlefield.

The focus of this book is primarily on the attitudes with which a community can approach the problem of hate groups within its midst, along with the methods by which the community can respond to such a threat. Some topics include "The Hate Message Online," "Community Organizing," "Recruitment and Radicalization," "Holocaust Education," and "Interfaith Efforts."

Marks, Kathy. 1996. *Faces of Right Wing Extremism*. Boston: Branden Publishing Company.
This book provides information on several less-well-known hate groups operating in the twentieth century. It is one of the best available books describing the typologies and histories of hate groups in the United States.

Maxson, Cheryl Lee, et al., eds. *The Modern Gang Reader*. New York: Oxford University Press.
The essays in this collection are presented under eight major themes: Defining and Studying Gangs, The Scope and Dynamics of Gang Involvement, Gang Structures and Gang Processes, Race and Ethnicity, Gender, Community Contexts, Crime and Victimization, and Responses to Street Gangs: Programs and Policies.

Miller-Idriss, Cynthia. 2020. *Hate in the Homeland: The New Global Far Right*. Princeton, NJ: Princeton University Press.
The author discusses the growing threat of far-right violence throughout the world and focuses on the mechanisms by which hate groups identify possible members and the techniques by which they recruit and educate members to become involved in hate activities.

Moore, Hilary, and James Tracy. 2020. *No Fascist USA!: The John Brown Anti-Klan Committee and Lessons for Today's Movements*. San Francisco: City Lights Books.
The rise of the third phase of the Ku Klux Klan in the mid-twentieth century inspired a corresponding reaction from antihate individuals. One manifestation of that reaction was the John Brown Anti-Klan Committee, formed in 1978 by a group of white antiracist individuals. The

committee remained active for more than a decade and, as this book shows, used methods that are still applicable in dealing with hate groups today.

Neiwert, David. 2018. *Alt-America: The Rise of the Radical Right in the Age of Trump*. London: Verso.
　　The author explores a series of events, ranging from the 9/11 disaster to the election of President Barack Obama to the present-day presidency of Donald Trump, that have led to the growth and empowerment of radical right hate groups.

Olsson, Peter Alan. 2014. *The Making of a Homegrown Terrorist: Brainwashing Rebels in Search of a Cause*. Santa Barbara, CA: Praeger.
　　This book focuses on the experiences of more than a dozen individuals who were brought into one or another hate group in the last few decades. It discusses the factors involved in "educating" a person in the hate group philosophy.

Patton, Ann. 2015. *Unmasked: The Rise & Fall of the 1920s Ku Klux Klan*. Tulsa, OK: APLcorps Books LLC.
　　The author provides a good overall description of the second phase of the Ku Klux Klan movement, set within a time period in the United States that was already revolutionary in other ways.

Pegram, Thomas R. 2011. *One Hundred Percent American: The Rebirth and Decline of the Ku Klux Klan in the 1920s*. Lanham, MD: Ivan R. Dee.
　　This very fine book provides an instructive and detailed history of the Ku Klux Klan during its second reincarnation, beginning around 1920.

Perry, Barbara. 2001. *In the Name of Hate: Understanding Hate Crimes*. London: Routledge.

This book is one of the best general works available on the general features of hate crimes. Some of the topics included are defining and measuring hate crimes, hate crimes among various characteristic groups, and ethnoviolence carried out by nation-states.

Perry, Barbara, and Ryan Scrivens. 2019. *Right-wing Extremism in Canada*. Cham, Switzerland: Palgrave Macmillan.
    The authors explore a topic to which relatively little attention has been paid, the history and present status of right-wing extremism. Of special interest is the influence of President Donald Trump's own thoughts and comments on the topic on Canadian thought and events.

Picciolini, Christian. 2017. *White American Youth: My Descent into America's Most Violent Hate Movement—and How I Got Out.* New York: Hachette Books.
    The author tells the story of how he became involved with hate groups, his experiences with such groups, and his gradual decision to disavow this lifestyle and become, instead, an antihate group activist.

Rawlings, William. 2017. *The Second Coming of the Invisible Empire: The Ku Klux Klan of the 1920s.* Macon, GA: Mercer University Press.
    In some ways, the most significant period of the Ku Klux Klan's existence was its so-called second phase, lasting from about 1915 to about 1945. Rawlings provides an excellent review of the Klan's rise during the second half of the nineteenth century, its demise in about 1871, its rebirth and rise to power in the third decade of the twentieth century, and its demise once again at the end of World War II.

Sanchezm Juan O. 2018. *The Ku Klux Klan's Campaign against Hispanics, 1921–1925: Rhetoric, Violence and Response in the American Southwest.* Jefferson, NC: McFarland & Company, Inc.

Although the Klan's violence against African Americans in the south is relatively well documented and known, similar actions against Latinos in the American Southwest are less so. This book provides an excellent review of that history for individual states of Arizona, California, Colorado, New Mexico, and Texas.

Saslow, Eli. 2018. *Rising Out of Hatred: The Awakening of a Former White Nationalist*. New York: Random House.

The author distills "hundreds of hours" of interviews with Derek Black, a former hate group member who eventually disavowed his membership and involvements within the white power movement.

Simi, Pete, and Robert Futrell. 2015. *American Swastika: Inside the White Power Movement's Hidden Spaces of Hate*. Lanham, MD: Rowman & Littlefield.

The authors provide important details about a special wing of hate groups in the United States, those with a neo-Nazi or Aryan focus. They discuss their structure and the ways they get their message across to sympathetic individuals and the general public.

Smolla, Rodney A. 2020. *Confessions of a Free Speech Lawyer: Charlottesville and the Politics of Hate*. Ithaca, NY: Cornell University Press.

The author draws on a lifetime of involvement in legal issues associated with hate groups. He uses the events of the Charlottesville riots of 2017 to go beyond the details of that specific event to a more general analysis of how and why changes in hate group activity have increased over recent years.

Stern, Alexandra Minna. 2019. *Proud Boys and the White Ethnostate: How the Alt-right is Warping the American Imagination*. Boston: Beacon Press.

The author explores the pathway by which white nationalist movements, regarded only a decade ago as relatively harmless fringe groups, have become "commonplace, normalized, and accepted—endangering American democracy and society as a whole."

Swanson, Doug J. 2020. *Cult of Glory: The Bold and Brutal History of the Texas Rangers*. New York: Viking Press.

It is not unusual for individuals, groups, and events to go down in history as historic experiences that earn those entities admiration and respect for decades into the future. Such is the story of the Texas Rangers, often seen as a law enforcement agency that brought peace and civilization to the American West, the territory and state of Texas in particular. But later scholarship often shows that these entities contain elements somewhat less than admirable. This book discusses such a case for the Texas Rangers. The author shows how the Rangers systematically carried out a war of attrition against Native American tribes, killing innocent people, burning whole villages, and committing what would be described today as war crimes. The book is a good illustration of the way in which the term "hate group" can be applied to an otherwise legitimate, legal, governmental agency.

Tenold, Vegas. 2018. *Everything You Love Will Burn: Inside the Rebirth of White Nationalism in America*. New York: Nations Books.

Shortly after the election of Barack Obama as president in 2008, Tenold embedded himself in three hate groups: the Ku Klux Klan, National Socialist Movement, and Traditionalist Workers Party. From this inside position, he followed the development of these organizations from relatively powerless, separate hate groups into a single powerful movement. He reports on his experiences in a wide range of settings, from their "conventions to backroom meetings with Republican operatives."

Valeri, Robin Maria, ed. 2018. *Hate Crimes: Typology, Motivations, and Victims.* Durham, NC: Carolina Academic Press, LLC.
The chapters in this anthology deal with topics such as hate groups, hate crime laws, hate and race, hate and religion, hate and gender, hate against the LGBT community, bullying, and "turning the tide of hate."

Waltman, Michael, and John Haas. 2011. *The Communication of Hate.* New York: Peter Lang.
The authors explore various ways in which hate groups use language to publicize their message in print and electronically. Chapters deal with topics such as the distinctive nature of hate language, hate speech and the Internet, nativist discourse, and antihate narratives.

Wells-Barnett, Ida B. 2016. *Southern Horrors and Other Writings: The Anti-lynching Campaign of Ida B. Wells, 1892–1900.* Boston: Bedford/St. Martins, Macmillan Learning.
Ida Wells won undying fame for her research and writings on the spread of lynching in the American South during the late nineteenth century. Her work was finally recognized by a Pulitzer Prize issued in 2020 for her historic work. Also see, Ida B. Wells-Barnett. 2020. *Crusade for Justice: The Autobiography of Ida B. Wells.* Chicago: University of Chicago Press.

Wendling, Mike. 2018. *Alt-right: From 4chan to the White House.* Halifax; Winnipeg: Fernwood Publishing.
The author traces the processes by which hate groups that were previously fringe elements in American politics have achieved a "place at the top" with their incorporation by President Donald Trump of their philosophy into his approach to governance.

Winter, Aaron. 2019. "Online Hate: From the Far-Right to the 'Alt-Right' and from the Margins to the Mainstream." In Karen Lumsden, and Emily Harmer, eds. *Online Othering: Exploring*

Digital Violence and Discrimination on the Web, 39–63. Cham, Switzerland: Springer International Publishing. https://www.researchgate.net/publication/332601405_Online_Hate_From_the_Far-Right_to_the_'Alt-Right'_and_from_the_Margins_to_the_Mainstream (Draft form).

The growth of the World Wide Web raised questions as to the need (or not) for control over the content published for free public consumption on the system. Hate groups at first tended not to appreciate the significance of this free access for their philosophies and programs. That situation changed quickly, and the Internet is now perhaps the most powerful of all forms of media by which hate groups get out their message. This chapter reviews the evolution of this phenomenon.

Articles

Reports and commentaries on hate groups tend to occur with relative frequency in some journals. The following titles are among those journals.

American Behavioral Scientist: ISSN: 0002-7642 (print); 1552-3381 (online)

Contemporary Sociology: ISSN: 0094-3061 (print)

Islam and Christian-Muslim Relations: ISSN:1469-9311 (print)

Journal of Applied Social Psychology: ISSN: 0021-9029 (print); 1559-1816 (online)

Journal of Applied Sociology: ISSN: 2008-5745 (print); 2322-343X (online)

Journal of Contemporary Criminal Justice: ISSN: 1043-9862 (print)

Journal of Criminal Justice Education: ISSN: 1051-1253 (print)

Journal of Gang Research: ISSN: 1079-3062 (print)

Journal of Hate Studies: ISSN: 1540-2126 (print); 2169-7442 (online)

Journal of Homosexuality: ISSN: 0091-8369 (print); 1540-3602 (online)

Journal of Interpersonal Violence: ISSN: 08862605 (print); 15526518 (online)

Violence and Victims: ISSN: 0886-6708 (print). 1945-7073 (online)

Adamczyk, Amy, et al. 2014. "Relationship Between Hate Groups and Far-Right Ideological Violence." *Journal of Contemporary Criminal Justice* 30 (3): 310–332.
  This paper is one of a series of articles on the connection between hate groups and hate crimes, with the exception that the latter, as used here, refer to the most serious examples of violent events. The authors conclude that "the existence of a hate group in a county is significantly related to the occurrence of far-right ideologically motivated violence."

Barnett, Brett A. 2016. "League of the South's Internet Rhetoric: Neo-Confederate Community-Building Online." *Journal of Hate Studies* 13 (1): 151–173. http://doi.org/10.33972/jhs.137.
  Recent hate crimes in the South have inspired the rise of neo-Confederate hate groups responding to what they see as an attack on the American South's history. This article examines the way in which the League of the South's Internet presence has attempted to present this belief to other neo-Confederates and sympathizers who are drawn by a desire to preserve Southern values and traditions.

Bartlomiej, Balcerzak, and Jaworski Wojciech. 2015. "Application of Linguistic Cues in the Analysis of Language of Hate Groups." *Computer Science* 16 (2): 145–156. https://pdfs

.semanticscholar.org/2a0e/ffac8214ca77a1a18d6e0d3e410f64
0a34e2.pdf

 The authors perform a linguistic analysis of the language used by hate groups in online posts to find ways of distinguishing between that type of communication and more normal, nonhate posts. The lay out certain characteristic features by which the two forms of communication can be distinguished from each other.

Bell, Jeannine. 2019. "The Resistance & the Stubborn but Unsurprising Persistence of Hate and Extremism in the United States." *Indiana Journal of Global Legal Studies* 26 (1): 305–316. https://www.repository.law.indiana.edu/cgi/viewcontent.cgi?article=1703&context=ijgls.

 The author argues that, although the far right has a long history in the United States, it has "come out of the shadows" with the election of President Donald Trump. She reviews specific events that have caused the emergence of violent hate groups and notes that "overt expressions of racism and racist violence are nothing new."

Benton, Bond, and Daniela Peterka-Benton. 2019. "Hating in Plain Sight: The Hatejacking of Brands by Extremist Groups." *Public Relations Inquiry* 9 (1): 7–26.

 The "hijacking" of well-known brands by hate groups has been known and studied for some time. The process occurs because it can give a hate group public exposure to a popular and well-liked product, supposedly adding legitimacy to the group. This study examines the process by which this occurs and its significance for both the hate group and the brand. For more on this topic, see Coren, Michael J. 2017, under Internet, below.

Blazak, Randy. 2011. "Isn't Every Crime a Hate Crime?: The Case for Hate Crime Laws." *Sociology Compass* 5 (4): 244–255.

The campaign to criminalize nonviolent hate crimes has long involved a debate between the First Amendment rights of those who use hate speech and those who argue that such speech is not protected by the U.S. Constitution. The author explores this ongoing debate and argues for the position that such hate speech does, in fact, sometimes quality as criminal behavior. The author has developed a teaching guide to be used in discussions of hate speech based on his article. See Randy Blazak. 2011. "Teaching and Learning Guide For: Isn't Every Crime a Hate Crime? The Case for Hate Crime Laws." *Sociology Compass* 5 (5): 392–394.

Castle, Tammy. 2012. "Morrigan Rising: Exploring Female-Targeted Propaganda on Hate Group Websites." *European Journal of Cultural Studies* 15 (6): 679–694.
A relatively modest amount of research has been conducted on the role of women in hate groups. In this study, Castle studied statements on the websites of nineteen hate groups for their view of women's role in such groups. She found that the majority of such statements reinforced traditional roles for women as wives, mothers, and supporters of their spouse or partner.

Chermak, Steven, Joshua Freilich, and Michael Suttmoeller. 2013. "The Organizational Dynamics of Far-Right Hate Groups in the United States: Comparing Violent to Nonviolent Organizations." *Studies in Conflict & Terrorism* 36 (3): 193–218.
This article explores differences in the threats posed to the United States by violent and nonviolent hate groups, the first of which operates on the assumption that violent actions are the appropriate way of achieving political goals, while the latter tends to eschew that view and focuses on propaganda, education, and other approaches to

anti-Democratic ideals and programs. The article is based on an earlier report by the authors in 2011. See Steven M. Chermak, Joshua D. Freilich, and Michael Suttmoeller. 2011."The Organizational Dynamics of Far Right Hate Groups in the United States: Comparing Violent to Non Violent Organizations," Final Report to Human Factors/Behavioral Sciences Division, Science and Technology Directorate, U.S. Department of Homeland Security. College Park MD: START. https://www.dhs.gov/sites/default/files/publications/944_OPSR_TEVUS_Comparing-Violent-Nonviolent-Far-Right-Hate-Groups_Dec2011-508.pdf.

Chung, Derrek Aaran. 2017. "What Creates Hate?: Examining the Motivations of Right-Wing Hate Groups In 2017." Doctoral Thesis, Georgetown University. https://repository.library.georgetown.edu/handle/10822/1055101.

The author explores factors that might be associated with the increase in the number of hate groups in the United States in 2017. He concludes that "the far-right may be shifting ideologically away from economic appeals and towards appeals that maximize social and cultural fear."

Cohen-Almagor, Raphael. 2018. "Taking North American White Supremacist Groups Seriously: The Scope and the Challenge of Hate Speech on the Internet." *International Journal for Crime, Justice and Social Democracy* 7 (2): 38–57. https://www.researchgate.net/publication/325485071_Taking_North_American_White_Supremacist_Groups_Seriously_The_Scope_and_Challenge_of_Hate_Speech_on_the_Internet.

This article has two foci: how hate speech is manifested on the Internet and whether there is a connection between hate groups and hate crimes. The author concludes, in the latter case, that a connection between these two does exist. This article follows another similar article on ways of combating hate speech on the Internet. See Raphael Cohen-Almagor. 2011. "Fighting Hate and Bigotry on the Internet." *Policy & Internet* 3 (3): 1–26. https://www.researchgate.net/publication/215660527_Fighting_Hate_and_Bigotry_on_the_Internet.

Crompton, Louis. 1976. "Homosexuals and the Death Penalty in Colonial America." *Journal of Homosexuality* 1 (3): 277–293. https://digitalcommons.unl.edu/cgi/viewcontent.cgi?article=1061&context=englishfacpubs.

Scholars are well aware of the number of hate crimes that were committed in Colonial America against people whom the society as a whole regarded as "unfit" or "evil." This article discusses the special case of hate crimes and the associated penalties for same-sex acts.

Dunbar, Norah E., et al. 2014. "Fear Appeals, Message Processing Cues, and Credibility in the Websites of Violent, Ideological, and Nonideological Groups." *Journal of Computer-Mediated Communication* 19 (4): 871–889. https://doi.org/10.1111/jcc4.12083.

This study attempted to discover differences in the language used by violent (hate), ideological, and nonideological groups in their online websites. The authors found that the first of these groups tended to rely more heavily on the use of fear to deliver their messages and were less inclined to provide reliable and credible information to users than were the latter two groups.

Flowers, Kory. 2017. "Inside the Antifa Movement: The Anti-fascist Movement Sounds like it Only Targets White Supremacy Hate Groups like the Klan and Neo-Nazis, but this Anarchist Group Has and Will Attack Law Enforcement Officer and People with Opposing Political Ideologies." *Police* 41 (9): 32–36.

The author of this article argues that the antifa movement that works against hate groups has, itself, many of the characteristic features of hate groups and are as inclined to attack law enforcement groups as readily as they do hate groups.

Gemignani, Marco, and Yolanda Hernandez-Albujar. 2015. "Hate Groups Targeting Unauthorized Immigrants in the US: Discourses, Narratives and Subjectivation Practices on Their Websites." *Ethnic and Racial Studies* 38 (15): 2754–2770.

>Members of hate groups, or individuals emboldened by such groups, may hold and act on strong beliefs about immigrants because of their feeling that formal governmental agencies are not acting forcefully enough to counteract the threat that immigrants are seem to pose to the United States. This article examines the basis and validity of this view of anti-immigrant hate groups.

Goetz, Stephan J., Anil Rupasingha, and Scott Loveridge. 2012. "Social Capital, Religion, Wal-Mart, and Hate Groups in America." *Social Science Quarterly* 93 (2): 379–393.

>The authors explore the question as to whether the presence of hate groups in a county in the United States is related in any way to the social structure of that county, religious organizations present in the county, and the number of WalMart stores there. They conclude that all three factors have an effect on the number of hate groups present in a county.

Hackett, Justin D., David Rast, and Zachary Hohman. 2020. Identification with the American South and Anti-Muslim Attitudes." *The Journal of Social Psychology* 160 (2): 150–163.

>The number of anti-Muslim hate groups tripled in the year prior to the election of Donald Trump as president. The researchers attempt to discover social, economic, political, and other factors that may have been related to this change in the American South. They find that the stronger Southerners adhere to a traditional view of their region, the stronger their anti-Muslim feelings are likely to be.

Hummel, Daniel. 2018. "Hate Groups and Muslim Population Changes in the Fifty States: Does the Presence of Muslims Encourage Hate Group Formation?" *International Journal on Minority and Group Rights* 25 (2): 317–332.

The author notes that there has been a recent increase in the population of the United States and the number of anti-Muslim hate groups. He attempts to determine if there is any relationship between these two variables. He finds no statistically significant relationship.

McCullough, Jolie. 2019. "Texas Executes John William King in Racist Dragging Death of James Byrd Jr." *The Texas Tribune*. https://www.texastribune.org/2019/04/24/texas-execution-john-william-king-james-byrd/.

One of the most widely known hate crime committed under the auspices of a hate group was the murder of James Byrd, Jr., a Black man from Jasper, Texas. This article provides the unpleasant details of that event, as well as the final punishment received by the Aryan members who carried out the crime.

McMillin, Stephen Edward. 2014. "Ironic Outing: The Power of Hate Group Designations to Reframe Political Challenges to LGBT Rights and Focus Online Advocacy Efforts." *Journal of Policy Practice* 13 (2): 85–100. https://www.researchgate.net/publication/272121561_Ironic_Outing_The_Power_of_Hate_Group_Designations_to_Reframe_Political_Challenges_to_LGBT_Rights_and_Focus_Online_Advocacy_Efforts.

The listing in 2010 by the Southern Poverty Law Center (SPLC) of thirteen religious groups, most referring to themselves as "traditional family values" groups, as "hate groups" drew widespread comment and condemnation by religious, social, political, and other groups. The author examines this event in view of the perception of LGBT rights and privileges suggested by the SPLC action and reaction to the listings.

McNamee, Lacy G., Brittany L. Peterson, and Jorge Peña. 2010. "A Call to Educate, Participate, Invoke and Indict: Understanding the Communication of Online Hate Groups." *Communication Monographs* 77 (2): 257–280.

This study explores the types of messages included in online messaging by twenty-one hate groups in the United States. The authors discover four major themes in these messages: "(a) education of members and external publics; (b) participation within the group and in the public realm; (c) invocation of divine calling and privilege; and (d) indictment of external groups including the government, media, and entertainment industries, and other extremist sects."

McNeel, Hillary D. 2014. "Hate Crimes Against American Indians and Alaskan Natives." *Journal of Gang Research* 4 (21): 11–21. https://ngcrc.com/journalofgangresearch/jgr.v21n4.mcneel.pdf.

Hate crimes against these two groups tend to receive less attention than hate crimes against other groups. The purpose of this essay is to explore the types of hate crimes "that are committed against American Indians and Alaskan Natives," and whether or not "tribal law enforcement agencies define hate crimes against American Indians and Alaskan Natives as a serious problem."

Medina, Richard M., et al. 2018. "Geographies of Organized Hate in America: A Regional Analysis." *Annals of the American Association of Geographers* 108 (4): 1006–1021.

The authors attempt to determine whether geographical factors are involved in the number and types of hate groups functioning in the United States. They do discover that such factors exist and show how they are connected to several social and economic variables.

Perry, Barbara, and Ryan Schrivers. 2018. "A Climate for Hate? An Exploration of the Right-Wing Extremist Landscape in Canada." *Critical Criminology* 26 (2): 169–187.

This article is a report on a three-year study of the environmental, social, and other factors conducive to the founding and operation of hate groups in Canada.

Sainudiin, Raazesh, et al. 2019. "Characterizing the Twitter Network of Prominent Politicians and SPLC-defined Hate Groups in the 2016 US Presidential Election." *Social Network Analysis and Mining* 9 (1): 1–15. https://link.springer.com/article/10.1007/s13278-019-0567-9.

This study is designed to determine any connection that may exist among the number of Twitter messages sent, received, and forwarded by major figures in the 2016 Presidential election and hate groups associated with those Tweets. The authors conclude that "[t]aken together, these findings suggest that Trump may have indeed possessed unique appeal to individuals drawn to hateful ideologies; however, such individuals constituted a small fraction of the sampled population."

Shibuichi, Daiki. 2015. "Zaitokukai and the Problem with Hate Groups in Japan." *Asian Survey* 55 (4): 715–738.

The rise of the Zaitokukai hate group in Japan has been one of the most significant events in hate actions in the world. The author here asks what factors have led to this rise of hate groups, what individuals are involved in the process, and what their motivations might be. For a similar article, see Daiki Shibuichi. 2016. "The Struggle Against Hate Groups in Japan: The Invisible Civil Society, Leftist Elites and Anti-Racism Groups." *Social Science Japan Journal* 19 (1): 71–83.

Simi, Pete, et al. 2017. "Addicted to Hate: Identity Residual among Former White Supremacists." *American Sociological Review* 82 (6): 1167–1187. https://doi.org/10.1177/0003122417728719.

The authors interview eighty-nine former hate gang members to discover why they remain with those groups even when they had decided to abandon the groups. They conclude that the process of escaping from a hate group is similar in structure to the struggles drug addicts experience in their efforts to abandon the practice.

Sternberg, Robert J. 2018. "FLOTSAM: a Model for the Development and Transmission of Hate." *Journal of Theoretical Social Psychology* 2 (4): 97–106.

The author has developed a model for explaining how hate groups originate, develop, manifest themselves, and spread. The acronym stands for Fear, License, Obedience to authority, Trust, Sense of belonging to a valued group, Amplification of Arousal, and Modeling. For a more complete discussion of this concept, see the author's book, *Perspectives on Hate: How it Originates, Develops, Manifests, and Spreads*. 2020. Washington, DC: American Psychological Association.

Strain, Christopher B. 2013. "Evil Black Guns: Hate, Instrumentality, and the Neutrality of Firearms." *Journal of Hate Studies* 11 (1): 51–72. https://www.researchgate.net/publication/333006485_Evil_Black_Guns_Hate_Instrumentality_and_the_Neutrality_of_Firearms.

The author examines the complex question as to how the availability of guns, public attitudes toward their use, and the rise of hate groups in the 2010s and 2020s may be related with each other. He concludes that the present problem in the United States is especially difficult and troubling because of the country's liberal gun laws (Second Amendment rights) and its protection of free speech (First Amendment).

Tusikov, Natasha. 2019. "Defunding Hate: Paypal's Regulation of Hate Groups." *Surveillance and Society* 17 (1–2): 46–53.

After the Charlottesville, Virginia, riots of August 2017, the online pay system, PayPal, removed some groups it determined to be hate groups from its programs. The author applauds the company for taking such an action, but asks whether such decisions should be left to private organizations, which may not always be sensitive to deal with "complex social problems" such as hate groups.

Waltman, Michael S. 2018. "The Normalizing of Hate Speech and How Communication Educators Should Respond. Wicked Problems Forum: Freedom of Speech at Colleges and Universities." *Communication Education* 67 (2): 259–265. https://www.tandfonline.com/doi/pdf/10.1080/03634523.2018.1430370.

The author notes that hate speech is hardly a new phenomenon in American society. But he suggests that the extent to which it has recently become "normalized" should be an issue of concern to communications educators (and the general public). He outlines some suggestions for the ways in which college teachers can help students understand the nature and threats of hate speech.

Weir, Kirsten. 2018. "Dismantling Hate." *Monitor on Psychology* 49 (1): 42–48. https://www.apa.org/monitor/2018/01/dismantling-hate.

This article reviews some of the progress psychologists have made in identifying the factors that lead to violent actions by hate groups and, as a side effect, some techniques that might be used in reducing the risk of such actions.

Woolf, Linda M., and Michael R. Hulsizer. 2004. "Hate Groups for Dummies: How to Build a Successful Hate-Group." *Humanity & Society* 28 (1): 40–62. https://doi.org/10.1177/016059760402800105.

These two experienced researchers on hate groups describe the steps by which a hate group begins to form and grow.

Reports

"Audit of Anti-Semitic Incidents 2019." 2020 (date varies). ADL. https://www.adl.org/audit2019.

> Like the SPLC, ADL publishes annual reports on various aspects of hate groups and hate crimes. This publication includes information on harassment, vandalism, and assaults, along with basic data on these and other aspects of anti-Semitic incidents.

"Center for the Study of Hate and Extremism: Data & Reports." 2020. California State University, San Bernardino. https://www.csusb.edu/hate-and-extremism-center/data-reports.

> This web page is a rich source of information on reports about hate groups and hate crimes. It consists of links both to agencies and organizations outside the center, as well as listings of reports produced by the center itself. Among the latter are reports on an illustrated almanac and decade summary of hate and extremist incidents in the United States, hate crimes in Los Angeles and other major cities in the United States, and extremism in California.

"Hate Crime Statistics." 2020. Federal Bureau of Investigation. https://www.fbi.gov/services/cjis/ucr/hate-crime.

> This website is the gold standard for data on hate crimes in the United States. The page listed here provides a detailed background of the FBI's work in this area, along with a link to all previous hate crime reports from 1996 through 2018.

"Hate-free Philanthropy: Identifying Opportunities and Obstacles to Safeguard the Sector." 2020. Council on American Islamic Relations; Southern Poverty Law Center. https://www.cair.com/wp-content/uploads/2020/03/Hate-Free-Philanthropy.pdf.

> This document summarizes a meeting held in August 2019 among representatives from the Council on American Islamic Relations, SPLC, and the American Muslim

Fund to discuss issues relating to the funding of hate groups by philanthropic organizations. The conference examined mechanisms by which more efficient of funds-withholding can be encouraged and can occur among such groups in the United States.

"Hate Groups." 2020. CQ Researcher. https://library.cqpress.com/cqresearcher/toc.php?mode=cqres-topic&level=3&values=Social+Movements%7EHate+Groups.

CQ Researcher is a publisher of detailed reports on a range of topics of general interest. It produces forty-four such reports each year. Among the reports on hate groups have been the *Ku Klux Klan* (1946), *Terrorism and Hatemongering* (1958), *Hate Crimes* (1993), *Hate Groups* (2009), *"Alt-Right" Movement* (2017), *Anti-Semitism* (2017), and *European Union at a Crossroads* (2019).

"Hijacked by Hate: American Philanthropy and the Islamophobia Network." 2019. Council on American-Islamic Relations. http://www.islamophobia.org/images/IslamophobiaReport2019/CAIR_Islamophobia_Report_2019_Final_Web.pdf.

This report provides evidence that some charitable foundations are being used to funnel donations to anti-Muslim hate groups. The report explains how this process occurs and names the organizations that may be involved in the practice.

Marzullo, Michelle A., and Alyn J. Libman. 2009. "Research Overview: Hate Crimes and Violence against Lesbian, Gay, Bisexual and Transgender People." Human Rights Campaign. https://assets2.hrc.org/files/assets/resources/Hatecrimesandviolenceagainstlgbtpeople_2009.pdf.

The Human Rights Campaign monitors and reports on hate crimes against lesbians, gay men, bisexuals, transgenders, and queer people. This report is the most recent document available outlining current information on this topic. It includes the following sections: Federal

Legislative Efforts, Predictors of Bias and Sexual Prejudice, Hate Crime Responders and Reporting, Bias Crime Reporting, and Best Practices for Hate Crime Reporting.

"Murder and Extremism in the United States in 2019." 2019 (date varies) ADL. https://www.adl.org/media/14107/download.
  The ADL publishes an annual "Murder and Extremism in the United States" report that includes information about hate groups and hate crimes. The major sections of the reports cover the murders, the perpetrators, the incidents, and policy recommendations.

"A National Epidemic: Fatal Anti-transgender Violence in the United States in 2019." 2019. Human Rights Campaign. https://assets2.hrc.org/files/assets/resources/Anti-TransViolenceReport2019.pdf.
  This publication provides an excellent overview of the statistics relating to hate crimes against transgender and gender nonconforming individuals in the United States. The specific data provided includes chapters on demographics, law and policy data, safety data, and reporting and enforcement data. The report concludes with a section on steps that can be taken to deal with the issue of transgender hate crimes.

"Preliminary Report on Neo-fascist and Hate Groups." 1954/2015. Committee on Un-American Activities. U.S. House of Representatives. London: Forgotten Books. HathiTrust. https://babel.hathitrust.org/cgi/pt?id=uiug.30112039713216.
  This early report presents an intriguing insight into the way that the U.S. Congress was thinking about the possible overthrow of the United States government by neo-Nazi, Communist, and other hate groups working underground in the country.

"Ten Days After." 2016. Southern Poverty Law Center. https://www.splcenter.org/sites/default/files/com_hate_incidents_report_2017_update.pdf.

The alleged relationship between the election of Donald Trump to the Presidency of the United States and the validation of hate groups and their expanded activities in the country has been the subject of considerable research and debate among experts and ordinary citizens alike. This report attempted to measure any possible statistical connection between the two variables. It found and discussed 867 discrete cases of hate-inspired harassment in the ten days following Trump's election. The report reviews eight general types of hate crimes uncovered in the study.

"To Protect and Slur." 2019. Reveal. Center for Investigative Reporting. https://www.revealnews.org/topic/to-protect-and-slur/.

A study by the organization found that law enforcement officers at all levels throughout the United States have participated in hate group activities by way of social media. The report is said to have been responsible for more than fifty police departments having begun investigation of the problem among their own officers.

"The Trump Effect." 2016. Southern Poverty Law Center. https://www.splcenter.org/sites/default/files/the_trump_effect.pdf.

The SPLC conducted a broad survey of schools across the country to determine what effect, if any, the election of Donald Trump as president may have had on the school environment and pupils in terms of hate-related events. More than ten thousand responses were received in the survey.

"2018 Annual Report." 2019 (dates vary). Southern Poverty Law Center. https://www.splcenter.org/sites/default/files/splc-annual-report-2019.pdf.

The SPLC annually publishes a detailed report about the status of hate groups and hate crimes in the United States. Among the most important features of these reports are new data on the number, location, and types of hate groups, along with descriptions of specific groups. Other topics covered tend to be similar (or the same) from year to year. These topics include teaching tolerance, economic justice, immigrant justice, criminal justice reform, children's rights, and LGBTQ rights.

"White Supremacist Prison Gangs in the United States: A Preliminary Inventory." 2016. ADL. https://www.adl.org/sites/default/files/documents/assets/pdf/combating-hate/CR_4499_WhiteSupremacist-Report_web_vff.pdf.

A poorly studied aspect of hate groups has to do with the number, kind, and activity of such groups in prisons. This report provides a detailed summary of all known prison hate groups in thirty-six states and federal (Bureau of Prisons) facilities. The report also includes a good summary of the origins, ideology, subculture, and activities of prison hate groups.

Internet

Abdelkader, Engy. 2015. "'Savagery' in the Subways: Anti-Muslim Ads, the First Amendment, and the Efficacy of Counterspeech." *Asian American Law Journal* 21 (1) https://ssrn.com/abstract=2264791.

This articles discusses the issue of the First Amendment right of speech for hate groups versus the harm that such rights can have for targeted minorities. The author concludes that verbal efforts to counteract such hateful speech are not a perfect, but still a promising, way of dealing with this form of hate against minorities.

"Amalgamated Foundation Launches Hate Is Not Charitable Campaign." 2019. Amalgamated Bank. https://www.amalgamatedbank.com/news/amalgamated-foundation-launches-hate-not-charitable-campaign.

This press release describes the creation of a new campaign, called "Hate is Not Charitable." The goal of the campaign is to discourage philanthropic groups from providing support to agencies that the SPLC has designated as "hate groups." The press release lists more than eighty groups that have joined in the campaign.

"The 'Anti-Hate' Group That Is a Hate Group." 2019. The Philanthropy Roundtable. https://www.philanthropyroundtable.org/home/resources/videos/videos/default-source/default-video-library/the-anti-hate-group-that-is-a-hate-group.

Scholars of hate groups rely heavily on the SPLC for basic information on organizations that qualify for that designation. Yet, several individuals and organizations have raised doubts about the center's fairness and neutrality in making such decisions. This video explains the basis for the concern about the center's activities.

Bernd, Candice, and Jordan Buckley. 2018. "How Texas Colleges Have Responded to the Hate Groups Behind All Those Racist Flyers." *Texas Observer*. https://www.texasobserver.org/nazis-go-school-texas-colleges-responded-hate-groups-behind-racist-flyers/.

One of the flyers read, "Now that our man TRUMP is elected and republicans own both the senate and the house—time to organize tar & feather VIGILANTE SQUADS and go arrest & torture those deviant university leaders spouting off all this Diversity Garbage." It was one of the several posted on the campuses of Texas State University, Rice University, the University of Texas at Dallas, and other state colleges and universities. This article explores the origin of those flyers and the response to their postings by administration, faculty, and students at several of the institutions involved.

Bohanon, Maria. 2019. "Universities Take Steps to Remain Vigilant of Hate Groups on Campus." Insight into Diversity. https://www.insightintodiversity.com/universities-take-steps-to-remain-vigilant-of-hate-groups-on-campus/.

This article focuses on the challenges facing colleges and universities by hate group speech on their campuses. Bohanon discusses some methods by which those institutions can deal with the problem in a manner that protects the groups' First Amendment rights of free speech.

Carter, Mike. 2017. "Resurgent Hate Groups Have Long History in Washington State, Northwest." *The Seattle Times*. https://www.seattletimes.com/seattle-news/crime/resurgent-hate-groups-have-long-history-in-washington-state-northwest/.

This article provides an interesting review of the long history of hate groups in one region of the country.

Clemmitt, Marcia. 2017. "'Alt-Right' Movement: Do its White-nationalist Views Have Wide Support?" *CQ Researcher* 27 (11). https://library.cqpress.com/cqresearcher/document.php?id=cqresrre2017031700.

This excellent report on the alt-right movement covers all basic aspects of the campaign. It concludes that it is too early to tell how wide the support is for this movement, but that its greatest strengths currently lie in the use of the Internet and social media to advertise its programs.

Cooney, Rosanna. 2018. "White, Male and Millennial: Hate Groups Tap Bro Culture to Recruit Members." The Center for Public Integrity. https://publicintegrity.org/politics/white-male-and-millennial-hate-groups-tap-bro-culture-to-recruit-members/.

This article discusses the changing face of hate groups in the United States, with trends toward the group of men described in the title. The greater part of the article is devoted to lengthy interviews with representatives of two such groups, Proud Boys and Identity Evropa.

Coren, Michael J. 2017. "A Complete List of Brands White Supremacists Have Given Their Unwanted Endorsement." Quartz. https://qz.com/1137806/a-complete-list-of-brands-white-supremacists-have-given-their-unwanted-endorsement/.

Alt-right groups sometimes adopt a connection with an otherwise legitimate, mainstream product or organization. The purpose of the practice is to gain legitimacy for the alt-right group. Some examples of this practice in the past have been unsolicited connections of such groups with Papa John Pizza, Taylor Swift, Tiki torches, and Pepe the Frog books.

Crockett, Zachary. 2016. "Most of America's Hate Groups Are Rooted in White Supremacy." *Vox*. https://www.vox.com/identities/2016/12/16/13861912/white-supremacist-groups-alt-right.

Discussions about hate groups often divide that overall category into smaller subgroups, such as anti-LGBTQ, anti-Muslim, neo-Nazi, and male supremacists. This article suggests that the majority of hate groups identified by the SPLC can be classified as white supremacist groups. The article defines each of the subgroups in this category, such as the Ku Klux Klan, neo-Nazis, neo-Confederate, and skinheads, shows where they tend to be located, and how their popularity has varied over time.

DeBruin, Claire. 2019. "Right-Wing Extremism in the United States." IdeaExchange@UAkron. https://ideaexchange.uakron.edu/cgi/viewcontent.cgi?article=2024&context=honors_research_projects.

The author attempts to explain how the number of hate groups and hate crimes has increased over the last decade, and what role the election of Donald Trump as president may have had in that trend. She concludes that available data "clearly demonstrat[e] the correlation between the President of the United States and the number of hate groups."

Desmond-Harris, Jenée. 2016. "How Journalists Are Shaping the Way Americans Understand Contemporary White Nationalism." *Vox*. https://www.vox.com/identities/2016/12/7/13826074/alt-right-white-nationalism-new-york-times-associated-press.

Words matter. They matter a lot when talking about hate groups. This excellent article explores the current problems about the use of terms such as *alt-right, nativism, white nationalism* in discussions about hate groups.

Eakin, Britain. 2017. "ACLU Won't Defend Hate Groups That Protest with Firearms." Courthouse News Service. https://www.courthousenews.com/aclu-wont-defend-hate-groups-protest-firearms/.

Following the riots at Charlottesville, Virginia, in August 2017, the ACLU decided to amend its long-held policy of defending hate groups' First Amendment right of free speech for those groups that choose to use firearms in their protests. For more background, see Farmer 2019.

Eddington, Sean M. 2018. "The Communicative Constitution of Hate Organizations Online: A Semantic Network Analysis of 'Make America Great Again.'" *Social Media and Society* 4 (3). https://doi.org/10.1177/2056305118790763.

The author explores the semantic connections that developed during the 2016 presidential campaign between Donald Trump's "Make America Great Again" campaign and the goals and beliefs over hate groups in the United States. He shows that the former became a constructive force in the rise and greater visibility and acceptance of the latter.

Farmer, Brit McCandless. 2019. "Why the ACLU Defends White Nationalists' Free Speech." 60 Overtime. https://www.cbsnews.com/news/why-the-aclu-defends-white-nationalist-free-speech-60-minutes

A companion piece to a 60 Minutes program on the ACLU's policy of defending hate groups, this article delves into the long history of that policy, as well as reasons for its origin and continued practice. Also see, Eakin 2017 for a change in this policy.

Fleetwood, Blake. 2020. AJC. Atlanta. News. Now. https://www.ajc.com/news/opinion/opinions-rights-hate-groups-deserve-protection-too/qCJqsqtLOdW5nhPrMLa9dN/.

> This opinion piece explains why groups like those that protested in Charlottesville in 2017 should not be prosecuted or criticized for their speech and actions because such activities are protected under the First Amendment of the U.S. Constitution.

Fording, Richard C., and John M. Cotter. 2014. "The Political Origins of Extremism: Minority Descriptive Representation and the Mobilization of American Hate Groups." *SSRN Electronic Journal*. http://doi.org/10.2139/ssrn.2487603.

> The authors review some existing theories as to the rise of hate groups in the early 2010s. They then offer their own explanation for the phenomenon, namely, that "white hate groups are best understood as a political movement, and that recent trends in white hate group activity can, to a large extent, be explained by contemporary changes in the political environment." Specifically, such groups are most likely to develop "when conventional political channels are perceived by racist extremists as ineffective at advancing their pro-white agenda."

"Former Alt-right Member Wants to Prevent Others from Joining These Hate Groups." 2019. YouTube. https://www.youtube.com/watch?v=PVQHKvAUS3E.

> This video presents an interview with a young woman who was formerly a member of a hate group, speaking about her experiences with the group and her reasons for leaving it.

Gerster, Jane. 2019. "The RCMP Was Created to Control Indigenous People. Can That Relationship Be Reset?" *Global News*. https://globalnews.ca/news/5381480/rcmp-indigenous-relationship/.

This interesting article draws some parallels between the way Indigenous people were treated by government forces in the United States and Canada during the formative years of both nations. The record suggests that, in both bases, those forces acted in ways that today might easily be called "hate groups."

Goldstein, Steve. 2020. "New Publication The Informant Focuses Hate Groups, Extremism In America." *KJZZ*. https://kjzz.org/content/1398271/new-publication-informant-focuses-hate-groups-extremism-america.

This news article introduces a new anti–hate group publication called *The Informant*. It includes a short interview with its founder as well as a link to the publication itself (https://www.informant.news/).

"Got Banned for Telling People to Stop Supporting Black Hate Groups." 2020. Reddit. https://www.reddit.com/r/WatchRedditDie/comments/gj25xg/got_banned_for_telling_people_to_stop_supporting/.

The debate continues as to what types of hate speech are covered by the First Amendment and which should be allowed to remain because of that protection. This website illustrates the decisions that one important online website has made about the use of hate speech on its platform.

Hall, Stephen. 2020. "Extremist Groups and Militias Are Using Protests to Take Aggressive Steps Toward Violence." *Ark Valley Voice*. https://arkvalleyvoice.com/extremist-groups-and-militias-are-using-protests-to-take-aggressive-steps-toward-violence/.

This report describes the involvement of hate groups in protests in favor of the reopening of certain parts of society during the new coronavirus pandemic.

"Hate Groups." 2020a. LGBTQ Nation. https://www.lgbtqnation.com/tag/hate-groups/.

This website provides links to news stories relating to the activities of anti-LGBTQ hate groups.

"Hate Groups." 2020b. Vice. https://www.vice.com/en_us/topic/hate-groups.

This website consists of news stories from a large variety of sources on the topic of hate groups. A good source for current information on the topic.

Holt, Thomas, Joshua D. Freilich, and Steven Chermak. 2017. "Can Taking Down Websites Really Stop Terrorists and Hate Groups?" *The Conversation.* https://theconversation.com/can-taking-down-websites-really-stop-terrorists-and-hate-groups-84023.

In September 2017, President Donald Trump recommended that hate groups be deprived of their use of the Internet to reduce their ability to deliver their message to actual and possible members, as well as the general public. The three experts in this discussion explain why such efforts are likely to be ineffective in achieving this goal and may, in fact, actually improve the ability of hate groups to get their messages out on the Internet.

Johnson, N. F., et al. 2019. "Hidden Resilience and Adaptive Dynamics of the Global Online Hate Ecology. *Nature* 573: 261–265. https://doi.org/10.1038/s41586-019-1494-7.

The study reported here involved an examination of the connections among hate groups worldwide. Researchers concluded that the Internet and social media made possible strong and active interactions among groups worldwide, and efforts so far to monitor or restrict in one area only increased their eventual successes in other areas. They say that this information provides some clues as to how the restriction of hate groups can be done more effectively in the future.

Jolly, Rajdeep, and Daryl Johnson. 2019. "Perspective: Don't Censor and De-platform Hate Groups—Monitor Them." *Homeland Security Today*. https://www.hstoday.us/subject-matter-areas/counterterrorism/perspective-dont-censor-and-de-platform-hate-groups-monitor-them/.

    These two writers argue that it will be counterproductive to try to remove hate groups from the Internet and social media because such actions will only drive them underground and make them more difficult to monitor.

Kotch, Alex. 2020. "Koch-Favored Donors Trust Keeps Funding Anti-Muslim and Anti-LGBTQ Hate Groups." *PRWatch*. https://www.prwatch.org/news/2020/01/13529/koch-favored-donorstrust-keeps-funding-anti-muslim-and-anti-lgbtq-hate-groups.

    An important issue in the discussion of hate groups is how these organizations are funded. Several researchers have attempted to discover possible links between various charitable organizations and groups designated as "hate groups" by the SPLC. This article summarizes the most recent information available on this topic.

Kunzelman, Michael. 2020. AP. "Virus Restrictions Fuel Anti-government 'Boogaloo' Movement." https://apnews.com/3783a0cdc0e6cc04b43fd28b6069e960.

    The author reviews actions taken by a specific hate group, Boogaloo, to use the coronavirus to advance its own hate-related agenda.

Laub, Zachary. 2019. "Hate Speech on Social Media: Global Comparisons." Council on Foreign Relations. https://www.cfr.org/backgrounder/hate-speech-social-media-global-comparisons.

    This article reviews the question as to when hate speech should and should not be allowed on social media sites and how countries around the world are dealing with that issue.

Levin, Brian. 2019. "Why White Supremacist Attacks Are on the Rise, Even in Surprising Places." *Time*. https://time.com/5555396/white-supremacist-attacks-rise-new-zealand/.

    Levin is the director of the prestigious Center for the Study of Hate and Extremism at California State University, San Bernardino. He summarizes the center's current research on the topic of this article, drawing special attention to the role that the election of Donald Trump has had in the changes described here.

Lewis, Danny. 2017. "How Hate Groups Recruit Online." WNYC. https://www.wnyc.org/story/how-hate-groups-recruit-online/.

    This short podcast provides an interview with Alice Marwick, an expert in the field of hate groups, discussing the techniques that hate groups use to recruit new members online and why these techniques tend to be successful.

Margolin, Josh. 2020. "White Supremacists Encouraging Their Members to Spread Coronavirus to Cops, Jews, FBI Says." *ABC News*. https://abcnews.go.com/US/white-supremacists-encouraging-members-spread-coronavirus-cops-jews/story?id=69737522.

    This article reveals a report sent by the FBI to local police agencies, warning that extremist groups were encouraging members to try to infect Jews, police, and other minority groups with the new coronavirus.

McKinney, Maureen Foertsch. 2020. "Stay-At-Home Protests Draw Extremists Groups, Anti-Hate Group Says." *NPR Illinois*. https://www.nprillinois.org/post/stay-home-protests-draw-extremists-groups-anti-hate-group-says.

    This article explores the current argument that hate groups are using the anti-stay-at-home movement to publicize and promote their own programs of hate against various minority groups.

Mulholland, Sean E. 2011. "Hate Source: White Supremacist Hate Groups and Hate Crime." *SSRN Electronic Journal.* https://papers.ssrn.com/sol3/papers.cfm?abstract_id=1760825.

    Researchers continue to be interested in the question as to how or to what extent hate groups are associated with hate crimes. Do groups encourage the number of crimes committed or do they serve as an outlet for members' concern and anger about minority groups. In this study, the author concludes that the presence of a hate group in a county accounts for an increase of 19.1 percent in hate crimes committed within that county.

Napoliello, Alex. 2020. "Feds: White Supremacists Using the Coronavirus Pandemic to Spread Hate." *Officer.* https://www.officer.com/on-the-street/news/21131024/feds-white-supremacists-using-the-coronavirus-pandemic-to-spread-hate.

    This article describes ways in which hate groups are making use of the coronavirus pandemic to stoke fear among minority groups, especially Jews and police officers. Also see Magolin 2020 for source document information.

Ouelleete, Jennifer. 2020. "The COVID-19 Misinformation Crisis Is Just Beginning, but There Is Hope." *Ars Technica.* https://arstechnica.com/science/2020/05/the-covid-19-misinformation-crisis-is-just-beginning-but-there-is-hope/.

    The emergence of the coronavirus pandemic of 2020 and the corresponding need for a vaccine for the disease has raised questions about the antivaccination movement in the United States. Some researchers are seeing interesting connections between the way antivaccinators and hate groups use social media and the Internet to get their messages out. The author asks how this association may affect the nation's future campaign to control the virus.

Pan, J. C. 2018. "Alternate History: The Tradition of Conspiracy Theories and Hate Groups Behind the Alt-right." *The New*

Republic 249 (3): 60. https://newrepublic.com/article/146916
/alternative-history.
 This review of David Neiwert's new book, *Alt-Right: The Rise of the Radical Right in the Age of Trump*, provides an excellent overview of this phenomenon in the United States since 2016. Also see the Neiwert reference in "Books."

Potok, Mark. 2017. "The Radical Right Was More Successful in Entering the Political Mainstream Last Year than in Half a Century. How Did It Happen?" Intelligence Report. Southern Poverty Law Center. https://www.splcenter.org/fighting-hate/intelligence-report/2017/year-hate-and-extremism.
 This article attempts to provide evidence for the role of President Donald Trump in the significant growth in hate groups as a result of his election and during his first year in office.

Reid, Shannon, and Matthew Valasik. 2020. "Why Are White Supremacists Protesting to 'Reopen' the US Economy?" The Conversation. https://theconversation.com/why-are-white-supremacists-protesting-to-reopen-the-us-economy-137044.
 The authors discuss possible reasons that hate groups are actively involved in the perhaps surprising protect against sheltering-in-place policies against the coronavirus pandemic of 2020.

"Responding to Hate Crimes." n.d. International Association of Chiefs of Police. https://www.theiacp.org/sites/default/files/2019-01/IACP-Hate_Crimes_Brochure.pdf.
 This brochure was published for use by law enforcement officers about appropriate ways of dealing hate crimes. It deals with differences between a hate crime and a hate incident, the most effective way of responding to hate crimes, the key indicators that a hate crime may have been

committed, the best ways of dealing with victims of hate crimes, and the ongoing role of police officers in working with victims and the community in general.

"The Roots of Racism and Hate Groups." 2017. Radio Times. WHYY. https://whyy.org/episodes/roots-racism-hate-groups/.
    This podcast is a discussion about the Charlottesville, Virginia, riot of August 2017 involving A.C. Thompson, a reporter for *ProPublica*, Washington University sociologist David Cunningham, and former white supremacist Christian Piccolini.

Sexton, Joe. 2019. "He Spent Years Infiltrating White Supremacist Groups. Here's What He Has to Say about What's Going on Now." *ProPublica*. https://www.propublica.org/article/he-spent-years-infiltrating-white-supremacist-groups-heres-what-he-has-to-say-about-whats-going-on-now.
    The title of the article says it all.

Singer-Emergy, Jacques, and Rex Bray, III. 2020. "The Iron March Data Dump Provides a Window into How White Supremacists Communicate and Recruit." *Lawfare*. https://www.lawfareblog.com/iron-march-data-dump-provides-window-how-white-supremacists-communicate-and-recruit.
    This detailed study of the online activities of the hate group Iron March (as well as the activities of its successor live group, Atomwaffen Division) shows how the Internet can be used as a powerful recruiting device for hate groups of their kind.

"The Southern Poverty Law Center (SPLC) and Its So-Called "Hate Groups." 2012. Family Research Council. https://downloads.frc.org/EF/EF12I53.pdf.
    One of the organizations named as a "hate group" by the SPLC explains why it believes that designation is wrong and improper.

Spies, Mike. 2015. "A Former Neo-Nazi on What Hate Groups See in Guns." *The Trace*. https://www.thetrace.org/2015/08/neo-nazi-hate-groups-guns-white-supremacists-extremists-skinheads/.

    This interview provides a look into the way that at least some hate groups view the importance and role of weapons in their work.

Stewart, Robert. 2020. "Firing over Mosque Tweet Merits Reflection on "Hate-Watch" Groups, Not Hate Speech." National Opinion Centre. https://www.nationalnewswatch.com/2020/05/12/firing-over-mosque-tweet-merits-reflection-on-hate-watch-groups-not-hate-speech.

    This article by a Toronto restaurant owner and politician explains the problems he has with the SPLC, and its Canadian partner, the Canadian Anti-Hate Network. An excellent overview of similar complaints about the objectivity and reliability of SPLC's work. A response from the Canadian Anti-Hate Network is included on the web page.

Stiffman, Eden. 2016. "Dozens of 'Hate Groups' Have Charity Status, *Chronicle* Study Finds." *The Chronicle of Philanthropy*. https://www.philanthropy.com/article/Dozens-of-Hate-Groups-/238748.

    The U.S. Internal Revenue Service has the practical problem of deciding when the speech of a supposed hate group if protected by the First Amendment and when it is "hate speech." That decision is a major factor in determining whether the organization can get "tax-free" status. The *Chronicle* found that fifty-five groups currently listed as hate groups by the SPLC have been given that status. That list of groups is included in this article.

Stone, Jeff. 2020. "Facebook Scrubbed Accounts Related to Qanon and a Designated Hate Group in April." *Cyberscoop*. https://www.cyberscoop.com/qanon-facebook-removal-vdare/.

This article provides a fascinating, in-depth explanation of Facebook's actions against two organizations that it believed to be hate groups.

Tolan, Casey. 2019. "Should We Police Online Hate Groups?" *Daily Democrat.* https://www.dailydemocrat.com/2019/09/01/white-nationalism-domestic-terrorism-social-media-presidential-candidates-beto-orourke/.

This article reviews some of the basic questions involved in the debate over First Amendment rights and hate group postings on the Internet and social media.

"An Update on Combating Hate and Dangerous Organizations." 2020. Facebook. https://about.fb.com/news/2020/05/combating-hate-and-dangerous-organizations/.

This web page explains Facebook's policies on the monitoring of groups it believes to be "hate and dangerous organizations."

Waqas, Ahmed, et al. 2019. "Mapping Online Hate: A Scientometric Analysis on Research Trends and Hotspots in Research on Online Hate." *PloS One* 14 (9): e0222194. https://journals.plos.org/plosone/article?id=10.1371/journal.pone.0222194.

The authors attempt to categorize the kind, distribution, and frequency of online hate presentations. They note that such programs occur most commonly in developed nations, especially in the United States and Europe, and that the number of hate publications available online has increased from about 50 in 2005 to more than 550 in 2018.

Ware, Jacob. 2019. "Siege: The Atomwaffen Division and Rising Far-Right Terrorism in the United States." International Centre for Counter-Terrorism. https://icct.nl/wp-content/uploads/2019/07/ICCT-Ware-Siege-July2019.pdf.

This article discusses a relatively small international hate group, active primarily in the United States, Atomwaffen.

The author calls the group "The Violent Face of American Neo-Nazism."

Watkins, Ali, and Josh Meyer. 2017. "Domestic Hate Groups Elude Feds." *Politico*. https://www.politico.com/story/2017/08/15/us-hate-groups-legal-protections-241653.

    The FBI and other state, local, and national law enforcement organizations often have their hands tied in the tools they can use to act against hate and other extremist groups. This article reviews what some of those problems are in dealing with hate groups.

Yahagi, Ken. 2019. "The Effects of Hate Groups on Hate Crimes." *Review of Law & Economics* 15 (3). https://doi.org/10.1515/rle-2017-0035.

    The author proposes a model to explain the connections (if any) between hate groups and hate crimes. He suggests that this model is consistent with recent empirical research on the topic.

Yarmouth, Aaron. 2020. "Implausible Deniability is GOP's MO." *Leo Weekly*. https://www.leoweekly.com/2020/05/implausible-deniability-gops-mo/.

    This columnist comments on the presence of a Kentucky state legislator at a rally also attended by hate groups, whose presence, she said, she was not aware of.

7 Chronology

Introduction

If one accepts the concept of state-sponsored and religious sect-sponsored hate groups, the number of items in this chronology could begin to approach infinity. For that reason, only a select group of such events are included here. Beyond those items, a larger number of specific events associated with the founding, operation, dissolution, and other activities of groups generally accepted as hate oriented are listed here. The author follows the generally accepted practice of using groups designated by the Anti-Defamation League (ADL) or the Southern Poverty Law Center (SPLC) as meeting the criteria of hate groups for the events listed here.

Some dates, especially those from earlier times, may be approximate and subject to controversy. Some events themselves have also been questioned as to their historical accuracy, or even the occurrence of the events themselves. The history of anti-Semitism is very long and complex. This chapter contains only a sample of events that fall under this category.

ca. 1200 BCE   In a tale with many uncertainties and disagreements among experts, the Jews are said to have been expelled from Egypt because they are "diseased" (leprosy) and unwanted

---

Members of the Right Wing Death Squad walk down Market Street in Charlottesville, Virginia on August 12, 2017. (Patrick Morrissey/Dreamstime.com)

in the country. One version of the story is told in the Book of Exodus in the Bible.

139 BCE According to some authorities and sources, Jews are expelled from Rome for proselytizing. This explanation is questioned by some authorities, and the presence of Jews there is also a matter of debate. The most important point about this event is that the story (and related stories) has become so fixed in the history of the Jewish people. Stories of the expulsion of Jews and Rome are also repeated, with more authority, in 19 CE by Emperor Tiberius and about 50 CE by Emperor Claudius. One recurring theme in these expulsions is the Roman view that Jews are "unfit" to live in the empire.

38 CE In one of the earliest known pograms, riots are held against the Jewish citizens of Alexandria (Egypt) because of their supposed lack of loyalty to the Roman emperor. Many Jews are killed in the riots, and survivors are restricted to a limited zone in the city.

613 CE Visigoth King Sisebut exiles all Jews from the portion of Iberia over which he reigns, excluding only those Jews who convert to Christianity.

1524–1525 One of the deadliest of all so-called religious wars in Europe in the sixteenth through eighteenth centuries, the German Peasants' War was a revolt by an extreme wing of Protestantism against the dominant Catholic Church. The death toll is thought to have exceeded one hundred thousand, the worst such event prior to the French Revolution of 1789.

1618–1648 The period covered by the Thirty Years War instigated by efforts to abolish and destroy Protestant sects that were growing in popularity. (The forces driving the conflict soon became much more complicated.) Experts place the number of deaths somewhere between three million and 11.5 million.

1782 Captain David Williamson of the Delaware militia orders his troops to bring members of the Delaware Indian tribe to a cooper shop where they are slaughtered two at a time. The event is now called *The Gnadenhutten Massacre*. It has been described by historians as an example of colonists "growing contempt for native people" (https://www.history.com/news/native-americans-genocide-united-states).

1794 English scholar Richard Brothers publishes a book *A Revealed Knowledge of the Prophecy and Times* in which he argues that residents of northern Europe and Great Britain are descendants of the lost tribes of Israel and the only correct leaders of government. That philosophy has continued to be influential among some hate groups ever since. Today, those groups are generally known as *Christian identity* groups. (Brothers was later committed to an insane asylum, where he spent the rest of his life.)

1830 The Indian Removal Bill authorizes the forced transfer of more than three dozen Indian tribes in the eastern United States to more distant central parts of the country. President Andrew Jackson explains the action by noting that "they have neither the intelligence, the industry, the moral habits, nor the desire of improvement which are essential to any favorable change in their condition. Established in the midst of another and a superior race, and without appreciating the causes of their inferiority or seeking to control them, they must necessarily yield to the force of circumstances and ere long disappear" (https://www.presidency.ucsb.edu/documents/fifth-annual-message-2).

The actual transfer of the tribes is now memorialized by the name of "The Trail of Tears."

1838 Missouri governor Lilburn Boggs issues Missouri Executive Order 44 against the state's Mormon population. The order declares that "the Mormons must be treated as enemies, and must be exterminated or driven from the State if necessary for the public peace—their outrages are beyond all description" (https://archive.org/details/factsrelativetoe00gree/page/n4/mode/2up). The order, also known as the Extermination Order, was issued in the midst of an ongoing battle with and violence against the small population of Mormons residing in the state. A rescission of that order was published by Missouri governor Kit Bond on June 25, 1976.

1843 A group of anti-Catholic, anti-immigrant form a new political party in the state of New York, the American Republic Party. The party agitated against both voters and office-holders of these persuasions. The party was very successful in local elections in New York City and Philadelphia in 1844. At that point, the party held a national convention, at which it changed its name to the American Native Party. In 1849, it changed its name once more to the American Party.

1849 The American Party (see **1843**) reconstitutes itself as the Order of the Star Spangled Banner. The party is open only to white, native-born Americans and creates a complex web of secret ceremonies. The party later becomes more commonly known as the Know Nothing Party.

1860 After substantial successes in the elections of 1854 and 1856, the Know Nothing Party suffers dramatic loses in the national elections of 1858 and 1860. By 1860, most members of the party had migrated to the new Republican Party or the Constitutional Union Party, and the Know Nothings were considered to have disbanded as a national party.

1864 Seven hundred troops under the command of Methodist minister and U.S. colonel John Chivington massacre about 160 members of the Cheyenne and Arapahoe tribes, mostly women and children at the Sand Creek Massacre.

1865 A group of former Confederate army veterans meets in Pulaski, Tennessee, to form a new social club, to be called the Ku Klux Klan (KKK).

1866 A riot breaks out in New Orleans when white law enforcement officials attack largely Black members of the

Louisiana Constitutional Convention. About 150 Blacks are injured, 44 of whom are killed.

1867–1871 The U.S. Congress passes a series of laws generally known as the Reconstruction Acts of 1867, 1868, and 1871. The legislation was designed to ensure that freed slaves would be granted and would receive the same rights and privileges of all citizens of the United States. The acts were never fully accepted by most white legislators and citizens of the South, and a broad-ranging program of discrimination against Blacks developed that was never fully addressed until the adoption of the Civil Rights Act of 1960.

1869 A federal ground jury declares the KKK to be a "terrorist organization."

1872 The U.S. Congress releases a report, "Report of the Joint Select Committee Appointed to Inquire into the Condition of Affairs in the Late Insurrectionary States, So Far as Regards the Execution of Laws, and the Safety of the Lives and Property of the Citizens of the United States and Testimony Taken," which includes extensive testimony on the activities of the Klan. In fact, the report is sometimes referred to as the "KKK Testimony."

ca. 1872 Aggressive actions by federal agencies concerning the actions of the KKK gradually have the effect of putting the organization out of business.

1886 Black minister Frank S. Cherry announces that he has had a revelation declaring African Americans to be the legitimate descendants of the twelve tribes of Israel. Cherry's announcement eventually became the founding philosophy of a long history of religious organizations based on that belief, the largest of which today is the Nations of Yahweh (Also see **1979**).

1890 Members of the U.S. Army's Seventh Cavalry massacre between 150 and 200 members of the Indian Ghost Dance spiritual movement at Wounded Knee, South Dakota.

1913 The Anti-Defamation League (ADL) is formed in response to a troubling increase in the number and severity of hate crimes against Jews.

1915 Failed physician and teacher, William Joseph Simmons, along with fifteen other "charter members" founds a new version of the KKK at Stone Mountain, Georgia. The rebirth of the organization has been credited to the appearance of a widely popular book on the earlier Klan, *The Clansman: A Historical Romance of the Ku Klux Klan* in 1905, and the very successful motion picture, "Birth of a Nation," in 1915.

1920s At the height of its influence, the KKK is estimated to have between four and six million members.

1921 White rioters in the city of Tulsa, Oklahoma, attacked predominantly Black residents of the Greenwood region of the city, home to one of the most prosperous Black neighborhoods in the United States. Estimates of deaths range as high as three hundred, with an estimated thirty-five blocks of homes and businesses also having been destroyed. The massacre has been described as the worst race-related event in the history of the nation.

1928 The KKK sues a former member of the organization for attempting to convince other active members to leave the organization, thus depriving it of an important source of funding. The court rules against the Klan noting that its activities do not in the least conform to its stated mission of carrying out beneficial social programs for its members.

1930 Wallace D. Fard Muhammad founds the Nation of Islam, a group whose purpose it is to improve the spiritual, mental, social, and economic condition of African Americans. The group continues to exist today.

1933 The German government establishes its first concentration camp outside the town of Dachau. The camp remains in existence for almost a decade. It is used for the incarceration of Jews, Roma (gypsies), homosexuals, political prisoners, and other "enemies of the state."

1933 The German government begins to adopt a series of laws that gradually exclude Jews (and some other "inferior" individuals) from all civic rights, including the right to vote, to own property, to teach, and to practice several professional occupations.

1938 An evening of violence by German troops against the Jewish population in Berlin, the so-called *Kristallnacht*, results in about ninety-one deaths, thirty thousand arrests, and the destruction of nine hundred synagogues and seven thousand Jewish businesses.

ca. 1940 The period known as Holocaust begins, a time during which Jews, Roma, criminals, homosexuals, and other "undesirables" were sent to concentration camps, where they usually were killed. An estimated six million individuals died by the end of World War II in Europe in 1945.

1954 The U.S. House of Representatives Committee on Unamerican Activities produces the "Preliminary Report on Neo-Fascist and Hate Groups." The report focuses especially on two groups, the National Renaissance Party and the newspaper *Common Sense*. The committee concludes that the two forces represent a threat to American democracy "from the extreme right." The report is available online at http://debs.indstate.edu/u588n4_1954.pdf.

1958 American businessman Robert W. Welch Jr. founds the John Birch Society in Indianapolis, Indiana. It soon became an important part of the Republican Party, opposing many of the progressive programs advocated and sometimes adopted by the federal government, most importantly perhaps, the Civil Rights Act of 1960 and related legislation.

1968 The U. S. Congress passes the first hate law in the country's history as an amendment to the Civil Rights Act of 1960.

The law criminalizes any acts of violence against a person on the basis of his or her race, color, religion, or national origin.

1969 In the case *Brandenburg v. Ohio* (395 U.S. 444), the U.S. Supreme Court rules that inflammatory speech cannot be punished by the law unless it is "directed to inciting or producing imminent lawless action and is likely to incite or produce such action." The action was brought as the result of a KKK rally held in rural Ohio, at which Klan members made threats against African Americans, Jews, and other groups that supported them.

1971 Alabama attorneys Morris Dees and Joe Levin combine to form the Southern Poverty Law Center (SPLC), specializing in civil rights law.

1971 Two Christian identity leaders in Oregon, William Potter Gale and Henry Lamont Beach, form groups called Posse Comitatus. The organization is only the most recent of a long line of similar groups that claim white Christians to be the only group with legal authority in a country, and that that authority resided in government at the country level. Most of the groups with this name are strongly anti-Jewish and anti-Black (For more details about this movement, see Kathy Marks. 1996. *Faces of Right Wing Extremism*. Boston Branden Publishing Company, 83–87).

1977 The Aryan Nations hate group is founded in Chillicothe, Ohio to promote a racist and anti-Semitic program. The group was disbanded in 2010.

1978 In the case of *Collin v. Smith* (578 F.2d 1197), the court ruled that the village of Skokie, Illinois could not prevent a group of neo-Nazis from parading through town wearing Nazi uniforms and carrying Nazi signs. It further ruled that town ordinance against such actions were unconstitutional under the First Amendment free speech provisions of the U.S. Constitution.

1979 Miami Black minister Hulon Mitchell Jr. (also known as Yahweh ben Yahweh) founds the Nation of Yahweh, an offshoot of the century-old Black Hebrew Israelite movement (also see **1886**).

1981 SPLC begins monitoring and reporting on the activities of the KKK.

1983 The Family Research Council (FRC) is founded in Washington, D.C. The organization was listed as a hate group in 2010 by the SPLC because of its negative comments about LGBTQ individuals. That listing produced a strong reaction from the FRC, a difference of opinion that remains today between the two organizations. See more on this topic at https://www.foxnews.com/politics/family-research-council-demands-apology-over-hate-group-label.

1985 The Center for Immigration Studies (CIS) is founded in Washington, D.C. The organization is listed as a hate group by SPLC in 2016, a designation to which CIS strongly objects, claiming that it is a legitimate scholarly institution interested in the study of immigration policy and activities. In 2019, CIS sued SPLC for this listing, a case that was thrown out of court before it could be heard.

1988 A group known as the Hammerskin Nation (also, just Hammerskins) is founded in Dallas, Texas, with the original name of the Confederate Hammerskins. The group was especially interested in racist and hate music. Since its founding, the group has broken into a number of new, but related, organizations, such as the Eastern Hammerskins, Northern Hammerskins, Outlaw Hammerskins, and Arizona Hammerskins. The ADL classifies the Hammerskins as "most violent and best-organized neo-Nazi skinhead group in the United States" (https://www.adl.org/education/resources/profiles/hammerskin-nation).

1990 The U.S. Congress passes the Hate Crime Statistics Act (28 U.S. Code 534), authorizing the Federal Bureau of Investigation to begin collecting data and statistics on the occurrence of hate crimes in the United States. The Bureau publishes the first such report in 1996.

1990 The SPLC begins tracking hate groups in the United States. In the first year of its work in the field, the Center lists twenty-eight groups associated with the KKK, the only group monitored at the time.

1992 In the case of *R.A.V. v. St. Paul* (505 U.S. 377), the U.S. Supreme Court ruled that an ordinance adopted by the city of St. Paul, Minnesota banning hate symbols such as burning a cross or exhibiting a swastika was unconstitutional because it violated an individual or group's right of free speech under the U.S. Constitution.

1992 The American Border Patrol is founded in Sierra Vista, Arizona, largely for opposing and acting against illegal immigration from Mexico to the United States. The group was designated as a hate group by SPLC in 2014.

1994 The Alliance Defending Freedom for Faith and Justice is founded in Scottsdale, Arizona. The group has been labeled an "anti-LGBTQ hate group" because of its efforts to recriminalize same-sex acts and to promote other anti-LGBTQ legislation and activities in the United States and worldwide.

1994 The Violent Crime Control and Law Enforcement Act establishes certain standards for the sentencing of individuals convicted of hate crimes in the United States.

1994 American historian and author Thomas Ernest Woods Jr. founds the League of the South.

1995 Former Gulf War veteran Timothy McVeigh commits the deadliest act of domestic terrorism in the United States prior to September 11, 2001 when he sets off explosives that kill 168 people at the Alfred P. Murrah Federal Building in Oklahoma City. Nearly seven hundred more people are injured in the attack. The attack came as a protest against U.S. domestic and foreign policy. McVeigh is put to death in 2001.

1996 Adopted largely in response to a series of arson crimes against mostly Black churches in the South, the Church Arson

Prevention Act (P.L. 104-155) provides definitions of such acts and the penalties to be applied for them.

1996 Said to be the largest of today's existing KKK groups, the Brotherhood of Klans (BOK) is formed in Marion, Ohio. In addition to its traditional racist and anti-Semitic views, BOK promotes an active program of anti-immigrant diatribe.

1998 A jury in South Carolina awards damages in the amount of $37.8 million (later reduced to $21.5 million) against the KKK for intentionally burning down the Macedonia Baptist Church in Clarendon County. The award is the largest ever given for a crime of this nature.

2000 An Idaho jury awards a judgment of $6.3 million to SPLC, acting on behalf of Victoria Keenan and her son. The two were attacked by security guards for the Aryan Nation after the Keenan's car backfire was misinterpreted as gunshots. The financial blow to the organization was largely responsible for its filing for bankruptcy and resulting demise shortly after the trial.

2001 Philanthropist William Regnery II founds the Charles Martel Society, an organization now designated by SPLC as a hate group. The society focuses primarily on the publication of hate-focused literature such as the journals *The Occidental Quarterly* and *The Occidental Observer*. The society also publishes books dealing with racist topics and related subjects.

2007 ACT for America is founded in Virginia Beach, Virginia, largely in response to the 9/11 attacks by Muslim extremists on New York City and other sites. The group has been classified as a hate group by the SPLC because "it pushes wild anti-Muslim conspiracy theories, denigrates American Muslims and deliberately conflates mainstream and radical Islam" (https://www.splcenter.org/fighting-hate/extremist-files/group/act-america).

2009 Former U.S. paratrooper Stewart Rhodes founds a group known as Oath Keepers. The group consists primarily of current and former members of the armed forces, police, and first responders. It emphasizes its commitment to the U.S. Constitution, rather than to any particular group of politicians.

2009 President Barack Obama signs the Matthew Shepard and James Byrd Jr. Hate Crimes Prevention Act (18 U.S. Code 249). The legislation is adopted at least partially in response to two horrendous murders based on the perceived sexual orientation of two men, for whom the act is named. The act adds new categories of bias to hate crimes laws, including religion, national origin, gender, sexual orientation, gender identity, and disability.

2010 Attorney David Yerushalmi drafts a model law called American Laws for American Courts. The law is designed to prevent the adoption of any type of "foreign" law by a state. It is intended, in particular, to prevent the introduction of any form of sharia in the American political system. Although that problem appears not to exist in the United States, twenty-three states have adopted some form of the law as of 2020.

2011 In the case of *Snyder v. Phelps et al.* (562 U.S. 433), the U.S. Supreme Court rules that hate speech used by Westboro Baptist Church members against certain groups of individuals, such as members of the military and LGBTQ people, is protected by the First Amendment right of free speech.

2011 *Snyder v. Phelps et al.* (562 U.S. 433) is the first case based on the Matthew Shepard and James Byrd J. Hate Crimes Prevention Act (**2009**). Defendants are found guilty of the crime of which they are accused and sentenced to five years (for two defendants) and eight and a half years (for the third defendant).

2011 An online neo-Nazi group called Iron March is created. When the site is disbanded about five years later, the live hate group Atomwaffen Division is created to carry on the traditions of the online site. Atomwaffen, in turn, was disbanded in 2020.

2013 Political activists Matthew Heimbach and Matt Parrott found the Traditionalist Youth Movement, a white supremacist hate group. The organization changes its name to the Traditionalist Worker Party in 2015. The party disbands in 2018.

ca. 2014 Wholesale actions by the Chinese national government against a Turkic-speaking Muslim minority, the Uighurs, begin. In a massive relocation program over the next decade, an estimated eight hundred thousand to two million Uighurs are moved to "re-education" or "vocational training" centers distant from their homes.

2015 Former U.S. Marine Dillon Hopper founds Vanguard America, a neo-Nazi, white supremacist hate group.

2015 Inspired by his interest in hate groups and their teaching about race, twenty-two-year-old Dylann Roof murders nine African Americans at the Emmanuel African Methodist Episcopal Church in Charleston, South Carolina. He is later sentenced to life imprisonment by the state of South Carolina and to death by the federal government.

2016 Donald Trump is elected President of the United States. Trump's political stance on a number of issues differs from that of his predecessor, Barack Obama, with some changes in activity among the nation's hate groups.

2016 Iraq war veteran Nathan Damigo founds Identity Evropa, a group that calls itself *identitarians*. They deny that they are racist, but are only interested in preserving Western culture. The group was classified as a hate group by SPLC in 2016. In 2019, the group changes its name to the American Identity Movement.

2016 Canadian British writer and political commentator Gavin McInnes founds Proud Boys, a group open only to males and committed to the use of violence, as needed, to carry out its political agenda.

2017 Members of several right-wing hate groups gather for a "Unite the Right" rally in Charlottesville, Virginia, on August 11–12. Violence ensues when a group of antihate group protesters confront members of the hate group, resulting in nineteen injuries and one death.

2017 A church group, D. James Kennedy Ministries, sues SPLC for religious discrimination because of its listing as a hate group. A district court rejects the suit saying that SPLC's actions were protected by the First Amendment right of free speech.

ca. 2017 Military forces of the government of Myanmar begin an intensive program of violence against a religious minority in the country, the Muslim Rohingya. Only the most recent of a centuries-long history of persecution by the national government, military forces use arson, theft of property, rape, intimidation, and murder to drive the Rohingya out of the country. By 2020, an estimated seven hundred thousand Rohingya, out of a million citizens of the country, had been forced to relocate outside the Myanmar borders.

2018 A new online hate group called Boogaloo is founded. It promotes a racist philosophy that includes calls for a second Civil War to restore the rights of white people. The group was especially active during the 2020 coronavirus pandemic, during which it attempted to promote its policies as an alternative to what it deemed as "repressive" stay-at-home recommendations against the virus.

2018 Unite the Right II is held at Lafayette Square in Washington, D.C., as a follow up to the first Unite the Right rally held in Charlottesville, Virginia, in November 2017 (see **2017**). The rally attracts an estimated twenty to thirty participants who face several thousand protestors to the march. One arrest is made in an otherwise peaceful rally.

2018 The Center for American Progress releases a detailed report on the ways in which hate groups use the Internet to carry out their activities. The report includes an extensive list of suggestions for ways in which companies can deal with this problem in the future.

2019 The CIS files suit against the SPLC claiming that the organization's listing as an anti-immigrant hate group had done irreparable harm to its fundraising capabilities. A local court ruled the suit invalid and declined to consider the case.

2020   The SPLC lists 940 organizations as hate groups for the year 2019.

2020   President Donald Trump announces that he intends to designate Antifa as a domestic terrorist group. Some questions arise as to whether he has the power to do so.

Glossary

Books, articles, web pages, and other resources on hate groups often use terminology that is unfamiliar or with somewhat different meanings than those of everyday life. This chapter presents several terms used in discussions of hate groups, most of which appear in this book. Other terms are also listed for the benefit of readers who wish to continue their research on this topic in other resources.

Accelerationists With regard to hate groups, the belief that existing governmental bodies in the West are inherently and irreparably corrupt, that they will eventually collapse, and that every effort should be made to increase the rate at which such a change will occur.

Ad hoc hate group A hate group formed spontaneously to express dislike or disapproval of some individual, group, or activity. The burning of a cross on the lawn of a new Black family in an otherwise all-white neighborhood might be the act of an ad hoc group, formed specifically for that purpose. Also called spontaneous hate group or informal hate group.

Aggravated assault *See* **assault**

Anti-Semitism Feelings or acts of hostility toward or discrimination of individuals or groups of Jewish heritage, religion, ethnicity, or racial group.

Arson The criminal act of specifically setting fire to another person's or organization's property. A common act of violence perpetrated by hate groups or members of such groups against their victims.

Aryan A racial concept that dates to the late nineteenth century based on the theory that Europeans constitute an identifiable, specific racial group that is superior to other racial groups, such as Blacks, Hispanics and Latinos, and Asians.

Assault A type of crime based on the aggressor's intent to cause bodily harm to his or her victim. Several types of assault are defined in the law. The lowest level is simple assault, in which there is little or no injury or violence involved. A much higher level is aggravated assault, in which more serious threats are involved, such as the use of a weapon in the assault.

Bias crime *See* **bias motivation**.

Bias motivation Any preconceived negative opinion, stereotypical assumption, intolerance, or hatred directed to a particular group that shares a common characteristic, such as race, ethnicity, language, religion, nationality, sexual orientation, gender, or any other fundamental characteristic. Also known as a bias crime or hate crime.

Black (African American) hate group/separatism Any collection of individuals who believe, in general, that people of African heritage will never be able to gain equal rights in the United States, and that they must form their own, separate governing bodies.

Bullying Any unwanted speech or act perpetrated by one person of greater strength, power, prestige, or other quality against another person with fewer or none of those qualities.

Christian identity group A group of individuals who accept a long-surviving belief that citizens of northern Europe and the British Isles are members of the "lost tribes" of Israel and are, therefore, the only individuals capable of leading a nation.

Ethnic cleansing The removal of some group of individuals from a particular area because of their ethnicity, race, religious beliefs, nationality, or other characteristics.

Flash demonstration A surprise event carried out, for example, by a hate group that occurs with little or no prior notice and lasts only a short period of time to protest or make a statement about some issue of concern to the group. A key element in the occurrence of flash demonstrations is the rapid and private exchange of information now available through social media and other platforms on the Internet.

Genocide The intentional, large-scale killing of individuals because of some basic characteristic different from that of the major population of a country or region, such as the slaughter of Jews by the Nazi party in Germany in the 1930s. *Also see* **ethnic cleansing**.

Graffiti Words or drawings inscribed illegally, usually in a prominent public place. Although used for some harmless, even artistic, purpose, graffiti is also used commonly to offend members of a disliked group by members of a hate group.

Gypsy *See* **Roma**.

Harassment Any continuous or repeated uninvited comment by an individual or group of individuals that serves no purpose other than belittling of the harassed.

Hate crime *See* **bias motivation**.

Hate group An organization whose primary purpose is to promote animosity, hostility, or malice against persons based on race, religion, disability, sexual orientation, ethnicity, gender, or gender identity which differs from that of the members or the organization.

Hate speech Any type of offensive spoken or written language that expresses hatred or prejudice against a person or group of persons of different race, ethnicity, sex, gender, gender identify, or other characteristic than that of the speaker.

Heretic An individual who rejects or does not accept the dominant views of some organization, most commonly, the religious dogma of a dominant religious sect.

Ideation The process that occurs when a person begins to think about, imagine, and, perhaps, plan some particular activity; often used in connection with suicide, as "suicide ideation."

Immigrant Any individual who leaves her or his native country and moves to a different country, with the intention of becoming a citizen of the new country.

Informal hate group *See* **ad hoc hate group**.

Inquisition A period in history that began about 1230 by edict of Pope Gregory IX, designed to ferret out, question, and punish individuals with heretical views. The practice waxed and waned with the rise and fall of Catholic, Protestant, and other views inimical to those of the Roman Catholic doctrine of the time.

Invisible hate crime A term sometimes used to describe hate crimes against individuals with a mental or physical disability. The term was invented to emphasize the fact that hate crimes against the disabled are not generally collected or reported, and many individuals seem to believe that the disabled are not a group worthy of being recognized as victims of such crimes.

LGBTQ An acronym used to express most possible types of sexual orientation, specifically, lesbian, gay men, bisexuals, transgender, and queer. The term is also expanded to include other groups, such as LGBTQQ, where the second Q stands for "questioning" (of one's sexual orientation).

Lynching The act of killing a person, usually as the result of mob action, most commonly by hanging, either with or without a legal trial.

Manifest Destiny A political doctrine based on the belief that America is fundamentally a nation of white Anglo-Saxon Protestants, created as superior to other nations and ethnic groups, as ordained by God.

Nativism The belief that native-born members of a nation are inherently superior to and entitled to greater consideration than individuals who have immigrated to the country.

Neo-Nazi hate group A hate group that believes in and adopts the principles and practices of the Nazi party that ruled in Germany in the 1930s and 1940s. Such groups are strongly anti-Semitic, racist, anti-LGBTQ, xenophobic, and generally opposed to anyone who is not of an Aryan heritage.

Othering   Treating people from another group as essentially different from and generally inferior to the group to which one belongs.

Pogrom   An organized mass killing of some group of individuals because of some characteristic of which the dominant population disapproves. The term is by far most commonly used by acts of violence by Christian groups against Jewish communities.

Populism   A political philosophy most commonly based on the beliefs by individuals or groups that their problems and priorities are being ignored by ruling members of the society.

Property damage   Harm caused to one's real or personal property, such as destruction of tomb stones in a cemetery by a hate group opposed to the religion of the cemetery.

Reconstruction   The period in American history between about 1865 and 1871 when efforts were made by the federal government to eliminate and reverse the evils of slavery and to integrate former slaves into the body politic of the country.

Roma   A member of an ethnic group who speaks the Romany language, tends to be migratory, and has traditionally been poorly regarded by other dominant ethnic groups. Also known as **gypsy** or **Sinti**.

Sexism   Any thought, feeling, act, or other state of mind based on the belief that women are inferior to men.

Sexual-orientation bias   A negative opinion or attitude toward a person or group of persons based on their actual or perceived sexual orientation.

Simple assault   *See* **assault**.

Sinti   Generally comparable to, and *see*, **Roma**.

Social media   Forms of electronic communication, such as websites, that can be used to develop online communities that share information, ideas, personal messages, and other content. Some familiar forms of social media are Facebook, Facebook Messenger, YouTube, TikTok, WeChat, Instagram, Twitter, Tumblr, Tieba, LinkedIn, Snapchat, Pinterest, and Reddit.

Sovereign citizen movement A collection of individuals who believe that at some time early in American history, the form of government established by the Founding Fathers was secretly replaced by a government run by and for a small group of privileged individuals. They believe that only sovereign citizens of the country can decide which laws to obey and which to ignore. The movement is historically racist and anti-Semitic.

Spontaneous hate group *See* **ad hoc hate group**.

State-sponsored hate crime A hate crime that is carried out with the tacit and understood approval or support of a national government, such as the conduct of pograms against Jews with the approval of Russia, or some other independent nation.

Verbal abuse The use of words, as in name-calling or the telling of offensive jokes, by one individual about another individual or group of individuals based on some characteristic of the victim(s).

White supremacy A social and political philosophy that individuals of the white race are superior to individuals of all other races and should, therefore, be responsible for the governance of nations and other governmental bodies.

Xenophobia Dislike, fear, or hatred of individuals from other countries or other cultures.

Index

Note: Page numbers in *italics* indicate photos; page numbers followed by *t* indicate tables.

Accelerationism, 83, 105–106, 108
ACT for America, 80, 311
Aid Worker Security Database, 41
Aid workers, violence against, 39–42, 220*t*
Alliance Defending Freedom for Faith and Justice, 138, 310
American Border Patrol, 310
American Civil War
  Battle of Glorieta Pass, 25
  Chivington, John, and, 25
  Confederate statues, 72
  history of hate groups and, 11
  history of the Ku Klux Klan and, 35–36
  history of white nationalists and, 71
  lynching and, 19, 205, 207
  second Civil War, 106, 314
  See also Neo-Confederate hate groups; Reconstruction Acts
American History X (film), 132, 160–163
American Identity Movement (formerly Identity Evropa), 74, 97, 313
American Islamic Congress, 186, 187
American Laws for American Courts, 312
American Party. *See* Know Nothing/American Party
Anti-Catholic bias and groups, 5*t*, 214*t*, 217*t*
anti-Italian hate groups, 32–33
Know Nothing/American Party and, 33, 34, 35, 304
Ku Klux Klan and, 37, 38, 62

323

Anti-Defamation League (ADL), 183–186
  activities and areas of focus, 185–186
  annual survey of hate group propagandizing, 97
  "Audit of Anti-Semitic Incidents," 43, 185, 280
  categorization of hate groups, 58, 59–60, 61
  Coughlin, Charles, and, 185
  database of hate symbols, 98, 185
  definition of hate group, 58
  Ford, Henry, and, 184
  history and founding, 183–184, 306
  Ku Klux Klan and, 184
  Livingston, Sigmund, and, 183, 184, 197–198
  on Nation of Islam, 68
  published documents, 186
  on racist skinheads, 76
  school curriculum programs, 186
  Shelley v. Kraemer and, 185
  on stages of hate group development, 91–94
  on trends in hate group activity, 43
  A World of Difference Institute, 143–145, 186
Antifa, 74, 109–110
  perspective from antifascist journalist, 178–181
  resources on, 273
  strategy and purpose of, 109
  Trump, Donald, and, 109, 110, 315
Antigovernment hate groups, 85–88
  conspiracy theories and, 86–87
  militias, 86–87
  Oath Keepers movement, 87, 311–312
  Patriot Groups, 85–86
  Three Percenters, 88
Anti-Hispanic immigrant hate crimes, 21, 173–176
Anti-immigrant bias and hate
  accelerationism and, 83
  American Border Patrol and, 310
  American History X and, 162–163
  anti-Hispanic immigrant hate crimes, 21, 173–176
  anti-immigrant hate groups, 76–78, 203
  anti-Italian hate groups, 32–33
  anti-Sikh hate and, 156–157

AZ Desert Guardians and, 83
AZ Patriots and, 83
Center for Immigration Studies (CIS) and, 59, 309, 314–315
Colorado Alliance for Immigration Reform and, 83
Dustin Inman Society in Georgia and, 83–84
Help Save Maryland and, 84
history of, 21–24, 31–35, 133–134
Know Nothing/American Party and, 33–35, 304
Ku Klux Klan and, 37, 38, 62, 311
nativism and, 21–22
Nazism and, 70
racist skinheads and, 75
Regnery, William H., II, and, 90
resources on, 274
Trump, Donald, and, 21–22, 25, 60, 82, 205
White nationalism and, 74
Anti-Indian groups, 168–172. *See also* Indigenous peoples
Anti-Italian hate groups, 32–33
Anti-LGBTQ bias and hate, 17–18

advocacy groups, 139–140
Alliance Defending Freedom for Faith and Justice and, 138, 310
American Family Association and, 138
anti-LGBTQ hate groups, 76–78, 136–140
anti-transgender hate, 78, 138–139, 195, 282
claims of anti-LGBTQ hate groups, 138
conversion therapy and, 138–139
Family Research Council and, 138, 309
Family Watch International and, 138–139
hate crimes against LGBTQ individuals, 27, 76–77, 78, 136–137, 138
history of, 17
laws and punishments, 17–18
Liberty Counsel and, 138
Pacific Justice Institute and, 139
Ruth Institute and, 139
Trump administration and, 77–78
Westboro Baptist Church and, 26, 136–137, 139
World Congress of Families and, 139

Anti-Mormon bias
  as FBI bias category used in hate crime reporting, 5*t*
  hate crime data, 214*t*, 217*t*
  Missouri Executive Order 44, 303–304
Anti-Muslim hate groups, 78–82
  ACT for America and, 80, 311
  hate crimes against Muslims, 78–79, 79*t*
  jihad and, 81
Anti-Semitism, 15–17
  in American higher education, 164–167
  anti-Semitic hate groups, 88
  German anti-Semitic laws, 307
  hate crimes, 17
  history of, 15–17, 301–302
  pogroms, 16
  The Protocols of the Learned Elders of Zion, 184
  See also Anti-Defamation League (ADL)
Anti-Sikh hate, 156–159
  Bellingham Riots, 156
  hate crimes against Sikhs, 157–159
  murder of Balbir Singh Sodhi, 157
Anti-transgender bias and hate, 78, 138–139, 195, 282. *See also* Anti-LGBTQ bias and hate
Aryan Nations, 92–93, 191, 203, 308
  Keenan v. Aryan Nations, 92, 203, 311
Atomwaffen Division, 69, 296, 298, 312

Barr, William, 105
Base, The, 108–109
Beirich, Heidi L., 188–190
  early years and education, 188–189
  published works and guest lectures, 189
  at Southern Poverty Law Center, 188, 189
Bias categories used by FBI in hate crime reporting, 5
Bias crimes, 153, 195. *See also* Hate crimes
Bias motivation, 214–215*t*, 216–219*t*
Birth of a Nation, The (film), 38, 306
Black Hebrew Israelite movement, 68, 308–309
Black Lives Matter, *210*
Black Panthers, 67
Black separatists and nationalists, 65–68

Black Hebrew Israelite
movement, 68,
308–309
Black Panthers, 67
definitions of, 66
Delany, Martin, and,
66–67
history of, 66–67
Nation of Islam, 67–68, 306
B'nai B'rith, 183–184,
197–198. *See also*
Anti-Defamation
League (ADL)
Boogaloo, 106, 292, 314
Brandenburg v. Ohio, 308
Bristow, Kyle, 94
Brotherhood of Klans
(BOK), 311
Bullying, 143–144, 159, 186,
200, 204
Bush, George H. W., 86
Butler, Richard, 92
Byrd, James, Jr., murder
of, 152, 154, 275.
See also Matthew
Shepard and James
Byrd Jr. Hate Crimes
Prevention Act

Carbone-Lopez, Kristin,
173–178
Catholic Church
Coughlin, Charles, and,
185
German Peasants' War
and, 302

history of hate groups and,
8, 12–13
Inquisitions, 8, 13
Know Nothing/American
Party and, 33, 34, 35,
304
Ku Klux Klan and, 37,
38
radical traditional Catholic
groups, 85
Ruth Institute (RI), 139
See also Anti-Catholic bias
and groups
Center for American
Progress, 102–103,
314
Center for Immigration
Studies (CIS), 59, 309,
314–315
Center for the Study of
Hate and Extremism
(CSU-SB), 195–197,
280, 293
Charles Martel Society,
90, 311
Charleston church shooting,
95, 99, 313
Charlottesville "Unite the
Right" rally, 60, 72–73,
102–103, 313, 314
Antifa and, 110
conventional dress of
participants, 103
impact of, 73, 85
National Socialist
movement and, 69–70

Charlottesville "Unite the Right" rally (*Continued*)
  neo-Confederate hate groups and, 85
  organizers of, 72
  Public Law 115–58 115th Congress and, 251–253
  purpose of, 72
  remarks by Donald Trump on, 163, 222–224
  resources on, 265, 278–279, 288, 289, 296
  Right Wing Death Squad at, *300*
  role of Internet in planning, 102
  Unite the Right II, 72–73, 102, 314
  White nationalists and, 71–72
Cherry, Frank S., 305
Christian identity groups, 61, 83, 91, 133, 303, 308
Church Arson Prevention Act, 107, 152
  amendment of Victims of Crime Act, 240
  appropriations, 240
  definition of religious real property, 240
  guaranteed loans, 240
  passage of, 310–311
  penalties, 239
  primary document, 239–240
  prohibitions, 239
  reauthorization of Hate Crimes Statistics Act, 240
  statute of limitations, 240
Citizens Equal Rights Alliance (CERA), 169–171
Civil Rights Act of 1871. *See* Third Enforcement Act (primary document)
Civil Rights Act of 1957, 63
Civil Rights Act of 1960, 63, 72, 201–202, 305, 307–308
Civil Rights Act of 1964, 164. *See also* Federal hate crime law (primary document)
Civil War. *See* American Civil War
Clinton, Bill, 152, 194
Collin v. Smith, 308
Concentration camps, 14, 306–307
Conspiracy theories, 86–87, 133, 138, 170–171, 311
Coronavirus pandemic (2020), 40
  Anti-Defamation League on, 186
  Boogaloo and, 292, 314
  hate crimes against aid workers, 41–42

protests and riots,
104–106
resources on, 290, 292,
293, 294, 295
COVID-19. *See* Coronavirus
pandemic (2020)

D. James Kennedy
Ministries, 58–59, 314
Daily Stormer, The, 61, 69
Damigo, Nathan, 74, 313
"Deep state," 86
Dees, Morris, 188, 190–192
early years and education,
190
influence of Clarence
Darrow on, 191
notable legal cases,
190–191
published works, 192
as Southern Poverty Law
Center CEO, 190, 191
Southern Poverty Law
Center cofounded by,
190, 201–202, 308
Dennis, Dawn A., 131–135
Duke, David, 60, 64, 74,
103, 134, 161

Education
ADL curriculum
programs, 186
anti-Semitism in American
higher education,
164–167

SPLC educational
programs, 203–204
on White nationalism, 106
Endean, Steve, 193–194
Ex-hate group leaders and
members, 159–163

Family Research Council
(FRC), 138, 296, 309
Faulkner, Ellen, 136–140
Federal Bureau of
Investigation (FBI)
bias categories used in hate
crime reporting, 5t
definition of hate group,
4, 57
Hate Crime Statistics Act
and, 234–236, 309
hate crime statistics
reported by, 7, 10, 26t,
78–79, 158, 280
objective evidence that
crime was motivated by
bias, 249–251
Federal hate crime law
(primary document),
232–234
on circumstances of
travel and commerce,
233–234
on hate crime acts,
232–233
on punishment, 233
on use of firearms, 233
Fillmore, Millard, 35

First Amendment
   Collin v. Smith and, 308
   hate groups and, 108, 137, 165, 166, 167
   resources on, 271, 278, 284, 285–286, 288, 289, 290, 297, 298
   Snyder v. Phelps et al. and, 245–246, 308
   SPLC's hate group listings and, 59, 314
Floyd, George, 105, *210*
Fogelman, Phil, 143–145
Ford, Henry, 184
Fort Pillow massacre, 36
Foundation for the Marketplace of Ideas, 94
Franklin, Benjamin, 31
Freud, Sigmund, 11

Gabriel, Brigitte, 80
Genocide, 15, 65, 101, 168–172, 180
German Peasants' War, 302
Gnadenhutten Massacre, 303
Gonzaga Institute for Hate Studies, 192–193
   activities and areas of focus, 192–193
   history and founding, 192
   Journal of Hate Studies, 147, 193, 269
   purpose of, 192–193

Griffiths, D. W., 38. *See also Birth of a Nation, The* (film)
Grossman, Joel, 147–150

Hammerskin Nation, 76, 91–92, 161, 309
   Arizona Hammerskins, 92, 309
   Eastern Hammerskins, 309
   Northern Hammerskins, 92, 309
   Outlaw Hammerskins, 91–92, 309
Hate Crime Statistics Act
   on areas of prejudice and types of crimes, 234
   on definition of sexual orientation, 235
   passage of, 309
   primary document, 234–235
   on publication of data, 235
   on use of data, 235
Hate crimes
   AAPI Hate and, 204–205
   against aid workers, 40–42
   against Asian Americans and Pacific Islanders, 204–205
   among select groups, 26*t*
   Anti-Defamation League and, 183, 185–186, 306
   anti-Semitism and, 15, 17, 43

bias categories used by FBI in reporting of, 5t
data by group and type, 214–215t
definitions of, 7
against disabled individuals, 28–29
fighting back against, 106–107
forms of, 30–31
hate groups and, 4–7, 57
against homeless individuals, 29–30
Human Rights Campaign and, 194–195
against immigrants, 21, 22–23, 32–33, 83, 173–176
invisible hate crimes, 28–30
Ku Klux Klan and, 35
legislation, 151–155
Levin, Brian, and, 195–197
against LGBTQ individuals, 27, 76–77, 78, 136–137, 138
against Muslims, 78–79, 79t
Not in Our Town and, 199–201
objective evidence that crime was motivated by bias, 249–251
by offender's race, ethnicity, bias, and motivation, 215–219t
resources on, 259, 260, 263–264, 267, 269, 270–271, 273, 275, 276, 280–286, 299
against Sikhs, 157–159
symbolism and, 99
trends and statistics, 7, 25, 26t, 212t, 213t
United States of America v. Paul Beebe, et al. and, 247–248
use of the term, 7
against women, 10
See also Federal hate crime law (primary document); Hate Crime Statistics Act; Matthew Shepard and James Byrd Jr. Hate Crimes Prevention Act; Violent Crime Control and Law Enforcement Act
Hate Crimes Sentencing Enhancement Act, 152
Hate groups
ADL's definition of, 58
in American history, 30–39
categories of, 61
characteristics of, 4, 12
coronavirus pandemic and, 104–106
counteroffensive actions and groups, 109–110
court cases, 107–108
definitions of, 4, 57–61
education about, 106

Hate groups (*Continued*)
   evolutionary change of, 93–94
   factors leading to rise of, 89–91
   FBI's definition of, 4, 57
   First Amendment rights and, 108, 137, 165, 166, 167
   founding and growth of, 91–94
   graduating in, 91
   hate crimes and, 4–7
   Internet use by, 99–103
   legal actions, 108–109
   legislation, 106–107
   names of, 93
   propagandizing of, 96–98
   signs and symbols of, 98–99
   SLPC's definition of, 58
   socialization and support in, 95–96
   splinter groups, 92–93
   violent activities of, 94–95
   working within the system by, 103–104
Health, impact of hate on, 147–150
   biochemical individuality and, 149
   dysregulation, 148–149
   emotional memories, 147–148
   flight-or-fight physiological response, 147, 148, 149
Henderson, Wade, 153
Hitler, Adolf, 13–14, 69, 77, 99, 101
Holocaust, 185, 307
   concentration camps, 14, 306–307
   denial groups, 85, 98
   nation-state hate groups and, 13–14
Human Rights Campaign, 193–195
   activities and areas of focus, 194–195
   Endean, Steve, and, 193–194
   history and founding, 193–194
   notable political successes, 194

Ideation, suicide, 27
Identitarians, 74, 313
Identity Evropa (later American Identity Movement), 74, 97, 313
Immigration. *See* Anti-immigrant bias and hate
Immigration Act of 1917, 157
Indian Removal Bill, 303
Indigenous peoples
   anti-Indian groups, 168–172

Citizens Equal Rights
  Alliance (CERA) and,
  169–171
 genocide and, 168, 172
 Gnadenhutten Massacre,
  303
 Montana Human Rights
  Network (MHRN) and,
  168–172
 Sand Creek Massacre,
  24–25, 304
 Trail of Tears, 303
 Willman, Elaine, and,
  169–171
 Wounded Knee massacre,
  305
Inquisitions, 8, 13
Internet, hate groups' use of,
  99–103
 anonymity and, 132
 Center for American
  Progress report on,
  102–103, 314
 election of 2016 and,
  131–132
 resources on, 258–259,
  269, 273, 276,
  278–279, 290, 293,
  296, 298
Iron March, 296, 312

Jackson, Andrew, 303
Jacoby, Jeff, 151–155
Jett, Joan, 162
John Birch Society, 307
Johnson, Andrew, 221–222

Johnson, William, 60
Journal of Hate Studies, 147,
  193, 269

Kaur, Aasees, 156–159
Kavadlo, Jesse, 159–163
Keenan, Victoria, 311
Keenan v. Aryan Nations, 92,
  203, 311
Kennedy, John F., 40
Kennedy, Ted, 152
*Knights of the Ku Klux Klan v.
  Strayer*
 background and case
  details, 229–230,
  306
 on charter of KKK, 230
 on KKK's practices and
  activities, 230–231
 on "Knight Riders," 231
 primary document,
  229–232
 ruling, 232
 on "unlawful organization"
  of KKK, 231
Know Nothing/American
  Party, 33–35, 304
Kristallnacht, 307
Ku Klux Klan (KKK),
  35–39, 62–65
 activities and rallies, 6, 36,
  96, 97
 Anti-Defamation League
  and, 184
 The Birth of a Nation,
  38, 306

Ku Klux Klan (KKK) (*Continued*)
- Brotherhood of Klans (BOK), 311
- *The Clansman: A Historical Romance of the Ku Klux Klan*, 306
- declared to be a terrorist organization, 305
- Duke, David, and, 60, 64, 74, 103, 134, 161
- first phase, 37–38, 62
- Forest, Nathan Bedford, and, 35–36
- fourth phase, 64
- hate groups, 64–65, 93
- history and founding, 35–36, 62, 63, 96, 304
- initiation ceremony, 2
- KKK Testimony, 305
- Klanwatch (SPLC program), 196, 202–203
- Knights of the Ku Klux Klan, 64, 65, 134, 229–232
- membership classes, 36–37
- membership statistics, 62–63, 306
- Metzger, Tom, and, 133–134
- naming of, 36
- organizational structure, 37
- political parties and, 36
- Reconstruction and, 36, 37–38
- recruitment of children and young adults, 38
- resources on, 258, 262–266
- second phase, 38, 62–63
- signs and symbols, 37
- Simmons, William Joseph, and, 38, 306
- Southern Poverty Law Center and, 309, 310
- Stone Mountain, Georgia, revival of, 38, 62, 306
- Third Enforcement Act and, 224
- third phase, 38–39, 63–64
- Women's Ku Klux Klan (Ladies of the Invisible Empire), 38
- *See also* Knights of the Ku Klux Klan v. Strayer

League of the South, 70, 84–85, 107, 269, 310
Levin, Brian, 195–197
- director of Center for the Study of Hate and Extremism at CSU-SB, 195, 196
- early years and education of, 195–196
- published works, 293

Levin, Joseph, 191, 201–202, 308

Livingston, Sigmund, 197–198
   Anti-Defamation League founded by, 183, 184, 197–198
   early years and education of, 197–198
   published works, 198
Lynching, 18–23
   antilynching activism of Ida B. Wells, 205–208, 267
   antilynching legislation, 138
   of Byrd, James, Jr., 152, 154, 275
   of Frank, Leo, 198
   history of, 18–21
   Ku Klux Klan and, 62, 63, 191
   mass lynchings, 18–23, 37

Macedonia v. Christian Knights of the Ku Klux Klan, 203, 311
Manifest Destiny, 31, 32
Manipulators, The (Hasson), 59–60
Marcus, Kenneth L., 164–167
Matthew Shepard and James Byrd Jr. Hate Crimes Prevention Act, 107
   on circumstances of travel, commerce, and firearms, 242
   history of, 136–137, 151–152
   Human Rights Campaign and, 194
   on offenses, 241
   passage of, 312
   perspective on punishment and, 151–155
   primary document, 240–244
   on punishment, 241
   on support for criminal investigations and prosecutions, 242–243
McAdam, Travis, 168–172
McInnes, Gavin, 73–74, 313
McVeigh, Timothy, 310
Mein Kampf (Hitler), 69
Metzger, Tom, 133–134
Minority threat, 174–175
Montana Human Rights Network (MHRN), 168–172
Mormon population. *See* Anti-Mormon bias
Muhammad, Wallace D. Fard, 67, 306
Munoz, Jorge A., 131–135
Muslim Rohingya population, 15, 314
Muslims. *See* Anti-Muslim hate groups

Nation of Islam, 67–68, 306
Nation of Yahweh, 68, 305, 308–309

National Socialist Movement, 69–70, 107
National Socialist (Nazi) Party, 13–14, 77, 319
Nation-state hate groups, 13–15, 44
Native Americans. *See* Indigenous peoples
Nativism, 21–22
Nazism
  American Nazi Party, 69–70
  National Socialist Party (Germany), 13–14, 77, 319
  signs and symbols, 88, 94, 98, 99, 134, 247, 248, 250, 308, 310
  See also Neo-Nazism
Neo-Confederate hate groups, 84–85
  Charlottesville "Unite the Right" rally and, 85
  League of the South, 70, 84–85, 107, 269, 310
Neo-Nazi National Alliance, 91
Neo-Nazism, 68–71
  Atomwaffen Division, 69, 296, 298, 312
  The Daily Stormer, 61, 69
  history of, 68–69
  Iron March, 296, 312
  National Socialist Movement, 69–70, 107
  neo-Nazi skinhead at rally, *56*
  Vanguard America, 71, 107, 313
  See also Nazism
New Orleans massacre of 1866, 221–222, 304–305
Not in Our Town, 139, 199–201
  history and origins of, 199
  Not in Our School (NIOS) program, 200
  Not in Our Town + Cops program, 200–201
  programs and activities, 199–200

Oath Keepers, 87, 311–312
Obama, Barack, 86, 99, 151, 153, 194, 241, 312, 313
Occidental Observer, The, 311
Occidental Quarterly, The, 90, 311
Office for Civil Rights, U.S. Department of Education, 164–167
Oklahoma City bombing, 310
Omar, Ilhan, 251–252
Order of the Star Spangled Banner, 33, 304. *See also* Know Nothing/American Party
Orlando nightclub shooting, memorial for, *130*

Orwell, George, 154
Other, the, 7–11
    antigovernment hate groups and, 85
    causes of othering, 8–9
    geography and, 11
    Inquisitions and, 8
    Ku Klux Klan and, 37
    lynching and, 18–19, 31
    Native Americans as, 8–9
    women as, 9–11

Pandemic. *See* Coronavirus pandemic (2020)
Patriot Prayer, 73, 134
Peace Corps, 40
Pence, Mike, 78
Phelps, Fred, 3, 136. *See also Snyder v. Phelps et al.*
Pogroms, 16
Posse Comitatus, 133, 308
Presidential statements on hate violence (primary document), 221–224
    Charlottesville "Unite the Right" rally and, 221, 222–224
    Johnson, Andrew, 221–222
    New Orleans massacre of 1866 and, 221–222
    Trump, Donald, 222–224
Propagandizing, 96–98
Protocols of the Learned Elders of Zion, The, 184

Proud Boys, 73–74, 101, 105, 133, 134, 179, 180, 265–266, 313
Public Law 115–58 Joint Resolution (primary document), 251–254
    condemnation of events in Charlottesville, 251–253
    "Condemning Anti-Semitism as Hateful Expressions of Intolerance," 253–254

Racist skinheads, 74–76, 93–94
    in Great Britain, 75–76
    SPLC on, 74–75, 76
    in the United States, 76
R.A.V. v. St. Paul, 310
Reconstruction Acts, 36–38, 305
Regnery, William, II, 90–91, 311
Religious wars, 302
Resources
    on Antifa, 273
    on anti-immigrant bias and hate, 274
    articles, 269–279
    books, 257–268
    on Charlottesville "Unite the Right" rally, 265, 278–279, 288, 289, 296

Resources (*Continued*)
  on coronavirus pandemic (2020), 290, 292, 293, 294, 295
  on First Amendment, 271, 278, 284, 285–286, 288, 289, 290, 297, 298
  on hate crimes, 259, 260, 263–264, 267, 269, 270–271, 273, 275, 276, 280–286, 299
  Internet, 284–299
  on Internet and hate groups, 258–259, 269, 273, 276, 278–279, 290, 293, 296, 298
  journals, 268–269
  on Ku Klux Klan, 258, 262–266
  reports, 280–284
  on Trump, Donald, 260, 263, 264, 267–268, 270, 274, 277, 282–283, 285, 287, 288, 291, 293, 295
Revealed Knowledge of the Prophecy and Times, A (Brothers), 303
Rhodes, Stewart, 87, 311–312
Rising Out of Hatred (Saslow), 160, 161, 265
Rockwell, George Lincoln, 69
Roof, Dylann, 95, 99, 313
Roper, Billy, 91
Rosenfeld, Richard, 173–178
Ross, Thomas, 162

Sanctuary policies (immigration), 176
Shelley v. Kraemer, 185
Shepard, Matthew, murder of, 136–137, 151–152. *See also* Matthew Shepard and James Byrd Jr. Hate Crimes Prevention Act
Signs and symbols of hate groups, 4, 98–99
  functions of, 98–99
  Nazism and, 88, 94, 98, 99, 134, 247, 248, 250, 308, 310
  numeric symbols, 98
Singh, Nikki, 156–159
Skinheads. *See* Racist skinheads
Smith v. YMCA, 202
Snyder v. Phelps et al., 312
  background and case details, 244–245
  on First Amendment, 245–246
  primary document, 244–247
  ruling, 247
Socialization and support, 95–96

Southern Poverty Law
Center, 201–204
  on antigovernment hate
    groups, 85, 86
  on anti-immigrant hate
    groups, 83
  on anti-LGBTQ hate
    groups, 76–77,
    137–139
  on anti-Muslim hate
    groups, 78, 80
  on anti-Semitic hate
    groups, 88
  on Black separatists
    and nationalists, 65,
    67–68
  categorization of hate
    groups, 58–62
  on Center for Security
    Policy, 104
  Dees, Morris, and, 190,
    191, 201–202, 308
  definition of hate group,
    58, 171–172
  educational programs,
    203–204
  on The Foundation for
    the Marketplace of
    Ideas, 94
  hate groups tracked by,
    132, 137, 310
  Hate Map, 201
  history and founding, 191,
    201–202, 308
  Intelligence Report, 64, 65,
    189, 201
  Keenan v. Aryan Nations,
    92, 203, 311
  on Klan hate groups,
    64, 93
  Klanwatch program, 196,
    202–203
  Ku Klux Klan and, 309,
    310
  Levin, Joe, and, 308
  Levin, Joseph, and, 191,
    201–202, 308
  *Macedonia v. Christian
    Knights of the Ku Klux
    Klan*, 203, 311
  on Neo-Confederate
    groups, 85
  on neo-Nazism, 69
  on racist skinheads,
    74–75, 76
  Smith v. YMCA, 202
  sued by Center for
    Immigration Studies,
    59, 309, 314–315
  sued by D. James Kennedy
    Ministries, 58–59, 314
  on trends in hate group
    activity, 42, 43*t*
  on White nationalists, 71,
    73
Spencer, Richard, 60, 72–73,
  90–91
Stacey, Michele, 173–176
Stop AAPI Hate, 204–205
Stryker, Kitty, 178–181
Suicide, 27–28, 143
Suicide ideation, 27

Suwaij, Zainab, Al-, 186–189
  American Islamic Congress cofounded by, 186, 187
  early years and education, 186–187
  honors and awards, 187–188
  joins uprising against Saddam Hussein, 187
Swastika, 88, 94, 98, 99, 247, 248, 250, 265, 310
Symbols. *See* Signs and symbols of hate groups

Third Enforcement Act (primary document), 224–229
  on authorization of military, 227–228
  on prohibitions against conspiracies, 225–227
  on redress, 225
  on suspension of writ of habeas corpus, 228–229
Thirteenth Amendment, 248–249
Thirty Years War, 302
Three Percenters, 88
Traditionalist Worker Party, 107, 312–313
Traditionalist Youth Movement, 312–313
Trends
  in hate crimes, 213*t*
  in hate crimes by various characteristics, 211*t*
  in hate group activity, 42–43
  in hate groups in the United States, 43*t*
Trump, Donald
  alt-right movement and, 260
  Antifa and, 109, 110, 315
  anti-LGBTQ hate groups and, 77, 138
  on "deep state," 86
  election of, 131, 313
  hate group leaders' responses to election of, 60–61, 70
  hate group trends and, 65–66, 77, 80, 86, 90–91, 111, 131–132
  immigration views and policies, 21–22, 25, 82, 205
  Internet forums dedicated to, 132
  photo op at St. John's Church, 135
  on protests for George Floyd, 105
  remarks about African Americans, 65–66
  remarks on Charlottesville, 163, 222–224
  resources on, 260, 263, 264, 267–268, 270, 274, 277, 282–283, 285, 287, 288, 291, 293, 295
Trump Effect, 22, 283

Tulsa race massacre, 306
Turner Diaries, The, 133

Uighur population, 15, 313
Unite the Right rally. *See* Charlottesville "Unite the Right" rally
United States of America v. Paul Beebe, et al. (primary document), 247–249
   background and case details, 247
   on McCulloch test, 249
   ruling, 248–249
   on Thirteenth Amendment, 248–249
U.S. House of Representatives Committee on Unamerican Activities, 307

Vanguard America, 70, 107, 313
Violence Against Women Act, 152
Violent Crime Control and Law Enforcement Act
   on definition of vulnerable victim, 237
   on hate crime motivation or vulnerable victim, 236–237
   passage of, 310
   primary document, 235–239
   on sentencing enhancements for hate crimes, 236

Walker-Barnes, Chanequa, 163
Wells, Ida B., 205–208
   anti-lynching activism of, 205–208
   in Chicago, 208
   early years and family, 206
   NAACP founding member, 208
   New York Times obituary, 205
   published works, 205, 207–208, 267
   travel of, 206–208
Westboro Baptist Church
   anti-LGBTQ bias and, 26, 136–137, 139
   Snyder v. Phelps et al., 244–247, 312
Western American history, hate groups and, 131–135
   Christian extremist groups and, 132–135
   dog-whistle politics and, 134–135
   Internet use and, 132, 134
   manifestos and conspiracy theories, 133–134
   religious myth-making and, 132–133

White American Youth (Picciolini), 160, 161–162
White nationalists, 71–74
American Identity Movement (formerly Identity Evropa), 74, 97, 313
Charlottesville "Unite the Right" rally and, 71–72
Damigo, Nathan, and, 74, 313
ex-hate group leaders and members, 161–163
Fraternal Order of Alt-Knights, 73
hate crimes and, 6
Hell-Shaking Preachers, 73
McInnes, Gavin, and, 73–74, 313
Patriot Prayer, 73, 134
Proud Boys, 73–74, 101, 105, 133, 134, 179, 180, 265–266, 313
Toese, Tusitala "Tiny," and, 73
Wilmington riots (1898) and, 71–72
See also Ku Klux Klan (KKK)
White Revolution, 91
White supremacists. *See* White nationalists
Wilmington riots (1898), 71–72
Witch hunts, 18
World of Difference Institute, A, 143–145, 186

Yerushalmi, David, 312

Zionist Organization of America (ZOA), 165

About the Author

David E. Newton holds an associate's degree in science from Grand Rapids, Michigan, Junior College, a BA in chemistry (with high distinction), an MA in education from the University of Michigan, and an EdD in science education from Harvard University. He is the author of more than four hundred textbooks, encyclopedias, resource books, research manuals, laboratory manuals, trade books, and other educational materials.

He taught mathematics, chemistry, and physical science in Grand Rapids, Michigan, for thirteen years; was professor of chemistry and physics at Salem State College, Massachusetts, for fifteen years; and was adjunct professor in the College of Professional Studies at the University of San Francisco for ten years.

Some of the author's previous books for ABC-CLIO include *Eating Disorders in America* (2019), *Natural Disasters* (2019), *Vegetarianism and Veganism* (2019), *Gender Inequality* (2019), *Birth Control* (2019), *The Climate Change Debate* (2020), *World Oceans* (2020), and *GMO Food* (2021). His other books include *Physics: Oryx Frontiers of Science Series* (2000), *Sick!* (4 vols., 2000), *Science, Technology, and Society: The Impact of Science in the 19th Century* (2 vols., 2001), *Encyclopedia of Fire* (2002), *Molecular Nanotechnology: Oryx Frontiers of Science Series* (2002), *Encyclopedia of Water* (2003), *Encyclopedia of Air* (2004), *The New Chemistry* (6 vols., 2007), *Nuclear Power* (2005), *Stem Cell Research* (2006), *Latinos in the Sciences, Math, and Professions* (2007), and *DNA Evidence and Forensic*

Science (2008). He has also been an updating and consulting editor on a number of books and reference works, including *Chemical Compounds* (2005), *Chemical Elements* (2006), *Encyclopedia of Endangered Species* (2006), *World of Mathematics* (2006), *World of Chemistry* (2006), *World of Health* (2006), *UXL Encyclopedia of Science* (2007), *Alternative Medicine* (2008), *Grzimek's Animal Life Encyclopedia* (2009), *Community Health* (2009), *Genetic Medicine* (2009), *The Gale Encyclopedia of Medicine* (2010–2011), *The Gale Encyclopedia of Alternative Medicine* (2013), *Discoveries in Modern Science: Exploration, Invention, and Technology* (2013–2014), and *Science in Context* (2013–2014).

CPSIA information can be obtained
at www.ICGtesting.com
Printed in the USA
BVHW030722140423
662322BV00001B/2